Luftwaffe
EAGLE
From the Me109 to the Me262

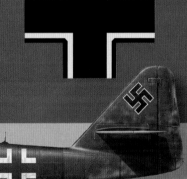

Walter Schuck

HIKOKI
PUBLICATIONS

This book is dedicated to all those of my
Geschwader comrades who were killed,
reported missing, or who died in captivity.

First published in 2007 by Helios Verlags und
Buchvertriebsgesellschaft

German ©Copyright Helios, Aachen, Germany

Translated by John Weal 2008

First published in English 2009 by
Hikoki Publications

ISBN 9 781902 109060

Printed in Singapore by Craft Print

Crécy Publishing Limited
1a Ringway Trading Estate, Shadowmoss Rd,
Manchester M22 5LH
www.crecy.co.uk

Publishers Note:
Research has brought to light many contemporary and
rare photographs of varying quality. They are
reproduced and have been enhanced as far as possible

Contents

Acknowledgements

My special thanks go to: Mrs Waltraud Girbig, Frau Ute Glöckner, Frau Nortrud de Vries, Herren Ferry Ahrlé, Kjetil Akra, Alfred Ambs, Robert Bailey, Klaus Blödorn, Manfred Boehme, Andreas Brekken, Wilhelm Bruhn, Peter W. Cohausz, John R. Doughty Jr, Michael Fluck, Ben Guthrie, Peter Hallor, Hajo Herrmann, Leslie Jantz, Waldemar Jung, Franz Kieslich, Josef Kunz, Christian Mayer, Gunter Mieth, Eric Mombeek, Ulrich Neuberger, Heinz Orlowski, Karl Ostwald, Johannes Otten, Joseph A. Peterburs, Peter Petrick, Eric Pilawski, Dr Gerhard Sarodnik, Bernhard Schäfer, Ernst Scheufele, Karl-Fritz Schlossstein, Günther Scholz, Kurt Schulze, Peter Seelinger, Barry Smith, Rudolf Stoll, Klaus Thiele, Raymond F. Toliver, Martin Villing, Dieter Vogel, John Weal, Dietrich Weinitschke, and to my biographer, Horst Kube, without whom this book would never have been written.

To all those persons or institutions who have contributed to the preparation of this book, but whose names have been inadvertently omitted from the above list, I would like to extend my apologies and assure them of my sincere thanks.

Late, but not too late, Walter Schuck has yielded to the promptings of his many friends and set down on paper the story of his life and times as a successful fighter pilot. In clear and factual language this book offers an insight into the special nature of the air war on the Arctic Ocean front, where the rhythm of life and operations was governed by the perpetual summer sun and the darkness of winter.

The ice-free ports of Murmansk and Kirkenes, on the Russian and German sides respectively, demanded the utmost from the young fighter pilots of the opposing factions whenever Allied convoys bearing war material put into the one, or German coastal supply convoys were making for the other. The result was a constant round of bitter air battles as each tried to destroy the enemy's vital supply lines – or protect their own.

For German fighter pilots these battles became ever harder as the war progressed. The Russians were soon producing machines that proved the equal to Germany's own, and the Airacobras, Hurricanes, Spitfires, Kittyhawks and Tomahawks supplied by the Western Allies outnumbered the Germans many times over.

Walter Schuck's remarkable success in combat came from his ability immediately to assess every situation with an alert eye, his total mastery of the Me 109 – which he could almost fly in his sleep – and his outstanding marksmanship, especially in dogfights. Nor does he forget to pay tribute to the 'black men', or groundcrews, who often had to carry out an engine change in temperatures of 40 degrees below, when describing the comrades he led into action against the enemy and with whom he shared both joys and sorrows.

This book also contains an important historic dimension with its detailed account of the true facts behind the *Tirpitz* tragedy, which at the time cast his Kommodore Heinrich Ehrler in such a false light.

The reminiscences of his youthful years growing up in the Saarland, his experiences while under training, the aerial battles on the Arctic Ocean front, his many adventures between operations, and his final missions flying the Me 262 jet fighter with JG 7 all combine to round out this impressive portrayal of Walter Schuck, fighter pilot.

I wish the book the success it deserves.

Ernst Scheufele

Oberleutnant Ernst Scheufele JG 5 and 14./ JG 4

In the pages of this book I have put down my own very personal memories of my time as a fighter pilot in the Second World War. It is not intended as a unit history, nor is it seeking to be measured against the many learned historical works already published on the wartime German Luftwaffe. And while on the subject, perhaps I may permit myself a few words to all the perfectionists out there: in my humble opinion it will never be possible to establish the true course of events of those days, and the background to them, down to the very last detail. Every day new revelations come to light, which appear finally to pin down the truth behind a particular happening, date or fact – only for this truth to be overturned again shortly afterwards by yet more new findings. This confusion then gives rise to the most divergent views and opinions, which, in turn, inevitably lead to constant disputes between historians and enthusiasts. At the very least, it may be stated with a fair degree of certainty that research into this period, like the labour of Sisyphus, will remain a task without end. As the wheel of history has turned quite a few more revolutions since the closing of the chapter on what was to have been the Thousand Year Reich, I would ask for understanding if, despite my best attempts to eliminate all errors, I am mistaken in any of the statements made herein.

It has not been my aim in this book simply to itemise and describe my aerial victories, nor do I wish in any way to give the impression that I was the archetypal invincible hero, fearless in the face of death. If truth be told, every day I climbed anew into my machine filled with the same almost unimaginable fear of death, serious injury or captivity that I had felt when I had clambered out of it at the end of the previous mission. And every night I tossed and turned in my bed, hardly able to sleep, going over and over again in my mind the details of every air battle fought, and waking in the mornings so bathed in sweat that my pyjamas would have to go straight into the wash basket. Even though, as the war progressed, a certain routine, possibly indifference, perhaps even a sense of callousness, set in, I simply could not shake off the feelings described above. They would remain with me until the last day of the war.

If, while penning these lines, stirred by the memories of events long past, I pause for a moment to consider why I survived my many air combats – and thus the war – relatively unharmed, three things spring to mind that may have had some bearing: the excellent flying training that pilots of my generation received, the unshakeable belief and trust in the dependability of one's comrades – and that famous smidgen of luck.

1 Early days and youthful years

'For goodness sake fetch the lad inside. It's snowing out there and if he's not careful he'll freeze his nose to the window,' Frau Kneip chided her husband Adolf as the pair of them stood in their bicycle shop.

'Yes. I've noticed him too – he's always hanging around here,' Kneip grumbled as he opened the door. 'Aren't you the young Schuck – Walter … Jakob's boy? Come in, you're all blue in the face. Why do you squash your nose flat against my window every day? Do your parents want to buy you a bicycle for Christmas? How old are you, by the way?'

For a shy youngster like myself these were quite a lot of questions that Kneip wanted answering all at once. 'Twelve,' I replied as I stumbled across the threshold in excitement.

A bicycle, no, that wasn't what I wanted at all. It was something quite different in his shop that was the object of my desire. Besides, in those days my parents couldn't have given me a bicycle for Christmas 'just like that'. My father was a coal-miner working in a colliery and my mother had her hands more than full bringing up my four siblings and myself. Our family actually came from Frankenholz, a coal-mining district in the Saarland which, after the First World War, numbered among the most economically disadvantaged regions in the whole of Germany. We had moved from there to Oberbexbach fairly recently. And it was only a few kilometres away, in the neighbouring village of Bexbach, that Adolf Kneip had his bicycle shop.

Kneip had been a pilot during the First World War, and towards the end of the 'twenties he had bought himself a biplane. Every day in the summer, whenever the weather was good, he would take off in this machine from a field close to the shop and carry out advertising flights to earn a bit of extra cash. Fluttering behind the tail of his aircraft was a long banner exhorting the populace to sample the products of a brewery in St Ingbert: 'Drink Becker's Beer'. The clattering of Kneip's biplane somewhere up in the heavens was the signal for every boy in the entire neighbourhood to drop whatever it was he happened to be doing and crane his neck skywards to wonder at the intrepid aviator up there in his flying machine. In order to save himself the cost of hangarage at Saarbrücken airfield, Kneip would dismantle his biplane in the late autumn and put its fuselage on display in his Bexbach shop during the cold winter months.

After I had been allowed to gaze my fill upon this marvel of technology from close up, and after Kneip had readily answered my many questions about the machine and how to fly it, I swaggered home in a state of euphoria. A pilot – that's what I would be one day too. Anything else was simply out of the question. To fling yourself about in the limitless expanse of the sky, free of school reports, free of the day's cares, there could be nothing more glorious than that in the whole wide world. Up there you don't need money and you don't have to look at people's glum faces all the time, I told myself as I neared my parents' house. At that time I didn't give a single thought to how I could achieve my ambition, or what it would cost to train as a pilot. Although times were hard and my father was the sole breadwinner and provider for our large family, we were brought up by mother to be decent and respectable, we wore clean clothes, and there was always food on the table, even if not exactly in abundance. At weekends father liked to go for walks in the nearby woods and regularly took us children along with him. It was during this time that I developed my respect and love for nature, which has remained with me into my present very ripe old age.

One result of the Versailles Treaty was to place the Saarland, with its rich coal-mines and important iron and steel works, into the hands of the French. Even before the First World War the miners of the Frankenholz region were among the most poorly paid in the whole of the Saar, and working conditions had always been appalling. In my youth people still talked of the great pit disaster of 1897, which had claimed the lives of almost sixty miners. The occupying French, however, went to considerable lengths to try to dispel their image as the enemy – which is how most people still regarded them in the aftermath of the war so recently lost – and were at great pains to make a good impression on the civil population. The workers were encouraged, for example, to send their children to state-sponsored French schools. But that only led to yet more tension between the Saarlanders and the French occupiers. My primary school friends and I regarded those German pupils being taught in French schools as 'Traitors to the Fatherland', which often led to brawls between the two factions.

Although the little community of Oberbexbach had fewer than 3,000 inhabitants in those days, it would produce no fewer than four of the Second World War's Knight's Cross winners: Edwin Thiel, the fighter pilot; Willi Rothaar of the Panzers; Karl Oberkircher of the mountain troops; and myself. My father never got involved in politics, but he did instil in me a healthy scepticism of the powers that be. If he did ever express an opinion on matters political, and then only in the family circle, he used to say: 'The state – in other words, the government – is the biggest criminal of all where the public is concerned. The people are squeezed to the last drop. Then the government is dissolved, a new lot get in, and the same rigmarole starts all over again.'

Hitler's assumption power in 1933 brought an increasing number of influences to bear on the Saarland. Those who had previously been all for reunification with Germany suddenly began to have second thoughts about the new regime. But for the majority of the population, the ruthless exploitation of the Saarland by the French, and the humiliation of living under a foreign occupier, far outweighed the fears of any changes a national-socialist government might introduce. And Hitler's social reform plans also played a large part in removing any lingering doubts there may have been about the new right wing party. One of the most popular measures was the introduction of free holidays for the children of less well-off families. My younger sister and I were among those chosen to benefit from this scheme. We spent a wonderful summer at the Baltic spa resort of Ahlbeck, not far from the later rocket-testing grounds at Peenemünde. During these holidays I got to know a pretty thirteen-year-old girl. It was a friendship that lasted until the day she died.

In primary school: the author is in the front row, fourth from left

In January 1935 a plebiscite showed a large majority of the population to be in favour of the incorporation of the Saarland back into the German Reich. A triumphal parade was held to mark the occasion in Saarbrücken, some 30km from where we lived. Nearly fifteen years old at the time, I myself never saw any German troops moving into the Saarland. But after reunification much changed in the area, and those changes were rapid. For one thing, we came to understand the true meaning of the word 'Gleichschaltung'. This innocuous term – 'coordination' – was used to describe the process of unifying the political, economical and social life of the nation under the control of the Nazi Party; in short, it was paving the way to dictatorship. I noticed that, although people were not necessarily more fearful, they were becoming somehow more careful. In conversation they watched what they said. And discussions, particularly about the Party and the Government, were avoided as far as possible. It was forbidden to tune in to foreign radio stations, and everyone was expected to listen only to the programmes of the Greater German broadcasting service. Most of the rights won by the unions were swept away and replaced by various social reforms. Workers' state benefits, for example, were something entirely new. These were particularly welcomed by the miners of the Saarland, whose economic situation during the recent French occupation had deteriorated even further.

During this period I was racking my brains as to how I could set about earning my own living and stop being a financial burden on the family. My father's low income ruled out any ideas I might have had of going to high school to further my education. After leaving primary school I tried, without success, to get an apprenticeship at the colliery in Frankenholz. All I could find in the end was a part-time job in a brickworks. The wages were laughable and I was only needed for short periods at a time anyway. I therefore saw the reintroduction of compulsory military service as offering me a possible career move. My father, who had been in the infantry in the First World War and had often described to me the hell he had experienced in the trenches, said: 'You've got to seize the opportunity and volunteer for military service. If you don't act now you'll find that, as the son of a miner – and one who has only been to primary school, at that – they'll draft you into the infantry. But if you go in as a volunteer, you'll be allowed to choose for yourself the branch of service you want to join. That's the only way you'll avoid ending up in the infantry.'

Seeing no chance of any other worthwhile career opening up for me, I came to the conclusion that father was right and that I should volunteer for the Luftwaffe as quickly as possible. Not only that, it would also provide the opportunity for me to realise my dream of becoming a flyer.

2 Into the Luftwaffe at sixteen

As soon as I was sixteen I applied to join the newly formed Luftwaffe as a volunteer. At the beginning of 1937 I received a letter informing me that I had been accepted. The only condition was that I would first have to complete six months Reich's labour service, which would then be followed by basic training in the Luftwaffe. In those days Reich's labour service was compulsory for all young men upon reaching the age of eighteen. It involved six months of manual labour allied to a form of paramilitary training. But those volunteering to join the Wehrmacht could be called up for their prior labour service at just sixteen years old. So life began for me in earnest on 3 April 1937. I was aware that Reich's labour service entailed heavy manual work: road building, for example, digging trenches, or constructing dykes, bunkers, fortifications and

During Reich's labour service (RAD)

the like. Because of my slight build, I had visions of falling at this first hurdle. But I needn't have worried. Despite my fears I got through my six months of labour service with relative ease.

For my subsequent basic training, which began in November 1937, I was sent to 2. Fliegerersatzabteilung 24 at Quakenbrück, and it was here that the easy life came to an abrupt end. Our course instructor, an Obergefreiter by the name of Dürr, was only happy when he could spend the whole day, from morning till night, putting his recruits through the wringer. Apart from all the dirty tricks he had up his sleeve for us during formal training and barracks fatigues, he really came into his own during field exercises. These were his special favourites. Needless to say, we invariably made our way out to the training area in full equipment, at the double, and wearing gas-masks. But this was not enough for him. While running, we also had to bellow a marching song loud and clear from underneath our masks. Once out on the training grounds, we exercised with our rifles, did knee-bends, or practised the various methods prescribed in the infantry manual for progressing across country. Our instructor liked methods Nos 3 and 5 the best. No 3, for some reason, entailed crouching down and waddling forward like a duck, while No 5 had us crawling flat on our bellies '5 centimetres below the level of the turf'.

In the middle of the area was a pond full of knee-deep stinking brown broth. And here the Obergefreiter gave full rein to his sadistic tendencies. At the edge of the pond we took off our field packs, gas-masks and helmets, and stacked our rifles. Then we had to wade into the brackish water, which immediately came over the tops of our boots and stained the white overalls we were wearing.

Basic training with 2. Fliegerersatzabteilung 24 at Quakenbrück

The author as a young airman

'Imagine the pond is a forest. And in this forest there are trees that you desperately want to climb. Right then, and I don't want to see anybody not making it all the way to the top. Now, up those trees, you monkeys – get climbing,' he ordered.

Any passer-by, seeing us standing in the middle of a pond making all sorts of weird climbing motions, must have thought it was the annual outing of the local insane asylum. It goes without saying that, once the exercises were over, it was back to the barracks at the double, our boots now full of mud and our overalls filthy dirty – but still with a merry song issuing from beneath our gas-masks. Shortly afterwards the Obergefreiter would carry out a room inspection, by which time everything had to be spotlessly clean again. If anything displeased him – and it didn't take much – we would be 'rewarded' with punishment drill, night guard duty or the cancellation of weekend leave passes. The fact that our paths crossed later in the war and I was able to get a little of my own back still gives me a great deal of pleasure even to this day. But more of that anon.

On 1 April 1938, when the six months of misery and oppression – officially known as basic military training – were finally over, I was transferred to Gütersloh to join the Flughafenbetriebskompanie of Kampfgeschwader 254. My company chief was a certain Hauptmann Schneidenberger. He had been born in what was then the German colony of South West Africa, today's Namibia, and was the son of a German soldier and a Chinese woman. He had inherited much of his mother's oriental looks, and so was far from being the fair Nordic type then being extolled by the Party as the Aryan racial ideal. Consequently, it was hardly surprising that he had few friends in the officers' mess and that most of its members cold-shouldered him.

Gunnery practice |

The primary task of a Flughafenbetriebskompanie – or Airfield Servicing Company – was, as its name suggests, to provide support and ground services to the flying unit based on the field. At Gütersloh this unit was IV./KG 254, commanded by Major Carl Rütger; it was later to be redesignated, first as II./KG 254, then as II./KG 28. The Geschwader was equipped with Junkers Ju 86D bombers. And at a time when most bombers were still biplanes, the diesel-engined Ju 86 was the most modern on the market. My own contribution to the company's services consisted at first almost entirely of guard duties. During the long boring hours of patrolling the field I would walk between the dispersed machines lost in admiration. One thing was firm in my mind – one day I would fly one of these mighty bombers.

After what seemed an endless period of pulling nothing but guard duty, I was assigned to a truck driver, a Gefreiter from Boppard on the Rhine, whose job was to collect bombs from the dump outside the field and transport them back to the armoury. Here the fuses would be removed, re-greased and checked for seating before being replaced. I got on very well with the driver, who was an avid reader of crime thrillers. Although I didn't possess a driving licence, he let me get behind the wheel from day one and taught me how to drive. The Mercedes 3½-tonner didn't have a synchromesh gearbox, of course, and whenever I made a mess of changing gear he would wallop me on the back of the head with his rolled-up crime magazine. Ultimately we both benefited from the arrangement: he could read his thrillers to his heart's content, and I learned fairly quickly how to handle the truck.

On 29 September 1938 IV./KG 254 was transferred to Neudorf in Upper Silesia, north of the border with Czechoslovakia. I was allowed to drive the truck for most of the long journey from Gütersloh down to Neudorf. Shortly before an intermediate stop en route, our vehicle was overtaken by the company chief on his motorcycle. When we pulled in to the next parking area to take a break, Hauptmann Schneidenberger came across to us. As I hadn't taken any official driving test – and thus didn't have a Wehrmacht driver's licence – I thought to myself, now you're going to get it in the neck good and proper. But to my surprise nothing of the sort happened – quite the opposite, in fact. Schneidenberger turned to the Gefreiter, clapped him on the shoulder, and said in a voice loud enough for everybody standing around to hear: 'Here's someone at least who understands the importance of teaching the youngsters new skills!' My willingness to learn to drive on my own initiative obviously impressed Hauptmann Schneidenberger. When the Sudeten Crisis – which had been the reason for our move to Neudorf – was over, he arranged for me to attend a glider-training course at Schüren. Now I knew that I really was going to be allowed to learn to fly.

The original glider training school at Schüren, in the hills to the south of the Arnsberger Forest and little more than a dozen miles from the now historic Möhne Dam, had been in existence since the 'twenties. In 1934 it was greatly enlarged. Due to the excellent wind conditions in the region, Schüren was, and remains to this day, one of the best gliding fields in Germany. It was here that I soared into the air for the first time, freeing myself from all

First hops in the glider

Schüren Glider School

earthly bonds. It was just as I had imagined it would be when I was a boy, and this is how old Kneip must have felt as he chuntered around above the meadows in his biplane. In Schüren I was given a thorough grounding in the rules of aerodynamics and the effects that different weather conditions could have on an aircraft's flying characteristics, lessons that would stand me in very good stead later in my career.

In the middle of November 1938, after competing my first few weeks of training, I left the glider school to return to Gütersloh. The next rung on the ladder to becoming a pilot awaited me in February 1939: the aviation technical school at Bonn-Hangelar. During the next three months I received a solid technical education that taught me, amongst other things, how to dismantle an aircraft engine and reassemble it again. With another course successfully completed, I was given a new posting, and this time I felt as if I was on the point of fulfilling my dream. Although the transfer took me back to Quakenbrück, it was not for another session of that miserable ground training. Instead, my destination was the station's flying training wing: the A/B Fliegerschule of Fliegerausbildungsregiment 82. The Luftwaffe's flying schools were divided into A and B courses, each of which trained pupils on different types of aircraft. First came the basic course. This was followed by A 2 training, which involved long-distance, overland, and formation flying, as well as emergency landing procedures and landings away from base. The B 1 and B 2 courses took things a stage further with advanced training in the above, together with pinpoint and night landings, type familiarisation and instrument flying, high-altitude and aerobatic flying, and learning how to control an aircraft in all conceivable emergency situations.

At flying training school: I am third from left

My instructor, a most affable type by the name of Brewes, knew how to get the best out of his pupils. He seems to have discovered in me a certain talent for flying that was perhaps down to the meticulous training I had received at glider school. Brewes decided that I was ready to go solo after only eighteen take-offs and landings. This caused quite a stir among the regiment's other instructors, as pupils were not normally entrusted to go up on their own until after they had made some thirty to forty dual-control take-offs. In the meantime war had broken out. Although the Western Allies had

been emphatically opposed to any further territorial demands on Hitler's part, he had still ordered the Wehrmacht to attack Poland on 1 September 1939. Germany had by now emerged as such a strong military power that Poland's forces were beaten in just a few weeks. When France and England declared war on Germany, however, I began to worry about my family living so close to the French border. And only a matter of days later French troops did, in fact, advance into the Saarland and occupy several villages. But nothing much happened after that. In October 1939 the French withdrew again and the western front was to remain remarkably quiet. The winter of 1939/40 was one of the coldest in living memory, but I flew as often as conditions allowed. The completion of the B 2 course coincided with the announcement on 10 May 1940 that the Wehrmacht had launched a major offensive against France, Belgium and the Netherlands. Fliegerausbildungsregiment 82, now under the command of Oberstleutnant Max Bauer, was transferred to Cottbus, about 90km to the south-east of Berlin. And it was here, on 14 May 1940, that I finally received the pilot's licence I had been longing for.

In contrast to some fellow pupils I had got to know at flying school and who wanted to become either dive-bomber or fighter pilots, I was more drawn towards long-distance reconnaissance. I had seen the slender, twin-engined Dornier Do 17, nicknamed the 'Flying Pencil', and, forsaking the Ju 86, now wanted above all else to fly one of these machines. I therefore remained with the Fliegerausbildungsregiment while awaiting a

At last, my Luftwaffe pilot's licence

posting to one of the C schools, where pilots were trained to fly multi-engined bombers and reconnaissance aircraft. But fate had something else up its sleeve for me. One day, not long after getting my pilot's licence, I was ordered to 'fly in' a single-seater Focke-Wulf Fw 56 Stösser. The expression 'fly in' meant to get to know an aircraft really thoroughly and to practise aerobatics in it. Designed as a fighter by Kurt Tank in 1933, this high-winged little machine was a lively performer and I loved flying it. On this day, with no other aircraft in the sky, I decided to indulge in a really daring display of aerobatics. I had just flown a succession of loops, one after the other, which had cost me a lot of altitude, and was roaring at low level across a village – something that was strictly forbidden – when I saw another machine appear over the horizon. The aircraft rapidly drew nearer and I recognised it as the Me 108 Taifun that our Fliegerausbildungsregiment used for courier flights. I realised at once that the occupants had observed my unauthorised low-level flying and that I was now in deep trouble.

When I landed back at Cottbus, instructor Brewes was already waiting for me with a worried look on his face. All that he could tell me was that the Me 108 had had a Major and three other officers of the regiment on board, and that I was to report to the company chief, an Oberleutnant Brunner, forthwith. The Oberleutnant was a regular officer and I sensed that, despite my good flying assessments, he would not be inclined to show me much mercy – and I was right.

'Gefreiter Schuck, you have contravened the rules of flying discipline in a most reckless manner. I am therefore referring the matter to higher authority. And I can tell you here and now what will happen then: you will have to answer charges before a court-martial.'

As I trudged back to the store to hand in my parachute, my eyes were filled with tears. The offence would undoubtedly mean the end of my flying career. The thought drove me to despair. I must have cut such a pathetic figure that a passing Obergefreiter hailed me: 'Hey, cry-baby, what's the matter with you then?' I found myself telling him about my illegal low-level flight, for which Oberleutnant Brunner was going to have me up in front of a court-martial. A broad grin spread across the Obergefreiter's features.

'So, the Herr Oberleutnant wants to hang you out to dry, does he? Well, how about this then: I take it you've heard about the ghost plane, the Heinkel Blitz that caused all the huge fuss a few weeks ago?'

I nodded. Everybody knew the story. It had been the major topic of conversation every day since. The hunt was still on for the mysterious Heinkel, and teletypes requesting information had been sent to all airfields in the vicinity. The pilot of the Heinkel had carried out a number of dummy attacks on a Junkers Ju 52 that was being flown by a trainee pilot on a blind-flying exercise. The Junkers pilot couldn't see the Heinkel as the windows on his side of the cockpit had been covered for the purposes of training. During one of the attacks the two aircraft had almost collided and the Junkers's trailing aerial had been ripped off. The instructor sitting next to the pupil pilot could just make out that the other machine was a Heinkel He 70 Blitz, but he could provide no further details as the attacker carried no registration markings. The teletype instructed all station commanders to report any knowledge of the machine being sought and the identity of its crew immediately – but so far without success.

'The pilot of the Heinkel was Oberleutnant Brunner,' rasped the Obergefreiter. 'I know that, because I happened to be the flight-engineer aboard the aircraft that day. The scoundrel made several dummy attacks on the Junkers and even tore its aerial off. Then he flew back to base, had the damaged paintwork on the Heinkel touched up and its registration markings re-applied. I'd already thought it best to forget the whole episode, but now that I hear you're to be punished for an offence when he's done something ten times worse, I don't see any reason to keep my mouth shut any more. There it is – use the information as you see fit!'

Greatly relieved, I made my way back to my quarters. Early in the afternoon Brewes dropped by to see how I was getting on. When he found me taking it easy on my bed, his brow furrowed.

'Tell me then, what happened?' he asked.

'I'm going to be court-martialled,' I replied quite unconcernedly.

Confused by my relaxed attitude, he left the room shaking his head. After a while he returned, sat himself down on a chair and tried again: 'Schuck, what's happening here? You're to go up in front of a court-martial, and yet here you are, stretched out quite happily on your bed and acting as if it's got nothing to do with you. Now, will you finally tell me what's going on?'

I explained to Brewes what I now knew about the Heinkel Blitz story. 'So, all well and good,' I said. 'I might be sentenced, but Oberleutnant Brunner must be prepared for me to tell the court everything I have learned about the incident involving the Heinkel Blitz.'

Things really started moving after that. Brewes went to see Brunner, who in turn went to talk to the head of the flying school. At six o'clock that evening I was ordered to report in full equipment – helmet, rifle, the lot – to the station commander. When I entered his office, he said, 'Remove your helmet, put your rifle over there and take a seat.' Then, in almost fatherly tone, he went on: 'Gefreiter Schuck, this is a nasty business. I won't allow my people to go up before a court-martial and, quite honestly, I would much prefer to let the whole matter drop. But as every single pupil in the school already knows what you have done, you will understand that I cannot let you get off scot-free. If you are not punished, flight discipline will be a thing of the past and every other pupil will consider he has the same right to fool around in the sky as you have done. Tomorrow morning you will report back to Oberleutnant Brunner. He will award you some form of legitimate punishment and then you are to forget the whole matter. Do we understand each other?'

Inwardly rejoicing, I left the station commander's office. The next morning I stood in front of a distinctly nervous Oberleutnant Brunner, who placed me under fourteen days arrest. When I reported to the guard commander, an Unteroffizier, I still had visions of two fairly untroubled weeks in the cells. But the Unteroffizier turned out to be a complete sadist who delighted in dreaming up new forms of physical exercise for the prisoners every day. For example, we would have to run round and round in a circle within the inner courtyard of the cell-block until we were on the point of collapse. And on one occasion he hit upon the idea of making us play 'ham-bashing'. This entailed one of the prisoners turning round, bending over and sticking his posterior out. Another prisoner, who was sitting on a stone in front of him, would hold the victim's head. And then all the others would take turns in hitting him as hard as possible on the backside. If he could guess who had just walloped him, that one would take his place. Among the prisoners was an enormous individual with arms as long as an ape's. He was suspected of manslaughter and was being held in the cells while enquiries were carried out. When it was my turn to be the guinea-pig, this criminal hit me with such force that I fell to the ground in a heap together with the prisoner who was supposed to be holding my head. Scrambling back to my feet, I pointed to the

ape-man and now he had to bend over. Instead of clouting him on the backside, however, I clenched my fist and punched my tormentor as hard as I could in the left kidney. He whirled round, eyes wild, and yelled: 'Who did that? Who the devil did that? I'll kill him, I swear I will!' Frightened of being blamed, one of the prisoners indicated that I was the culprit. The guard commander managed to pull the enraged giant off me just in time.

As I didn't want to run the risk of meeting my opponent again, or to take part in any more of the commander's exercises, I resolutely refused to leave my cell in the days that followed. Even when the commander threatened to report me for refusing to obey orders I stayed put; not appearing even once for meals. When a couple of friends came to my cell window to find out if there was anything they could do for me, I asked them to fetch the chocolate bars that were in the locker next to my bedspace. I had bought the chocolate in Prague during the course of a practice cross-country flight in a Focke-Wulf Fw 58 Weihe a few days before my arrest. It now came in very handy and allowed me to sit out the rest of my sentence in my cell without going hungry. Upon my release I had to report to the station commander again.

'Gefreiter Schuck, I just don't know what's got into you,' he said. 'First you show above-average flying abilities and gain your pilot's licence quicker than any of the other pupils on your course. Then suddenly you turn into the black sheep of the whole school. You flout flying regulations, want to denounce an Oberleutnant, and now, while under arrest, refuse to obey the guard commander's orders. What have you got to say for yourself?'

There was no other option. I would have to tell the station commander all about the events while I was under arrest; the 'ham-bashing' episode and the threats made by the prisoner awaiting a charge of manslaughter. The result was that the Unteroffizier was immediately suspended from duty.

'As you may well imagine,' the station commander added, 'you are not exactly popular with some people around here. I am therefore now having papers made out to get you posted elsewhere. When they come through you will be transferred to the nearest fighter training school.'

That was the reason why I missed out on becoming a reconnaissance pilot and ended up at the Jagdfliegerschule Werneuchen instead.

3 At fighter training school

On 16 June 1940 I arrived at Werneuchen, the home of Jagdfliegerschule 1. My transfer had been so hasty that I arrived three days before the rest of the new intake of trainee fighter pilots turned up. Situated in the province of Brandenburg to the north-east of Berlin, the Werneuchen fighter training school had been established in November 1937 and had since built up a good reputation. Upon my arrival I reported for duty with 3. Staffel to my future instructor, an Oberfeldwebel, or Flight Sergeant, by the name of Hobe. He had already read the unfavourable remarks in my records and said in an unfriendly tone of voice: 'Gefreiter Schuck, we don't want any troublemakers here. I'll be going up for a practice flight with you tomorrow and straight afterwards, let me assure you, you'll be packing your bags again.'

When we taxied our two trainers out next morning, I was determined to show him how good I was. I didn't want to lose my place in the school, for if I washed out now I would be thrown out of the Luftwaffe altogether and would almost certainly end up in the infantry. I had already been taught how important it was when flying for the wingman to keep close station on his leader, and I therefore concentrated my whole attention on this one basic rule.

As most school machines didn't carry radios in those days, instructor and pupil communicated by means of hand signals. But I deliberately 'overlooked' Hobe's signal to keep a greater distance away from him, as I didn't want to give him the chance to lose me. Hobe now began to throw his aircraft around wildly, but I stuck to him

Werneuchen fighter training school: a Focke-Wulf Fw 56 Stösser

like a leech. From our machines we could see that a group of pupils had gathered on the airfield below and were staring up at us. It was the new intake, together with Oberleutnant Klaus Quaet-Faslem, the Kapitän of the school's 3. Staffel. Quaet-Faslem was an experienced pilot, who had already taken part in the Polish campaign. Hobe went through all sorts of aerobatic manoeuvres, but I doggedly maintained position. After a final flurry of stunts that, under normal circumstances, would only have been attempted by two pilots fully familiar with each other's flying skills, Hobe decided to land. While I was still taxiing in to the dispersal area, Hobe had already leapt from his machine and was running towards me. Before I could climb out of my own aircraft he was yelling at me: 'You imbecile, you obviously don't know the most basic rules of flying. That was the last flight you'll ever make – I'm getting you removed from here immediately!'

I was pretty well exhausted by the effort of keeping station during the manoeuvres he had just put me through, and although I was drenched in sweat beneath my flying overalls, the instructor's tirade hit me like a cold shower.

What neither of us knew then was that, in the meantime, Oberleutnant Quaet-Faslem had been telling the trainees: 'Watch those two aircraft carefully. They are being flown by two highly experienced instructors. You'll only be ready for front-line service when you can fly like that!' Quaet-Faslem heard the fuss that Hobe was kicking up over at dispersal and came across to us.

'Oberfeldwebel, what's going on? Why are you ranting at your colleague like that?'

'Herr Oberleutnant, this is no colleague,' Hobe retorted angrily. 'This is an undisciplined beginner who only arrived here yesterday. I gave him clear signals to keep his distance. But he took not the slightest notice of them, and that's why I'm going to do my utmost to make sure that he's taken off the course.'

'But we can't do that,' Quaet-Faslem replied. 'I've just made a special point of telling my new pupils to watch your demonstration and learn something from it. Besides, we can't afford to lose such a talented pilot as the Gefreiter here.'

Then he turned to me, saying: 'Gefreiter, I congratulate you on your flying abilities, but next time pay more attention to your instructor's hand signals!'

With these words he turned on his heel and left us. Once again, my flying career had been saved.

A ground-attack aircraft in the Spanish Civil War, then a trainer: a Henschel Hs 123

It was at Werneuchen that I first made the acquaintance of a sharp little single-seat fighter, the Messerschmitt Me 109. Because of its narrow-track undercarriage it displayed some critical tendencies during take-off and landings, and was difficult to manoeuvre when on the ground. But on my first flight I lifted off fairly cleanly and, once in the air, discovered that the machine was a pure delight to fly. At first I trained on an Me 109B-2, which was powered by a 690hp twelve-cylinder Junkers Jumo 210D in-line engine driving a two-bladed wooden propeller. It was not long, however, before we received the Me 109E-1, which was fitted with an engine of almost double the power, the 1,175hp Daimler-Benz DB 601A, and featured a three-bladed metal propeller. The output of the DB engine could be increased even more, albeit only for a few minutes, by injecting a mix of water and methanol into the supercharger. In addition to take-offs and landings, we practised all kinds of formation flying, tactical manoeuvring and attacks on target aircraft.

To complete the course there were three days of consecutive gunnery practice with the Me 109 at a military training ground. Here we fired at a ground target that comprised a screen some 1.5 metres square, which was set up at a slight angle and had a number of rings

painted on it. On the first day's shooting I scored sixty-five hits with my machine-guns, and on the second I got eighty-six. My score on the third day was ninety hits in the rings, but two bullets smashed into the target's wooden framework. On this last occasion I had flown so low that my slipstream had knocked the screen over. When I landed I was still fuming about this mishap. Now at last I had given Hobe the chance he had been waiting for – I was certain in my own mind that the Oberfeldwebel had not forgiven me for the earlier incident. As I had made something of a laughing stock out of him, he would no doubt welcome the opportunity to get rid of me. But this time my fears proved groundless.

'Over ninety per cent hits! That's the highest score anyone has ever achieved here on the firing range,' the armourers informed Hobe.

Upon finishing the course at the Jagdfliegerschule, I was now officially numbered among the Luftwaffe's fully trained fighter pilots. However, on 2 September 1940 I was posted to 3. Staffel of the Ergänzungsjagdgruppe Merseburg. This was a sort of operational training unit, where I was received by a combat-experienced Unteroffizier, who had himself joined the Gruppe only a short time earlier after having claimed six victories on the Channel front. He greeted me in an almost friendly manner.

A Bf/Me 109B-2 with the Jumo 210D engine and a two-bladed wooden propeller

'I see from your records that not all your previous superiors were exactly delighted with you.' He read aloud: 'Personal characteristics – unsuitable.' Then he laughed and said: 'Unsuitable characteristics, I know what that means – you didn't suit theirs! But that doesn't matter to me; I didn't hit it off with my superiors either. They were all jealous because I was more successful than they were. My Staffelkapitän couldn't stomach the fact that I'd got six kills and had been awarded the Iron Cross, First Class. He, on the other hand, only had two victories, and that's probably why he had me transferred here.'

The Unteroffizier was temporarily in command of a flight of six Me 109s. Operating out of Merseburg, its role was to provide aerial protection for the barrage balloons guarding the huge synthetic oil refineries of the Leuna works. Over the following weeks the Unteroffizier with the six victories taught me a lot of flying tricks that stood me in good stead during my later combat career.

After a few weeks, however, the protection flight was disbanded and I received my next posting. This took me on 6 October to the Ergänzungsstaffel of Jagdgeschwader 3, which was based at St Omer-Wizernes, an airfield on the French Channel coast not far from Calais. The Wehrmacht's rapid successes against Belgium, Holland and France had encouraged the leadership to launch an air offensive against the British Isles in August 1940. But very soon the name 'Adlertag' – or 'Eagle Day' – had

proved to be just so much eye-wash: right at the start of the Battle of Britain the Me 109E had revealed its Achilles heel – a range that was much too short. At that stage long-range fuel tanks had not yet been introduced, so the time available for combat with the Hurricanes and Spitfires, which were taking off from their home soil, was limited to only about 15 minutes. This shortcoming had been of no great significance during operations over Germany's neighbours Poland and France, but now, with the English Channel having to be crossed, our fighters were faced with a stark choice: they could either leave the bomber crews to their fate shortly after arriving over the target area, or they could run out of fuel themselves and come down in the 'drink'. The outcome was that one of the most important prerequisites that had to be achieved if an invasion of England was to stand even the remotest chance of success – namely, air superiority – could not be attained. The cross-Channel operations had cost the Luftwaffe so much blood that this failure must be regarded as the first indication that the war could never be won.

As the name again implies, the Ergänzungsstaffel, or reserve training squadron, was not a front-line unit. The job of its experienced members, who had already seen operational service, was to teach combat tactics to the newcomers in its ranks. At St Omer-Wizernes the Ergänzungsstaffel shared the field with I./JG 3. Our training Staffel consisted of some ten newly qualified fighter pilots, who were taught by several ex-operational types now serving as instructors. For this purpose the Staffel was equipped with a number of Me 109Es drawn from other elements of JG 3. Our CO was Hauptmann Dr Albrecht Ochs, a friendly officer and one of the so-called 'Old Eagles'. Although he was almost blind in one eye, he was a larger-than-life individual, bursting with energy, who had flown on operations with Kampfstaffel 20 in the First World War. Later he had joined 22. Staffel of the famous Bombergeschwader 7, led by Hauptmann Kastner, where he flew Albatros and Gotha bombers. On 3 January 1918 his Albatros was attacked by a mixed formation of French Spad and Nieuport fighters, one of which he managed to shoot down. For this exploit he and his gunner were awarded the Honour Cup of the Imperial German Flying Service by the Commander-in-Chief, General von Hoeppner.

With Ergänzungsjagdgeschwader 3

The combat-experienced pilots of the Ergänzungsstaffel not only instructed us in all the various ways of formation flying, but also taught us tactics and many other things important to our survival in the air. These included, for example, how a flyer could orientate himself by the differences in the terrain below; how to escape from ground fire; the best evasive action to take when attacked by the enemy; how to watch one's speed and altitude while doing so, and at the same time keep an eye on one's opponents, the instruments and the surrounding airspace; how to carry out low-level attacks; and a host of other practical tips and advice.

'The highest priority of all,' the instructors drummed into us time and time again, 'is to have the upper hand in the existing combat situation and keep a constant watch on the entire airspace in both the vertical and horizontal planes. Always remember: the victor in an air battle is usually the pilot who spots the enemy first.'

I soon discover that I was blessed with particularly good eyesight. This ability was my passport to many future aerial victories and often proved a life-saver too, for I was able to spot my opponents long before they had seen me. With its narrow cockpit and a canopy enclosed in a fairly substantial metal framework, the Me 109 did not offer the best in all-round visibility. In order to improve my vision, I always used to fly with the seat fully forward. Being less than 5ft 6in tall, this meant I almost disappeared below the cockpit sill, which became a standing joke among my comrades: 'If you see a Messerschmitt flying past and there's no one sitting in it, then that was Schuck.'

I enjoyed the time at St Omer-Wizernes and soon felt myself to be a proper fighter pilot. But it was still relatively peaceful, and so there were no scrambles, operations or air battles. On two or three occasions we were permitted to accompany the instructors to bars or cinemas in St Omer. At the end of October 1940 the operational pilots of I./JG 3 were transferred with their Me 109s to an airfield in Belgium, from where they were to fly an escort mission over the province of Namur. At the time none of us knew the reason for this move: Hitler would be flying through Belgian airspace after a meeting with foreign heads of state. Once the front-line Staffeln had left St Omer, our Ergänzungsstaffel took over their duties. Now for the first time we were regularly called to cockpit readiness. On one occasion a report came in that a formation of

English aircraft would soon be crossing the French coast, whereupon an emergency scramble was ordered. The still inexperienced pilots began to take off from their dispersal areas in all directions – it was a scene of complete and utter confusion. Because of the Me 109's long engine cowling, the view ahead from the cockpit when on the ground was severely limited. In order to be able to see the runway at all, the pilot had to weave from side to side while taxiing. But some of the new boys had obviously forgotten this fact in the excitement of their first real scramble.

The inevitable occurred. The Messerschmitts began heading towards each other from all corners of the field. When I saw another machine coming straight at me, I tramped hard on the rudder pedal in an attempt to avoid a collision, but there was a loud bang and my Me tipped over on to its side. When I regained consciousness I found myself in station sick quarters with concussion. My machine, an Me 109E-3, was now just a pile of scrap metal, but at least the pilot of the other Messerschmitt, whose name I never did discover, had come out of the collision without a scratch thanks to my swerving away at the last moment.

On 1 December 1940, shortly after being allowed to leave sick-bay, I was promoted to Unteroffizier, and a little more than two months later, on 10 February 1941, I was again on the move, to 10. Staffel of Ergänzungsjagdgruppe 3, which had just been set up at Brombos, north-west of Paris. I therefore departed St Omer in an Me 109 and headed for Brombos, which was situated roughly halfway between Paris and the Channel coast.

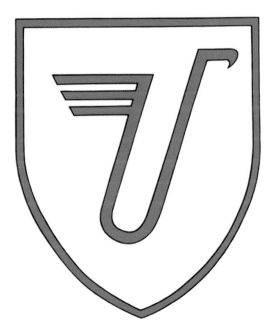

The emblem of Jagdgeschwader 3

4 Still all quiet with JG 3

As I approached Brombos airfield heavy rain had set in. The runway was a sodden, slippery stretch of grass and I only narrowly avoided standing the aircraft on its nose. As flying control told me later, a number of pilots who had come in earlier had faced serious problems and several machines had crashed on landing. I reported to my new Staffelkapitän. He was a wiry Oberleutnant who had come from JG 54 and was the possessor of a good family name: Hans-Curt Graf von Sponeck. His father was the Army General Hans Emil Otto Graf von Sponeck, whose air-landing divisions had captured the bridges and airfields around Rotterdam and The Hague on the first day of the campaign in the west. For this exploit he had become one of the first soldiers in the Wehrmacht to be awarded the Knight's Cross.

At that time 10./JG 3 was a sort of cross between an Ergänzungsstaffel and a front-line Staffel. We were expected to undertake two forms of activity: if, for example, Reichsmarschall Hermann Göring travelled anywhere in his special train, we had to provide aerial cover for it; the rest of our time was taken up in learning the finer points of combat tactics. Although NCOs and other ranks were forbidden to visit Paris, the officers always brought back a whole lot of goodies from their trips to the French capital. We rarely encountered a single enemy aircraft during our regular patrols. This was perhaps due to the fact that the English had not yet begun to 'lean' into German-occupied northern France, while we, for our part, had been ordered not to fly more than halfway across the Channel. During March and April we spent a few weeks at St Jean-d'Angély, an airfield in south-west France not far from Cognac and La Rochelle. While we were there,

Oberleutnant Rudolf Freiherr von Metzingen, who had previously been the German military attaché in Turkey and was now brushing up his flying skills with JG 3, took us younger pilots under his wing in a special way: he derived a great deal of amusement from teaching us proper table manners! Among the things he showed us was how, in high society, one ate lobster with mayonnaise, including the correct way to hold a lobster fork.

In mid-April 1941 our Staffel was redesignated as 1./Ergänzungsjagdgruppe JG 3 and transferred to Cracow in Poland. It was a long flight and we made various stops along the way: Paris-Le Bourget, Metz-Frescaty, Mannheim-Sandhofen, Langensalza, Berlin-Tempelhof and Cottbus. On Cracow airfield I saw another diesel-engined Ju 86, the type of machine that had aroused my interest during my time with the Flughafenbetriebskompanie at Gütersloh. While walking around the aircraft, I got into conversation with the Ju 86D's flight engineer. He explained to me that this was a special variant with a heated pressurised cockpit and extended wingspan. 'We can climb up to 11,000 metres in it,' the mechanic chuckled. 'We fly over Moscow quite undisturbed, and the Ratas can't even make it as high as 8,000 metres!' At the time I couldn't quite fathom out why the Russians would want to climb up after a German aircraft flying over Moscow. I had thought that all was peaceful since the signing of the non-aggression pact between the Soviet Union and Germany in August 1939; after all, Germany was receiving regular shipments of grain and other commodities from Russia. Of course, I didn't know then of the preparations and planning that our leaders had embarked

The mysterious Ju
86D with its
pressurised cabin
and extended
wingspan

upon prior to the Wehrmacht's forthcoming march into Russia. The Ju 86 that I had seen, and about which the talkative mechanic had perhaps said a little bit too much, belonged to an Aufklärungsgruppe that was carrying out a systematic aerial reconnaissance of Russian territory. The intelligence thus gained was to play an important part in the opening rounds of Operation 'Barbarossa', the invasion of the Soviet Union launched upon Hitler's orders on 22 June 1941.

The ex-fighter instructor Oberleutnant Walter Dahl spent some time with us at Cracow. After serving at a training school, he had been transferred to the Geschwaderstab of JG 3 and had shot down a Soviet fighter on the first day of the German attack on Russia. He was probably bored by our persistent requests for his views on the tactical and strategic situation on the eastern front, his impressions of the enemy's actual strength, and of his feelings before, during and after his combat missions. We hung on his every word when he described his aerial battles, and in our imaginations we were up there flying the missions with him. Occasionally, either to take our minds off the war or perhaps because he himself was keen on architecture, he would conduct a group of six of us into the picturesque old inner city of Cracow. I still remember with pleasure one of these sightseeing trips when he showed us the ornately decorated buildings and Cracow's imposing cathedral. I continued to follow the flying career of the later Sturm pilot and Oak Leaves winner Walther Dahl throughout the war and the years thereafter until his death at the much too early age of 69. At one of our last get-togethers he gave me a beautifully worked silver ring with a black stone containing a Luftwaffe eagle inlaid in silver. It had been presented to him, he said, by some 'bigwig or other of the Flak arm' on the occasion of his being awarded either the Knight's Cross or the Oak Leaves.

The victory reports coming in from the eastern front made a huge impression on us. It seemed as if the Soviet colossus would be collapsing in very short order. Most of our pilots were grousing because we were an Ergänzungsgruppe and, as such, not yet officially classified as operational and therefore not allowed to fly front-line combat missions. Instead we continued with our endless programme of training, and that was all. A close comradeship developed between myself and some of the other pilots, such as Franz Strasser and August Braun. Among this

'Papa' Franz Dörr, right, playing cards with mechanic Kargerhuber

circle there was a very special man: the then 'ancient' twenty-eight-year-old Unteroffizier Franz Dörr from Mannheim. We hit it off from the day of our first meeting. Our friendship outlasted the war and even now, although he is no longer with us, he is often in my thoughts. Perhaps back in those days he took me under his wing because, having only just turned twenty-one, I looked more like a young scamp than a dashing fighter pilot and he probably thought I needed protecting against the big bad world. Be that as it may, he acted like a father towards me and started calling me 'Sohndel', or 'laddie'. The older pilots immediately picked up on this nickname, of course, and so 'Sohndel' I remained until the end of the war.

About a week after the invasion of Russia we were ordered to transfer back to the west, this time to Bergen-aan-Zee in Holland. From here JG 3 carried out a few routine coastal patrol flights and these enabled me to feel more and more at home in the cockpit of an Me 109. It was also in Holland that I again finally found the time to indulge in my hobby of jazz. I had first developed an enthusiasm for this type of music during my boyhood days in the Saarland when the French and English radio stations used to broadcast American jazz. In Germany at that period such music was very much frowned upon and it was almost impossible to get jazz records. But in Holland there was no such problem. I rummaged around in the little Dutch radio shops and bought as many records as I could afford. Within a short while I had amassed a collection of over a hundred discs which, often to the distress of my room-mates, I would play one after the other until lights out.

Myself and mechanic Kargerhuber

With a girlfriend
and record player
at Bergen-aan-Zee,
Holland, summer
1941

It was towards the end of summer 1941 that our unit first made the acquaintance of the enemy. After the heavy losses suffered by the Luftwaffe during the Battle of Britain, and the subsequent transfer of most of its units to the eastern front, a strengthened RAF went over to the offensive. At the beginning of August 1941 a number of British bomber formations flew low-level sweeps over Holland. On 20 August several pilots of our Staffel took off to combat another of these incursions. After landing, Leutnant Joachim Kirschner reported his – and the unit's – first victory. And on the following morning, 21 August, our pilots tangled with some Spitfires of 130 Squadron RAF, which were escorting two waves of Blenheim bombers. Over the west coast of Holland Unteroffizier Werner Schumacher brought down the Spitfire flown by William Roy Bloyce; another of the Spitfires fell victim to Flak.

In the meantime English bombers were also regularly undertaking harassing attacks and night raids on Germany's towns and cities. On one occasion, while carrying out an early-morning patrol with Franz Dörr, I spotted a low-flying aircraft beneath me in the dawn light. It was heading west and proved to be a four-engined bomber. After Dörr and I had identified the machine as a Handley-Page Halifax, we dived to the attack. My short bursts of fire hit the bomber's right wing, causing it to stream a white trail of some escaping liquid or other. To avoid further damage, the Halifax dived even lower into a thick layer of cloud

only about 50 metres above the surface of the sea. Just as I had made out its shadow and was about to open fire again, Franz Dörr's voice came over the R/T: 'Sohndel, I've got a problem with my machine – the oil temperature is much too high and it's still rising!'

If an engine is overheating, especially when flying over water, there is only one course of action to take: head straight back to base without delay. On the one hand, I desperately wanted to finish off the bomber; on the other, it was clear that I had to escort my friend and leader back home immediately. I quickly carried out another attack on the Halifax, setting its right wing and starboard outer engine on fire. Unfortunately, as Franz Dörr was fully preoccupied with his ailing Messerschmitt, he was unable to observe my second attack. I would dearly have liked to return to base with my first victory. The burning bomber could not have remained in the air much longer, that's for sure, but whether the crew ever got back to their homeland again will remain one of the many unsolved minor mysteries of the war. We left the scene of the action and flew back to our field.

Shortly after the RAF's incursions over Holland had become the daily norm, we were transferred up into an altogether quieter Denmark. We touched down at Esbjerg, our new base, at the beginning of September 1941. In addition to my cherished record collection, I also took along a portable record

Cockpit readiness with Erg./JG 3. Our Me 109s were already wearing the later Staffel badge of 7./JG 5

player and, for safety's sake, a plentiful supply of replacement needles. At this stage of the war the RAF was leaving Danish airspace pretty much alone, so it must have been pure coincidence that the English happened to send over a small formation of bombers one night in October to attack Esbjerg harbour. Franz Dörr, in the meantime promoted to Feldwebel, described to me how he shot down a Wellington. After this the Denmark of 1941 sank back into a state of such tranquillity that it might just as well have been peacetime.

Staffelkapitän Oberleutnant von Sponeck didn't let us ease up on our training, however. Flying and fighter practice continued unabated, and we soon began to regard ourselves as the absolute experts on the Me 109. Although I was already fed up to the back teeth with the monotony of training, I am still convinced to this day that the constant round of dry-run exercises – we used to call them 'Graf Sponeck's aerial numbers' – increased my chances of survival in later air combat many times over.

Quiet days while still with JG 3 in France: in the centre is Staffelkapitän Hans-Curt Graf von Sponeck

After the death of Generaloberst Ernst Udet, who committed suicide on 17 November 1941, the name of this legendary flyer was enshrined in the new title of our unit: 'Jagdgeschwader 3 Udet'. By now the offensive of our forces on the eastern front had come to a grinding halt. On the southernmost flank of the Russian front Generaloberst Graf von Sponeck, the father of our Staffelkapitän, was commanding an Army Corps at Kerch on the eastern tip of the Crimean peninsula. At the end of December 1941 the Soviets carried out an amphibious landing on the southern coast of the Crimea to the rear of his armies. Because he considered the position untenable, the General – contrary to High Command's orders to hold the positions – instructed his troops to pull back. The Reich's leadership interpreted this as cowardice in the face of the enemy. General von Sponeck was relieved of all of his duties and put before a court-martial. He was sentenced to death, but this was later commuted to imprisonment and he was incarcerated in Germersheim military gaol.

On 29 December 1941 Ergänzungsjagdgruppe 3 received an order from Reichsmarschall Göring. Our Staffel was now to be made operational and, with effect from 1 January 1942, was to be redesignated to become 7. Staffel of Jagdgeschwader 5. Göring's teleprint further instructed Staffelkapitän Hauptmann von Sponeck to transfer the unit at once to Bodø in Norway. We were all confined to base, and those who happened to be away on leave were ordered to report back immediately.

The family coat-of-arms of the Counts von Sponeck became the Staffel badge of 7./JG 5

Christmas 1941 at Esbjerg: on the wall is the coat-of-arms of Staffelkapitän von Sponeck, front row, third from left

5 Transfer to the far North

The 7. Staffel of the III. Gruppe of Jagdgeschwader 5 was made up primarily of NCOs and other ranks. Hauptmann Graf von Sponeck and Leutnant Fritz Simme were the unit's only officers. The backbone of the Staffel was composed of Feldwebeln Franz Dörr and Franz Strasser, Unteroffiziere August Braun, Hans Link, Helmut Klante, Kurt Philipp, Werner Schumacher and myself, and the two Obergefreiter, Richard Steinbach and Kurt Scharmacher. All preparations for the transfer to the north were carried out with the utmost haste. Early in the afternoon of 30 December 1941 our Staffel lifted off from Esbjerg for the last time. We crossed the Skagerrak at an altitude of 500 metres. After following Norway's mountainous south-western coastline for a short distance, we turned in towards the little town of Kristiansand, whose airfield, situated right on the coast, boasted a concrete runway.

As I entered the landing pattern I saw Hauptmann Sponeck's machine on its final approach. He was the first to land. Touching down, he rolled smoothly along the runway, but suddenly he started to slide to one side and ended up standing his aircraft on its nose. The second Messerschmitt landed, and the same thing happened again. Then the third repeated the whole sorry process. By the time it was my turn to put down, I had realised what the trouble was: the entire runway was one huge sheet of ice. I therefore let my aircraft roll almost the whole length of the runway before gently applying the brakes.

From the left, Link, myself, Schumacher, Scharmacher, and Klante

Even so, my Me performed a ground loop before finally coming to a stop. Although no one was seriously hurt in these accidents, von Sponeck was beside himself with rage and stormed off to flying control. We subsequently learned that at all airfields situated directly on the coast in these northern latitudes sudden side winds were an ever-present threat, particularly so at this time of the year when the winds blowing off the sea could turn the damp runways into skating rinks in a matter of moments. As repairs to the machines took several days, we were able to join in the New Year's celebrations in the NCOs' mess at Kristiansand before setting off on 2 January 1942 on the second stage of our journey, which would take us to Stavanger. Two aircraft were still not yet fully airworthy so had to be left behind with their pilots; they were to follow us a few days later.

The airfield at Stavanger, further along the south-west coast of Norway, possessed a large maintenance hangar, where we had the tailwheels of our machines locked in place. This meant they could no longer swivel from side to side while taxiing, and our Me 109s would be less susceptible to crabbing sideways during take-offs and landings. The few days we spent at Stavanger passed fairly quietly. There were emergency scrambles now and again, but no enemy aircraft were ever encountered. Instead, we were treated to magnificent aerial views of the Norwegian landscape. As I had always been a lover of nature, the wonders I got to see during these flights made a deep impression on me: the blue and emerald-green waters of the fjords, rivers and lakes standing out against the snow-covered mountains, the seemingly endless vistas of forests, broken here and there by clearings, each with a small red-painted hut so typical of the region. With such scenes of natural unspoilt beauty, Norway must be one of the most attractive and peaceful countries on earth, I thought to myself. After leaving Stavanger we continued our journey northwards along the Norwegian coast. We crossed the broad expanse of Hardanger Fjord and prepared to put down on the island airfield of Herdla, close to Bergen.

'This time I don't want to see any landing accidents,' Staffelkapitän von Sponeck had warned us prior to taking off from Stavanger. Despite this admonition, the last machine but one to touch down ended up on its nose. The pilot was uninjured, however, and the Me 109 only slightly damaged.

At the end of January 1942 we were given a number of Messerschmitts that had previously seen service with other units. Even though these were only Me 109E-7 variants, which were already obsolescent when compared to the new F models, they nonetheless helped to bring our Staffel up to the not inconsiderable strength of some fifteen Messerschmitt 109s.

Heavy snowfalls and persistent fog kept us on the ground at Herdla for several days then, when the skies cleared, we resumed our flight to Bodø. Our next stop en route was the airfield at Trondheim-Vaernes. Equipped with ventral fuel tanks, we made the approximately 450km hop in one go. We didn't stay long at Trondheim, merely putting down to refuel. On 1 February 1942 we landed at what was initially intended to be our final destination, Bodø, an airfield some 1,000km to the north of Kristiansand. During the coming weeks our Staffel was entrusted with a threefold task: to patrol the Narvik-Lofoten Islands airspace to

Transfer to the Far North: the flight legs were Esbjerg-Kristiansand-Stavanger-Herdla-Trondheim-Bodø

The island airfield of Herdla near Bergen

the north of Bodø up to a distance of 50km out to sea and protect it against enemy air and sea incursions; to provide protection for our own naval units in the same area; and to defend an important industrial plant situated on the shores of a fjord close to the Arctic Circle. To carry out these duties the Staffel was placed on constant readiness: every day a Schwarm of four machines was held at three-minute cockpit readiness, another Schwarm placed at fifteen-minute readiness, and the remainder of the Staffel kept on standby.

During this time our Staffelkapitän learned to his great relief that, on 22 February 1942, Hitler had repealed the death sentence against his father and commuted it to six years'

confinement in a military fortress. But this was to prove nothing more than a respite. For later, after the 20 July 1944 plot to assassinate Hitler, factions within the SS accused the General of being in league with the group of conspirators around Graf von Stauffenberg. Before he was executed on Himmler's orders on 23 July 1944, General von Sponeck is reputed to have said: 'For forty years I have served my beloved Fatherland as a soldier and an officer. Today I end my life in the hope of a better Germany.'

As winter drew to a close all Luftwaffe units based in Norway under the command of Generaloberst Hans-Jürgen Stumpff were reorganised. At the beginning of 1942 the various fighter units in the Luftflotte 5 area had

An RAF aerial reconnaissance photo of Bodø, showing the airfield and harbour area

been amalgamated into one formation: Jagdgeschwader 5. Major Gotthard Handrick, who had won the gold medal in the modern pentathlon at the 1936 Berlin Olympics, was appointed as the Geschwader's first Kommodore. Since the outbreak of the war with the Soviet Union, those elements of Luftflotte 5 serving under Generalleutnant Alexander Holle, the Fliegerführer Nord, had been responsible for the outermost northern flank of the eastern front. The Fliegerführer's forces consisted of bombers, dive-bombers, reconnaissance aircraft and a Gruppe of fighters. It was this latter Jagdgruppe that had been redesignated to become II. Gruppe of Jagdgeschwader 5. The unit's 6. Staffel, led by Oberleutnant Horst Carganico, was to achieve widespread fame. Meanwhile, the new III. Gruppe was being formed around Hauptmann Graf von Sponeck's 7. Staffel. Command of III./JG 5 was entrusted to the very experienced Hauptmann Günther Scholz, who had arrived on the Arctic Ocean front fresh from service with Jagdgeschwader 54. On 22 April 1942 7. Staffel, of which I was a member, landed at Petsamo airfield.

A Lapp boot on the cross of Finland: the Gruppe badge of III./JG 5

The badge of JG 5, the 'Eismeer' or 'Arctic Ocean' Geschwader

The transfer of 7. Staffel from Bodø to Petsamo, seen here during the stop en route at Banak

Hauptmann
Günther Scholz,
first Kommandeur
of III./JG 5

Major Gotthard
Handrick, first
Kommodore of JG 5

General Holle,
Fliegerführer Nord

General Stumpff, GOC Luftflotte 5

6Petsamo

The Norwegian coastline, with all its many fjords, bays and peninsulas, stretches over a total length of several thousand kilometres. The climate varies from the temperate weather zones in the south to the inhospitable conditions of the far north. In those days the northernmost tundra regions of Norway and Russia were separated geographically by the Finnish corridor, 30-60km wide, which afforded northern Finland access to the Barents Sea. It was through this corridor that the Petsamo Joki, or River Petsamo, flowed from south-west to north-east before emptying its cold waters into the Barents Sea. Today, Norway and northern Russia share a common border through the tundra region. Where the River Petsamo widened out into an inlet lay the tiny community of Petsamo, now known as Pechenga, in an area which encompassed the strategically important ice-free port of Liinakhamari and some of the richest iron and nickel ore deposits in the world.

Slightly further upstream to the south-west, on the left bank of the Petsamo Joki, stands an ancient, orthodox monastery dating back to the 16th century. Close by was a large area of open meadow that the Luftwaffe had selected for what was, at first, intended to be a temporary landing ground. This would be my 'home base' for the next 2½ years. By the time of our arrival the airfield already had two runways. One was simply a stretch of the natural terrain, which, when the snow melted during the spring thaw, became so soft as to be completely unusable. The other was surfaced with thick wooden planks to a width of some 50 metres and a length of 1,400

| Petsamo, circa 1942

metres, and was flanked on either side by protective walls of snow 3 metres high. In those early days all the field's facilities were still completely primitive. Our 'quarters' were nothing more than large holes blasted out of the ground like bunkers, over which were stretched octagonal Finnish Army tents to provide accommodation for up to six people. In the middle of each excavation was an iron stove that in winter, or whenever it rained, caused the tent to steam up, adding an almost unbearably high humidity to the already stiflingly musty smell.

Here I was then, in what must have been one of the bleakest and most desolate places on earth. The only point worth mentioning is that Petsamo was, at that time, the largest community in the Finnish Corridor, although most of its roughly 2,000 inhabitants had already been evacuated because of the war. The next largest settlement in the area was the Norwegian fishing port of Kirkenes, which was home to just over 2,500 people. Compared to Petsamo, the Soviet port of Murmansk, some 130km away to the east and with a population numbering more than 20,000, was absolutely huge.

In the left foreground is the bunker accommodation with a Finnish tent stretched on top; on the right is the Petsamo ops room hut

The Arctic Ocean highway through Petsamo, with the airfield on the right

In between operations there were far fewer options for rest and relaxation than we had been accustomed to in France or Holland. The two main alternatives for whiling away our free time were playing table-tennis and sleeping. I soon noticed that up here, far removed from the influences of the Reich, the outlook and behaviour of the front-line pilots was quite different from those in the units I had previously served with – much more free and easy, and a lot less military. I first experienced this when we were invited to dine with our comrades of 6. Staffel. 6./JG 5, also known as the 'Expertenstaffel', had been the first fighter unit in this sector. It had already achieved a remarkable number of victories here on the Arctic Ocean front, and news of its prowess had quickly spread throughout the Luftwaffe. The unit's Kapitän was the Knight's Cross-winner Oberleutnant Horst Carganico, who already had forty kills under his belt. We new boys eagerly soaked up the stories with which the 'veterans' regaled us, although in some cases I got the distinct impression that there was quite a lot of exaggeration involved in their telling.

After we had taken our places at table, two of the 6. Staffel pilots disappeared into another room. 'You must understand,' explained one of those still seated, 'we know the local Ivans very well. They've got a powerful transmitter set up on a mountaintop close to the Kola Inlet, and whenever it's time for a German news bulletin, they drown out our broadcast with their propaganda.' He had hardly finished speaking when the radio, which had been playing music in the background, fell silent. Then a crackling noise came from the loudspeaker and all conversation in the room was stilled.

'Pay attention!' somebody shouted and everyone cocked their ears. Even Hauptmann Graf von Sponeck, who was sitting off to one side with Oberleutnant Carganico, was listening intently. Then we heard a strident voice speaking in German, but with a heavy Russian accent: 'Here is a message for our enemies. We are finally fed up to the back teeth with one of your accursed Messerschmitt pilots!' The voice then sank lower and took on a threatening tone. 'We are referring to Oberleutnant Horst Carganico.' We stared at each other, appalled, then all eyes turned on

Oberleutnant Carganico, Staffelkapitän of 6./JG 5, the 'Expertenstaffel'. Whenever Carganico was shot down, he regularly lost his shoes. On his aircraft Mickey Mouse is holding them tightly by the laces

A barefoot Oberleutnant Carganico arrives back safely after having been shot down

Oberleutnant Carganico – the Russians even know our names! 'This Carganico will pay for everything he has done to us. We'll soon have him in our hands, and then things will get really nasty for him!'

Startled, Carganico jumped up from his chair. 'Herr von Sponeck, did you hear that? It's unbelievable – they're trying to put the wind up me. They're trying to frighten me, so I'll do it in my pants and never fly across the front line again!'

When the other pilots of 6. Staffel started to roar with laughter, we were at a complete loss. I didn't understand what was going on at all. But the explanation was not long in coming: the two pilots who had earlier left the room had patched themselves through to the loudspeaker via a microphone outside. The whole thing had been a stupid prank, and when the man with the 'Russian voice' came back in, tears of laughter were rolling down his cheeks. Personally, I didn't find this nonsense all that amusing, but apparently this was 6. Staffel's

way of demonstrating to us their devil-may-care attitude to the war and front-line operations.

There were, of course, other means of making our free time more bearable at this desolate outpost in the back of beyond. On the banks of the Petsamo Joki there was a sauna that we visited once a week. Also, I was overjoyed when I heard that there was a Leutnant in 6. Staffel who shared my enthusiasm for jazz music. His name was Heinrich Ehrler and he introduced us to the hit tune 'Carry me back to old Virginny'. This song soon became a sort of national anthem for us at Petsamo.

Under the command of the Fliegerführer Nordost, the Luftwaffe units on the Arctic Ocean front had been assigned a wide variety of tasks:

Support of the Finnish Army; our allies in the fight against Russia.

Protection of our shipping convoys coming from the North Cape and sailing round the Varanger Peninsula on their way to the ice-free ports of Kirkenes and Petsamo to bring supplies to our troops.

Escorting our bombers and dive-bombers during their attacks along the Kola Inlet, on the harbour installations at Murmansk, and on the Kirov railway line skirting the White Sea.

Destruction of the Allied Arctic convoys coming in across the Barents Sea – to the north and east of the Rybachi, or Fisherman's Peninsula – en route for the Kola Inlet and the ice-free port of Murmansk bringing Lend-Lease supplies of aircraft, tanks, trucks, munitions, spare parts, etc.

Providing aerial support for General Dietl's 20th Mountain Army along the River Litza front.

Defence of the large iron-ore and nickel mines in the Petsamo region.

I./StG 5, a dive-bomber Gruppe equipped with Ju 87s, was employed in carrying out attacks on the harbour installations at Murmansk and on the Kirov railway line that connected the port with the Russian hinterland. In addition, the unit's Stukas were tasked with knocking out the Soviet airfields surrounding Murmansk and with relieving the pressure on our ground troops by low-level strikes on Soviet positions. Twin-engined Ju 88s of KG 30, the 'Eagle' Geschwader, mounted constant attacks on enemy convoys and on Murmansk. Anti-shipping operations were also sometimes flown by the torpedo-equipped He 111s of I./KG 26, but these mostly took place far out over the Barents Sea. In order to perform its primary task of flying escort to the bombers and dive-bombers, as well as to the slow Henschel Hs 126 tactical reconnaissance machines of 1.(H)/32, Jagdgeschwader 5 had at its disposal five Staffeln of Me 109s: the fourth, fifth, sixth, seventh and eighth. These Me 109 Staffeln were dispersed on a number of fields including, among others, Petsamo, Rovaniemi, Salmijärvi and, somewhat further to the south, Alakurtti. The twin-engined Me 110 Zerstörer of 13.(Z)/JG 5 were based at Kirkenes. Along the line of the River Litza, which ran some 45km to the south-east of Petsamo airfield, the troops of General Eduard Dietl's 20th Mountain Army

were facing the 14th Soviet Army, together with marines and other units of the Soviet Northern Fleet. Unlike most of the other sectors on the eastern front, the fighting in this area of the Arctic had frozen into a form of static or trench warfare. But with Murmansk not far to their rear, the Soviets at least had the advantage of home territory at their backs. As their only ice-free port in the Far North, this town was of the greatest importance to the Russians. Since the autumn of 1941 the Allies had been delivering a constant stream of war material to the Soviet Union, and Murmansk was the only port where unloading could continue throughout the long winter months.

In 1942 the German Luftwaffe was still numbered among the world's most modern air forces. Nonetheless, certain shortcomings were already beginning to make themselves felt, and often these could only be made good by resorting to improvisation. For example, we were often sent into regions that were completely unknown to us, and had to fly missions without any prior opportunity to familiarise ourselves with the terrain. To try to keep one's bearings over the desolate wastes of the tundra with none of today's modern navigational aids was more than adventure enough in itself. There were hardly any houses or settlements, very few roads and no railway

A Junkers Ju 87 Stuka of I./StG 5

Reconnaissance
machines of
1.(H)/32: a Focke-
Wulf Fw 189 in
foreground, and a
Henschel Hs 126
behind

lines to provide points of reference. The inhospitable landscape was dominated by vast tracts of treeless tundra, and from the air one could see that the entire wilderness was a confused maze of lakes, swamps, moors, hills and mountains. Wherever one looked, the surface of the sterile and stony soil was littered with a haphazard scattering of rocks and boulders. In wintry weather orientation became the biggest problem of all. Icy storms, extreme cold, thick fog and the Polar darkness made our life on the ground bad enough, but in the air such conditions often got us into severe difficulties, sometimes even into hopeless situations. Upon my arrival at Petsamo at the end of April 1942, snow still lay thick on the ground. When I first saw the terrain below from the cockpit of my Me 109, it seemed as if I was flying over a snow-covered moonscape. But after a while I began to be able to find my way around, using distinctively shaped hills, lakes and rocks to pinpoint my position. In addition, the fixed front line between ourselves and the Russians could be distinguished fairly easily from the air by the craters left by the never-ending artillery duels.

There were three ways of getting from Petsamo to Murmansk on the Kola Inlet. The first was to follow the rocky coastline eastwards. This took you across the neck of the Rybachi Peninsula and along the shores of Motovski Bay to the north of the River Litza. After about another 50km to the east, the shoreline made a sudden sweep southwards to form the entrance to the Kola Inlet. From here you simply flew south along the hilly banks of the Kola until Murmansk appeared in front of you. The second, more direct, route was to follow the dirt road that linked Petsamo to Ura Guba on the Russian side of the border. From the air in winter, this road looked for all the world like a brown line somebody had drawn

in the snow. If neither of these two options was feasible, the only alternative was to navigate by compass. This had to be done whenever a ground mist suddenly swept in from the Arctic Ocean, which happened all too often in this region of changeable weather. But we didn't trust our compasses up here so close to the Pole, and certainly not when flying over the iron-ore mines, which made the compass needles go haywire. Lying parallel to our airfield was a long, low hill. Such was our relief when we saw this ridge rising up out of the mist as we returned to base on instruments that we christened it 'Salvation Mountain'.

Our opponents were organised into various Soviet commands. The largest of these was the air force of the Soviet Northern Fleet, which, at the time of my arrival in Petsamo, comprised some two hundred aircraft of every type and kind. Murmansk also had its own aerial defence units totalling about another hundred machines dispersed on several fields close to the town. At first the Russians flew their ageing Ratas, which were markedly inferior to our Me 109s. But the numbers and types of Soviet-flown aircraft were to increase within a very short space of time. Much of the war material supplied to the Soviet Union by the Western Allies under the terms of the Lend-Lease agreement was delivered by Arctic convoys rounding the North Cape. The destination for the vast majority of the ships involved – and in winter for every single one of them – was the ice-free port of Murmansk, where they were unloaded. But before the supplies they had delivered could be despatched southwards to the main fighting fronts, the local Soviet air fleet commander up here in the north appropriated a large proportion of the newly arrived Hurricanes, Kittyhawks and Airacobras to supplement his own strength. However, these Western fighters didn't pose too serious a threat to us either.

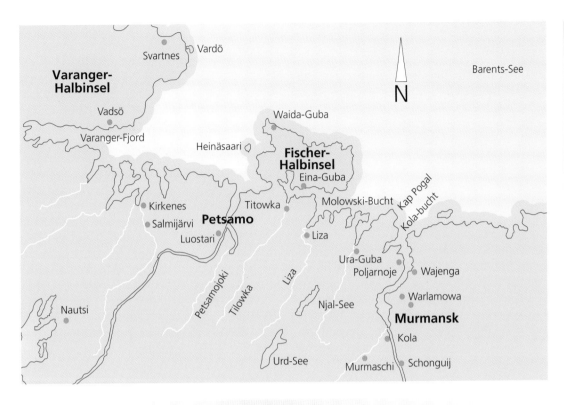

Operational areas around Motovski Bay, the Kola Inlet, Murmansk and the Varanger and Rybachi (Fisherman's) Peninsulas. The German areas are marked in blue with the Russian areas being in red

'Salvation Mountain', the ridge overlooking Petsamo airfield

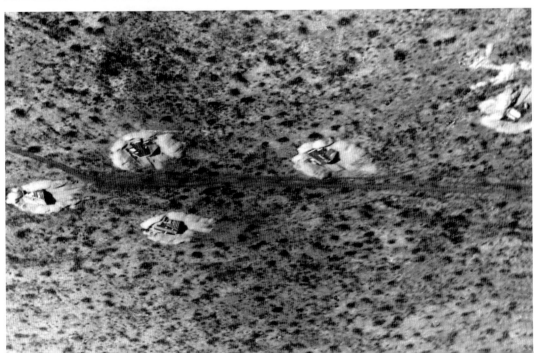

The tundra 'moonscape', showing enemy positions

While we were still flying the Me 109E-7, the experts of 6. Staffel had already been equipped with new Me 109Fs and were using them to mount 'freie Jagd' sweeps, or free-ranging patrols, over Russian territory. Almost every day they would return to Petsamo waggling their wings to indicate yet more aerial victories. We asked ourselves time and time again why the Russians made it so easy for us to shoot them down, and why they sacrificed their pilots so needlessly. For an explanation to make any sense, there had to be other factors involved. Initially, Russian pilots were quite poorly trained; their schooling was clearly of much shorter duration than the training we were given. The air combat tactics drilled into them by their flying instructors were long out of date. But the Russian pilots stuck rigidly to what they had been taught, even when they found themselves involved in a fight that demanded a rapid rethink of their situation. Thus we could usually rely on enemy aircraft always to approach at the same altitude, and always to engage us in the same inflexible formations. The mystery was cleared up when a number of Russian pilots shot down and subsequently captured told us that they didn't belong to a front-line unit at all, but were just ferry pilots. The job of these men, who had probably never been to a fighter training school in their lives

and didn't know the first thing about air combat tactics, was simply to fly the Allied machines unloaded at Murmansk to airfields in the Russian rear areas or to some other critical sector of the eastern front. Instead, they had been 'press-ganged' by the air arm of the Soviet Northern Fleet and thrown into battle in our region. Although there must have been any number of very experienced Soviet pilots, the majority of our opponents at this time were complete novices. Little wonder that most encounters ended in our favour.

Because of the unimaginable quantity of aircraft supplied by the Allies, however, our early air superiority was not to last for long. According to my information, by the war's end the western powers had delivered more than 11,000 fighters to the Russians: this included Hawker Hurricanes, Curtiss P-40 Kittyhawks and Warhawks, Vickers Supermarine Spitfires and Bell P-39 Airacobras. In addition to this, they also supplied more than 3,700 Douglas Boston and North American Mitchell bombers. Soon the Russians were also introducing newer and more dangerous variants of their own indigenous LaGG, MiG and Yak fighters, which they likewise sent to the front in huge numbers.

During our first weeks at Petsamo, however, there were only a few confrontations between our 7. Staffel and the Russian enemy. Staffelkapitän Graf von Sponeck had selected

Rocky terrain in the Far North

Unteroffizier Werner Schumacher as his wingman. Schumacher was an outstanding fighter pilot and excellent table-tennis player, but it was his relaxed attitude and typical Berliner's cheek that seemed to appeal to the Staffelkapitän. When the pair set off on a freie Jagd on 23 April the result was a couple of Hurricanes, one for each of them, to add to the Staffel's scoreboard. Five days later Schumacher was credited with two more Hurricanes. The rest of us weren't permitted to fly freie Jagd sweeps all that often. Our duties consisted in the main of rendezvousing over the Litza front with bombers or Stukas returning from raids on Murmansk and escorting them back to base, or operating in pairs as fighter cover for reconnaissance aircraft.

of 8. Staffel got another. My first Stuka escort mission to Murmansk almost took my breath away: as we approached the harbour area the whole sky was nothing but a mass of black clouds from exploding anti-aircraft shells. It hardly seemed possible to me that any aircraft could survive in such an inferno. Yet while we were flying a wide arc to avoid the worst of the barrage, the Stukas had somehow managed to penetrate this black wall and hit their targets. It appeared that on this occasion the Russian anti-aircraft gunners, normally so dangerous and rightly feared, had somehow failed to concentrate their fire properly.

The greatest problem of all was the lack of darkness during the short summer months. This was the 'land of the midnight sun' where,

Towards the end of April and beginning of May I flew several missions escorting Ju 87 Stukas attacking a small Russian force that had carried out an amphibious landing on the shores of Motovski Bay. During one such operation on 9 May my friend Franz Dörr and Unteroffizier Kurt Philipp claimed a Hurricane apiece, and on 14 May Feldwebel Heinz Beyer

from the middle of May until the end of July, the sun never set. During my first summer in the Far North I found it almost impossible to sleep, let alone get used to its being daylight around the clock. Then at the beginning of May 1942, much to everyone's surprise, it started to snow again. When it thawed, the ground, mainly covered in sphagnum moss –

Staffelkapitän Hauptmann Graf von Sponeck (right)

Feldwebel Heinz
Beyer of 8. Staffel

From the left, Klante, Dörr, Schumacher,
Scharmacher and Steinbach

known up here as reindeer-moss – turned into a swamp. And before the onset of the really hot summer weeks, this brought something else to plague us – mosquitoes and gnats, which appeared in enormous swarms and fell upon everything and anything that had blood running through its veins.

On 15 May I was one of eight pilots ordered to cockpit readiness. Although it was already getting on for evening, the sun was still creeping along the horizon and resolutely refused to disappear into the sea. Our two Schwärme of 7. Staffel had been briefed to fly escort for the Ju 88s of KG 30, the 'Eagle' Geschwader, in a raid on Murmansk, and we were to take off when the bombers overflew the Petsamo area. There followed a long wait, during which we occupied ourselves by hunting for mosquitoes. I could see my wingman, Gefreiter Richard Steinbach, slowly losing patience.

At last we heard the welcome drone of the Ju 88 bombers, followed by the shouted order 'Scramble!' Our Daimler-Benz engines coughed into life, cockpit canopies were slammed shut, and we began to gather speed along the runway. As my Messerschmitt lifted off I was filled with a feeling almost of exuberance. We climbed to an altitude of 3,000 metres and set off in a south-easterly direction in the wake of the bombers, which would soon be crossing the front line. My wingman and I had been ordered to fly close escort to the bombers, while Oberfeldwebel Franz Dörr and Unteroffizier Kurt Philipp were responsible for top cover. Ten minutes after take-off Kommandeur Hauptmann Scholz reported oil pressure problems. He passed the lead over to the Gruppen-Adjutant, Staffelführer Oberleutnant Rudolf Lüder, and headed back to Petsamo. Although it was bitterly cold in the cockpit, I was so excited that sweat was trickling down my forehead. We were now only about 30km from the target area and would soon be meeting the enemy. I scanned the skies while our bombers continued serenely to hold course for Murmansk. Then suddenly I saw them below us to the right: a formation of eight Russian fighters patrolling at a height of some 1,000 metres above the tundra. 'This is White 6, Indians, 90 degrees, one thousand!' There was no reply from the Staffelführer. He appeared not to have heard my message, for he flew blithely on without acknowledging it. Now of all times, with the Russian fighters having spotted us, his R/T had to go on the blink. But with or without permission, I signalled to my wingman, tipped the machine onto its right wing, and dived down.

From the left, Franz Dörr, myself and Richard Steinbach

Oberleutnant
Rudolf Lüder
(second from left)

Oberleutnant Lüder (left) and Staffelkapitän
Graf von Sponeck

A quick look at the altimeter: 1,800 metres. I then turned my full attention back to the Russian fighters. Another glance at the altimeter: 1,500 metres. During the descent my Me 109 had built up so much excess speed that I was frightened I was going to overshoot the slower enemy machines. I eased back on the throttle and tried to pull my aircraft out of its dive as quickly as possible. Although I was exerting all my strength, the stick felt like a ton weight and was extremely slow to respond. After levelling off at about 500 metres, I got my machine under control again and the Messerschmitt began to climb. I was absolutely furious with myself: anybody watching that little demonstration would think I was a complete beginner. The fact that I hadn't already been shot down was due in no small measure to the Russian machines' poor performance. From their long noses I took them to be MiG-3s, accompanied by a number of Hurricanes. While several of the MiGs tried to gain height and get above us, the slower Hurricanes were attempting to form a defensive circle. But one or other of them was always just that little bit too slow getting into position and the circle failed to close. Wringing the last bit of power from the Daimler-Benz engine, I went after the MiGs. As I approached them they scattered in all directions. I selected one of the enemy fighters and opened fire from a distance of 50 metres. The MiG broke away, but I reduced my speed and remained behind it, slightly to the right. When I had it full in my sights again, I let fly at the enemy's tail with all barrels. As I was by this time only about 30 metres away, I could see my HE rounds exploding all over its rear fuselage. At first nothing at all happened: the MiG flew on for a bit longer seemingly quite unconcerned. Then it turned over onto its back, went into a vertical dive trailing black smoke, and smashed into the tundra below.

The battle had taken me back down nearly to ground level again and only now did I realise that I was flying much too slowly. Tracer bullets suddenly began whizzing past my cockpit. I banked hard left and, when the firing stopped, threw a belated glance to the rear, but all I could see behind me was another Messerschmitt – Steinbach's! Had he mistaken my machine for a Russian fighter? Somewhat wound up, I yelled at him over the R/T: 'Richard, stop shooting at me!'

'That wasn't me – I've just shot down the other MiG that was sitting on your tail,' Steinbach replied as cool as you please. I must have turned deathly pale at that moment.

Shortly afterwards we heard the Staffelführer's voice in our headphones. Lüder, who was still flying at 3,000 metres and apparently hadn't noticed the slightest sign of our fight down close to the ground, reported: 'I've had a problem with my electrics. Something must have been going on down there – I saw two aircraft crash and burn. Why did you break formation? Close up again immediately.'

'We've been busy shooting down two Russians,' was Steinbach's casual response.

Although this was my first aerial victory, I derived no real pleasure from it. Instead, I reproached myself bitterly for my carelessness. The torment was slow to release me from its grasp. During the nights that followed I lay awake, tossing and turning in my bed and replaying over and over again in my mind the combat that could so very easily have been my last. 'That was such a close thing, and if Steinbach hadn't been there…' It was only too obvious that I had made every stupid beginner's mistake that there was to be made. I had forgotten to check my tail and had neglected to watch either my height or my speed. I swore to myself never to make the same errors again. In every combat in future I would always do my utmost to regain height as quickly as possible. And I remembered the words of advice an experienced instructor had drummed into me during training: 'Speed is half the key to survival.' For our first victories Kurt Philipp, Richard Steinbach and I were each awarded the Iron Cross, Second Class, on 19 May 1942.

In front of 'White 6' after my first victory

Abschrift.

7./Jagdgeschwader 5
(Dienstgrad, Name, Truppenteil)   Gefechtsstand, den...15.5.42......

1/ Abschussmeldung / Zerstörungsmeldung.

1.) Zeit, (Tag, Stunde, Minute) Gegend d. Abschusses: Höhe:.....15.5.42.
.....18.18 Uhr, Quadrat 37 Ost 20872, 600 m

2.) Durch wen ist der Abschuss / Zerstörung erfolgt:....................
........Uffz. Schuck mit Bf 109 takt. Nr. weiße 6.................
Flugzeugtyp des abgeschossenen Flugzeuges:....Mig 3................

3.) Werknummer bzw. Kennzeichen:......Sowjetstern...............

4.) Staatsangehörigkeit des Gegners:.russisch.................

5.) Art der Vernichtung:
    a) Flammen mit dunkler Fahne, Flammen mit heller Fahne
    b) Einzelteile weggeflogen, abmontiert (Art der Teile erläutern
    ....
    c) Zur Landung gezwungen, diesseits oder jenseits der Front
       glatt bzw. mit Bruch

6.) Art des Aufschlages, nur wenn dieser beobachtet wurde.
    a) diesseits oder jenseits der Front
    b) senkrecht, flachen Winkel, Aufschlagbrand, Schneewolke
    c) nicht beobachtet

7.) Schiksal der Insassen (tot), mit Fallschirm abgesprungen,
    nicht beobachtet

8.) Gefechtsbericht des Schützen ist in der Anlage beigefügt.

9.) Zeugen: Luft: .....Ogfr. Steinbach.....Erde:......./.........

1o.) Anzahl der Angriffe, die auf das feindliche Flugzeug gemacht
     wurden:......1 Angriff

11.) Richtung, aus der der Angriff erfolgte:....hinten rechts.........

12.) Taktische Position, aus der der Abschuss angesetzt wurde:.hinten oben

13.) Entfernung, aus der der Abschuss gemacht wurde:....50 - 30 m.......

14.) Ist einer der feindlichen Bordschützen kampfunfähig gemacht worden:
     ....

15.) Verwandte Munitionsart:.Pmk., SmkL., B-Patr., M 90 gr., Spreng L 115 gr.

16.) Munitionsverbrauch:......60 Schuß M.G., 52 Schuß Kanone

17.) Art und Anzahl der Waffen, die bei dem Abschuss gebraucht wurden:..
     ....2 M.G. 17, 2 Kanonen 2 cm

18.) Typ der eigenen Maschine:....Bf 109 F7

19.) Weiteres taktisch oder technisch bemerkenswertes:........./.......

2o.) Treffer in der eigenen Maschine:.....keine...............

21.) Beteiligung weiterer Einheiten, auch Flak:....../.................

F d R.d.A.

Oblt. u. Offz.z.b.V.

gez. Graf von Sponeck
Hauptmann und Staffelkapitän

Opposite: The official report of my first victory
on 15 May 1942

My Messerschmitt
Bf 109 E-7 'White
6'. With this
aircraft I achieved
my first victory on
15 May 1942. *Kjetil
Akra, 2008*

The Iron Crosses,
2nd Class, awarded
on 19 May 1942.
From the left are
Kurt Philipp, myself,
and wingman
Steinbach

7 First aerial victories

The Allies were organising more and more convoys bringing fresh supplies of war material to the Russians, and the air battles out over the Arctic Ocean now began to heat up. In addition, the Russians were intensifying their bombing raids on all our airfields in the area. These were intended not only to destroy our installations, but were also designed to keep our fighters close to their bases. This meant that they would be unable to maintain the same high degree of protection for our bombers as they had been providing during the anti-shipping operations against the Allied convoys to date. On the late afternoon of 28 May 1942 the Russians selected our airfield at Petsamo as their target. Ilyushin DB-3 and Petlyakov Pe-2 bombers were despatched to plough up our runways and pulverise our ground facilities. Not long before, Stukas and Ju 88s had attacked one of their Arctic convoys almost continuously over a two-day period, and now the Russians were aiming to rectify their mistake of having failed to pin our forces to the ground much earlier.

That afternoon one of our forward air observation posts reported the Russian bombers, escorted by I-16 Ratas and Hurricanes, as they overflew the front lines. Our 7. Staffel was given the order to scramble. On this occasion Gruppenkommandeur Hauptmann Scholz was the first to spot the enemy and I heard his voice in my earphones: 'Achtung! 110 degrees, suspected enemy aircraft. Hold formation and follow me!'

I looked to my right and there, sure enough, a number of tiny black dots were visible against the horizon. Scholz, canny tactician that he was, led half of the Messerschmitts in a long sweeping curve to the left, placing us in position between the Soviet bombers and the sun. The other half of

the Staffel was ordered to fly top cover against the Russians' escorting fighters and remained some 1,800 metres above them. We approached ever closer to the enemy until the bombers suddenly realised we were right on top of them. Without giving a second thought to the fighter escort, we put our noses down and dived on the bomber formation.

Feldwebel Bruno Strasser aimed for the leading machine and set it on fire. Even as this first Ilyushin was falling away, disgorging a thick plume of smoke, Unteroffizier Schumacher pounced on a second, riddling it with bullets and sending that down too. After this Schumacher went after a Pe-2 and, once this was successfully dealt with and had exploded on the ground, he turned his attention to the escorting fighters. Before the action was finally over he had added two Hurricanes to his score. This brought his total for the day to six, for he had already been in a fight with Hurricanes in the morning and had claimed two of their number. Our determined attacks must have rattled the remaining bomber crews so much that they jettisoned their bombs and turned away. I chased after one of the fleeing DBs, crept up close to it and manoeuvred until I had it exactly centred in my reflector sight. Suddenly something rose up out of the bomber's fuselage. The dorsal gunner had got to his feet and was shooting back at me with his machine-gun! A hail of red tracer bullets came at me and I quickly decided that things were getting a bit too hot. I side-slipped to the left, put the Messerschmitt into a dive and, after completing a full 360-degree turn, went after the bomber again. I was now about 400 metres behind him, much too far away to open fire really, but I gave him a burst anyway. More by luck than judgement I hit the Ilyushin, my salvo ripping

Robert Bailey ©2002

'Petsamo Scramble':
a painting by
Robert Bailey
depicting an
emergency
scramble as Russian
fighter-bombers
attack Petsamo
airfield

Gruppenkommandeur Hauptmann Scholz

open the upper surface of the wing between the fuselage and the starboard engine. The engine began to burn and I watched as the pilot fought desperately to crash-land the stricken bomber. Then, as I looked around for another enemy target, there was a sudden loud crack and a stream of ice-cold air poured into the cockpit. A small hole had appeared in the roof of the canopy. I had just registered the fact that I was being shot at when Steinbach's voice came over the R/T: 'Walter, watch out! Indians behind you!' A rapid glance over my shoulder – two enemy fighters, which I identified as Hurricanes, were jockeying into position and preparing to open fire again.

I immediately clawed for height, the Daimler-Benz engine screaming under full power. Below me the two Hurricanes accepted the challenge and climbed up after me. I tried to make my ascent as steep as possible, while at the same time being careful not to exceed the angle at which I knew the aircraft would stall. My two pursuers were still firing at me, but their shots were going wide of my tail. Frustrated, both Soviet pilots pointed the noses of their machines ever more steeply up into the sky, presumably hoping at least for a lucky hit. This was just what I had been banking on. For a few seconds the pair of Hurricanes seemed to hang motionless in the sky, then each tumbled over into a stall.

Recovering and picking up speed in the dive, they were now heading down towards a solitary Messerschmitt flying straight and level. It was Feldwebel Bruno Strasser, who must have momentarily neglected to keep a sharp eye on the airspace around him. From my position above Strasser and the two Russians I could see the danger he was in. I quickly winged over into a dive myself and shouted a warning to Strasser. In sliding to the left to get into a better firing position behind Strasser's fighter, one of the Russians sacrificed some of the speed he had built up. This gave me the chance to close up on him and get on his tail. After a short burst of fire, long strips of metal peeled away from his ailerons and the enemy machine went spinning down out of control. Not waiting to see what happened to him, I now went for the other Hurricane. In order to be able to follow his evasive manoeuvres I had to ease off the throttle. But that robbed me of so much speed that when the Russian pilot suddenly put his heavier machine into another dive he began to pull away from me. I tried to chase after him but soon gave it up as hopeless. When we returned to base the groundcrews greeted us ecstatically. Not only had we successfully foiled the enemy's attempt to bomb our airfield, we had also done so without loss to ourselves and had claimed eight victories into the bargain.

The trackless wastes of the tundra regions combined absolute solitude with a silence so total that it was almost frightening. Between operations I never ceased to be amazed at how quickly the harshly inhospitable conditions of the winter months could change with the advent of

From the left, Franz Dörr, Bruno Strasser and myself

spring. The vegetation up here consisted in the main of low-lying juniper bushes, shrub-like bilberry plants, birch trees, stunted pines, reindeer-moss and lichen. As the days grew longer, it became almost impossible to remain in this area for any length of time, for it was then, especially when there was no breeze, that hundreds and thousands of mosquitoes and gnats went on the warpath. During one of my exploratory walks beyond the airfield perimeter I came across a patch of ground that was covered in mushrooms, each one as big as the palm of my hand. I told the Staffelkapitän of my find and persuaded him to let me borrow his Kübelwagen and driver to go and gather them. When we returned, the jeep-like vehicle was filled to the brim with mushrooms, which I handed over to our head cook, Jupp Heinrichs. He prepared several portions for us to enjoy straight away, but most were hung up to dry as provisions for the winter. Jupp Heinrichs was a fat, cheerful character who, because of his bulk, needed two chairs to support him comfortably when he sat down. I used to enjoy kidding around with him and once even threatened to climb into the boxing ring with him. At this he fairly exploded with laughter, his huge stomach wobbling as though it would never stop: 'Just watch your step, you little half-pint. All I've got to do is take a deep breath and you'll be dangling under my nose like a moustache!'

At the beginning of June the wind turned and brought moist air in from the sea. Thick fog hampered operations for several days. During this period Luftflotte 5 decided it was time to put a stop to the unloading of Allied supplies at Murmansk once and for all. The destruction of the port and harbour installations was given top priority. On the

afternoon of 13 June, after the skies had cleared, we took off on a mission to escort Stukas and Me 110 Zerstörer on their way to Murmansk. During the course of the operation Werner Schumacher shot down a MiG-3 and I got a Hurricane. Shortly prior to this 6. and 8. Staffeln had also returned from a similar mission, with Feldwebel Rudi Müller, the new ace of the Expertenstaffel, having added three more enemy fighters to his score and Heinrich Ehrler claiming one. I was greatly concerned, however, that my friend Unteroffizier Josef Kaiser was missing. But he turned up not long afterwards, on foot and unwounded, explaining that engine damage had forced him to make a belly-landing just before reaching base.

Because of Murmansk's massed anti-aircraft defences, the bomber and Stuka raids on the town's harbour facilities had not achieved the success hoped for. So on 18 June wave after wave of bombers ceaselessly showered the centre of Murmansk with incendiaries. For days afterwards a huge pall of black smoke, towering 6,000 metres into the sky, was visible from afar. It was astonishing what little response these heavy attacks on the town provoked from the Russian fighter units stationed in the area. On 19 June Generaloberst Stumpff, GOC Luftflotte 5, visited us at Petsamo and awarded Feldwebel Rudi Müller with the Knight's Cross. Afterwards he handed out Iron Crosses, First Class, to a number of other pilots, including myself.

On 22 June we ran into a force of about twenty Russian fighters to the east of Murmansk. Although it was already well past 22.00 hours, the light of the midnight sun still enabled us to see the clouds of dark smoke hanging over the town from the fire raids of four days earlier. The

Murmansk after a Stuka raid on the harbour installations

Feldwebel Rudi Müller (right), the ace of 6. Staffel, and Leutnant Heinrich Ehrler

The award certificate of the Iron Cross, 1st Class, signed by Generaloberst Stumpff, GOC Luftflotte 5

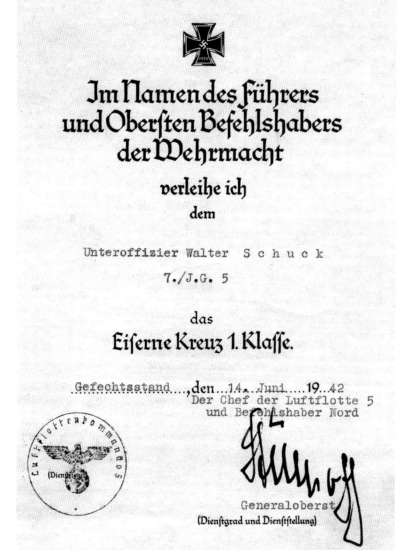

Im Namen des Führers und Obersten Befehlshabers der Wehrmacht

verleihe ich

dem

Unteroffizier Walter Schuck

7./J.G. 5

das

Eiserne Kreuz 1. Klasse.

Gefechtsstand...,den...14...Juni.....19..42
Der Chef der Luftflotte 5
und Befehlshaber Nord

Generaloberst
(Dienstgrad und Dienststellung)

Soviet formation, consisting of Hurricanes and Polikarpov I-180 fighters, immediately turned towards us. Because of its light weight, the I-180, powered by an 1,100hp engine and armed with four 7.62mm machine-guns, was very fast and extremely manoeuvrable. It had already given us a lot more problems than the slower Hurricanes. By this time Unteroffizier Kurt Scharmacher had been appointed my regular wingman. He was the epitome of what I then imagined a typical East Prussian to be: rough, abrupt, boorish and taciturn. But when he did choose to say something in his broad, almost unintelligible dialect, his words held meaning, or they contained a dry humour that took some little while to understand and appreciate. At all events, he was a kind-hearted character and one of the most dependable comrades I ever got to know. Whatever happened, I could always rely on his keeping station and guarding my back during a fight. On this occasion, just as I was concentrating on attacking a Hurricane, another Russian fighter tried to sneak up on my tail. But Scharmacher was fully on top of the situation. The moment I heard his warning yell, 'Walter, break right – now!', I immediately took evasive action as directed. Then his inimitable East Prussian dialect sounded in my headphones again – 'Got him!' – and I saw an I-180 going down in flames. I confirmed Scharmacher's victory, then tucked in behind another of the I-180s and sent that one down too. Five minutes later I claimed a Hurricane, after which our 7. Staffel, having achieved seven victories without loss, returned to base at Petsamo.

One day we received an invitation from our comrades in the Navy, whose destroyers had just escorted a supply convoy into Kirkenes. As they had to wait for the transports to be unloaded before shepherding them back around the North Cape, they had apparently decided to ask us aboard one of their ships as a kind of 'thank you' for the help and support we provided in the air. By the time we realised that the true purpose behind the Navy's invitation was to get us Luftwaffe types roaring drunk, it was already too late for the majority. Days later a number of our pilots were still suffering terrible headaches, and we began to consider ways of getting our own back.

The opportunity didn't arise until the autumn, when we invited the Navy to pay us a visit at Petsamo. After enjoying a meal together, I marched off into the kitchen and started mixing up a brew that we had christened 'Turks' blood'. First I emptied twenty bottles of red wine and eight bottles of corn alcohol into a large cauldron. Next I added a generous amount of sugar and stirred the mixture until the sugar had completely dissolved. The whole lot was then decanted into jugs, which were taken to the table, where several bottles of sparkling wine were poured over them. Because the taste of the red wine masked the sweetness of all the sugar and the aroma of the corn schnapps, the Navy people found the delicious concoction very much to their liking and downed copious amounts of it. Later in the evening, when they were all thoroughly plastered and dancing around the mess hall, the ship's dentist tripped and fell heavily to the floor. Our MO, Dr Schulz-Gericke, diagnosed a broken arm and immediately arranged for his naval colleague to have the fracture put in plaster. This meant, of course, that he would be unable to carry out any dental work in the immediate future. But when he rang a fortnight later to enquire how long his arm would have to remain in plaster, Dr Schulz-Gericke laughingly informed him: 'You can remove it and start pulling your people's teeth again whenever you feel like it. Your arm wasn't broken at all. It was just pay-back time for the thick heads you and your men gave us when you invited us on board your ship!'

The summer may have brought milder temperatures, but there was also a constant strong wind blowing in from the ocean. After the combination of sun and wind had dried out the breeding grounds of the mosquitoes and gnats, these pests seemed to disappear into thin air. In the summer light all the colours of the sky and the landscape suddenly became that much more intense. The previous grey-green waters of the lakes now shimmered a deep, dark blue and the reindeer-moss took on a rich green hue. But there was no time to study the beauty of nature more closely, as the war continued with unabated ferocity. On 28 June there were further heavy attacks by our bombers on Murmansk. During the first of these I flew cover for our Stukas and succeeded in bringing down a Hurricane. My wingman on this date was Unteroffizier Steinbach, who went one better than me by shooting down a Rata and a Hurricane during the second mission of the day. But the laurels once again went to Unteroffizier Werner Schumacher, who ended the day with five victories.

At the beginning of July a battle-damaged Ju 88 landed on our airfield. While the crew of the bomber tucked into a meal, they regaled us fighter pilots with an account of how they had wiped out an entire Allied supply convoy. Their story was confirmed shortly afterwards by a Wehrmacht communiqué, which reported the sinking of more than twenty merchantmen and a heavy cruiser in our area. This time the transports took with them to the bottom of the sea all the war supplies so desperately needed by the Russians, and that gave us something of a breathing space.

Ordered to fly a freie Jagd patrol of the region to the west of Murmansk on 8 July, I bumped into a gaggle of Curtiss P-40 Kittyhawks and shot one of them down. Later in the same engagement the starboard side of my Me escaped by a hair's breadth from being rammed by another Kittyhawk. I instinctively put on hard left rudder, while at the same time yanking the stick in the opposite direction. It was just enough to side-slip the machine to port and the Russian flashed past perilously close to my right wing. When we got back to Petsamo one of our aircraft was missing. It was my friend from JG 3 days, the Austrian Feldwebel Franz Strasser. A search party found his remains near the wreckage of his fighter about halfway between the front line and Petsamo.

The summer of 1942 was hot and dry. The temperatures soared to the mid-eighties and the sun never stopped shining. Above the hills the sky was stained with smoke from burning bushes, birch trees and stunted spruce. Throughout this period we flew practically around the clock. As the sun was still above the horizon at 4.00am, there was hardly any let-up and we were kept at near constant readiness.

8Interlude at Kirkenes

In mid-July 1942 my wingman Scharmacher and I were ordered to Kirkenes as part of a small detached Kommando provided by III./JG 5. Kirkenes airfield was located north-west of the township on a tongue of land jutting out into the waters of the Höybugtmoen, or Bøk Fjord. From the heights above the field there was a marvellous view of the surrounding inlets and the harbour town of Kirkenes itself. A constant sea wind swept across the surface of the airfield, and although this didn't bother the base's resident Me 110 Zerstörer, it made take-offs and landings in our spindly legged, narrow-tracked Me 109s somewhat tricky. The task of the small group to which I was attached was to defend the airspace above Kirkenes harbour. As there were no roads or railway lines up here in this area, all the supplies from our southern depots had to be shipped in by coastal convoys around the North Cape to the harbours of Petsamo-Liinakhamari and Kirkenes. This was a mammoth logistical undertaking, for its wasn't just our airfields that needed supplying; the 40,000 men of the Mountain Army and naval coastal batteries in the area also required provisions, weapons, ammunition, spare parts, etc. Thus our major role at Kirkenes, as at Petsamo, was to protect our own shipping convoys against attack from Russian bombers and torpedo aircraft.

Kirkenes airfield seen from the surrounding heights

As well as Scharmacher and myself, five other pilots made up our group, all of them newcomers from the Reich. Although I was only an Unteroffizier, I was placed in command of the little detachment on the strength of my previous experience. Shortly after our arrival small formations of Russian Petlyakov Pe-2 dive bombers had begun attacking our convoys and the harbour of Kirkenes. Even though these raids were at first little more than pin-pricks, we were given orders to put a stop to them. On 19 July a number of our ships were busy unloading at Kirkenes; others lay at anchor in the fjord outside the harbour awaiting their turn to discharge their cargoes. I considered it highly likely that the Pe-2s would show an interest in these proceedings and held my group at readiness. As expected, the enemy put in an appearance early on the morning of 20 July, whereupon Scharmacher, two of the other pilots and myself took off and started climbing eastwards. As we crossed Kirkenes at about 5,000 metres we saw swathes of smoke hanging above the harbour. It was evident that the Russians had already done their work and that we were unfortunately too late. Shortly afterwards we spotted three bombers over Litza Bay. They were 2,000 metres below us and on an easterly heading, obviously making for home. Ordering the other Rotte, or pair, to stay high and provide top cover, I led Scharmacher down to attack the Pe-2s. My first rounds buried themselves in the lead bomber's starboard engine, and it started to go down, burning like a torch. But long before it hit the ground it was rent by a tremendous explosion and blown to pieces in mid-air.

In the weeks that followed, Kirkenes was spared further attack. Before July drew to a close we were involved in several emergency scrambles, none of which resulted in contact with the enemy. One day Gruppenkommandeur Hauptmann Scholz, whom I greatly respected and got on well with, came to visit us at Kirkenes. He gave us all the news about what had been going on at Petsamo and I could scarcely believe my ears when he said that three pilots of my 7. Staffel – Unteroffiziere Werner Schumacher and Kurt Philipp, and Leutnant Bodo Helms – had just been reported missing during a transfer flight. I did not discover the details behind their loss until much later.

A Rotte (pair) of Me 110 Zerstörer of 13.(Z)/JG 5

At the beginning of August our ground forces, together with Finnish troops, had attempted a breakthrough in the Kestenga-Loukhi area. This sector lay close to the Gulf of Kandalaksha, an arm of the White Sea, some 300km to the south of Murmansk. As the few roads in the region allowed for no major troop movements, the war in the almost primeval forests of northern Karelia was fought between small units of men. To the south-west of Kestenga-Loukhi, near Pontsalenjoki, the Russians had established an airstrip in the middle of the woods, which had been captured by our troops. But after sustained air and ground attacks by the Soviets, it had had to be abandoned again. Then we wrested it back from the Russians; and so it had gone on, with the field exchanging hands several more times.

It was an order calling for the transfer of elements of 7./JG 5, together with a Staffel of Ju 87s of StG 5, down to Pontsalenjoki during one of our periods of occupation that led to the loss of the three pilots mentioned above – Schumacher, Philipp and Helms. Having taken off on 5 August for the flight south, the Me 109s made an intermediate stop at Rovaniemi for refuelling. But when a request was made for the machines' auxiliary belly tanks to be refilled as well, this was refused by Rovaniemi flying control on the grounds of the current shortage of aviation fuel. The second leg of the flight exacted a terrible toll. In order to reach the Pontsalenjoki airstrip with the fuel they had been given, the three Me 109s had to fly at economical cruising speed and thus fell easy prey to the enemy. Schumacher's machine was hit by Russian anti-aircraft fire. Wounded in the thigh, he was forced to make an emergency landing in a forest clearing. Not wanting to abandon his comrade to his fate, Leutnant Helms put down alongside him and tended Schumacher's injury as best he could. Then he prepared to set off on foot through the forest with Schumacher, in the hope of reaching the nearest Finnish positions. Meanwhile Kurt Philipp circled overhead, keeping watch on them until his own fuel ran out and he too was forced to land. All three were subsequently picked up by a Russian patrol. Werner Schumacher, one of our best and most courageous pilots, the former wingman of Staffelkapitän von Sponeck, died in a Russian prisoner-of-war camp early in 1943.

When Hauptmann Scholz arrived for his visit, Scharmacher and I happened to be at readiness. He asked us how long it would take us to get into the air in the event of an emergency scramble.

'According to regulations, three minutes, Herr Hauptmann,' I replied.

'Really?' he responded with feigned interest. Then he changed the subject. Later, when we were sitting chatting in the ops room hut, Scholz suddenly looked at his watch and said quietly, 'Emergency scramble.'

I had already guessed that something of this sort was going to happen, that Hauptmann Scholz would put us to the test, when he had asked me earlier how long it would take to get off the ground. That's why, when Scholz wasn't looking, I had motioned to Scharmacher to stay by his machine. I had also taken the precaution of opening the hut window and placing a chair beneath it. Hardly had Scholz murmured 'Emergency scramble' than I was out of the window and racing to my aircraft yelling, 'Alarm! Immediate emergency scramble!'

I reached my machine in a flash, climbed up onto the wing and swung myself into the cockpit. Two men turned the crank of the inertia starter and I pulled the starter handle. The engine spat out a few puffs of smoke, sprang suddenly into life, and the canopy was slammed shut. Without bothering to buckle my parachute or fasten my seat harness, I released the brakes of the Messerschmitt and poured on the gas. Scharmacher, who had been ready before me, followed hot on my heels. As we roared along the runway, airfield control sent up a volley of red flares indicating that we had not been given permission to take off. Too late – I already had the throttle fully forward and the tailwheel of the Me 109 was off the ground. If I eased off the power and braked now, I would almost certainly either swing off the runway or ground-loop and stand the aircraft on its nose, maybe even write it off completely. Our Messerschmitts lifted off and as we banked away more flares arced into the sky – green this time, the signal to land immediately. After we had done so and taxied across to our dispersal area a delighted Hauptmann Scholz was already there waiting for us.

'Well, Schuck, how long did it take you?' he asked.

'Inside the required three minutes, I would guess, Herr Hauptmann,' I replied.

'Three minutes? You did it in less than two. That's very good, I must say. In fact, it's excellent!' Then he enquired whether I wanted to return to 7. Staffel. I knew, however, that Scharmacher and I had already been selected to join the newly activated 9. Staffel, and therefore requested permission to fly with the ninth after I got back to Petsamo.

An armourer working on the MG 17 nose machine-guns

For us pilots of the 7./JG 5 detachment at Kirkenes, August 1942 also remained unusually quiet. In contrast, the crews of the field's resident Me 110 Staffel had their hands more than full. They were flying escort missions for Ju 88 bombers, Ju 87 Stukas and the aircraft of the region's air-sea rescue services, and carrying out low-level bombing raids along the Litza front, over the Varanger, Rybachi and Kola Peninsulas, against the enemy's airfields around Murmansk, and along the Kirov and Murmansk railway lines. They were also flying land and sea reconnaissance, undertaking meteorological flights, anti-submarine patrols, and providing air cover for our own supply shipping. As there was no sign of Russian fighters in the Kirkenes area during this period, we single-engined pilots were rarely called upon to scramble.

However, I didn't want to get rusty, so I used the time to further my mastery of the Me 109. Under simulated combat conditions I participated in mock dogfights, I tried out new aerobatic manoeuvres, practised how best to shake an enemy off my tail, and how to keep a watch on the surrounding airspace at all times, even in the hardest fight. During any violent manoeuvre, such as a flick roll for example, enormous centrifugal forces are created and the rudder pedals become extremely heavy. To control an aircraft in a really savage dogfight or during high-speed aerobatics a lot of physical strength is required. If my strength proved insufficient during a steep climb, say, I would pull back on the stick with my right hand as usual, but support it with my left forearm. In certain manoeuvres I would also make full use of the large tailplane trim wheel down beside my seat. Spinning this wheel rapidly would, admittedly, cause the whole aircraft to shudder and vibrate badly, but it gave me an extra edge during sharp turns.

The sudden transition from a steep climb into a dive didn't just give the pilot a momentary feeling of weightlessness, it also filled the cockpit with all the dirt and muck that had gathered on the floor. Even if the groundcrew

An Me 110 on the landing approach over Heu Bay, Kirkenes

Wireless operator/air gunner Gerhard Sarodnik

swept the cockpit clean before every flight –
there were no vacuum cleaners up here on the
Arctic front – the pilot couldn't avoid bringing in
fresh dirt on his boots when he next climbed
into the aircraft. And in winter there would be
snow, mud and water as well. It was particularly
unpleasant if, when looping or rolling, all this
accumulated filth flew into your face, covered
your goggles and oxygen mask, and got down
your collar and neck. That is why I took to
wearing a yellow scarf – it wasn't just to look
'snappy'. Besides, the bright yellow colour
might also help the air-sea rescue services to
spot me if I were shot down over the sea and
found myself floating about in the water.

While at Kirkenes I also took the
opportunity to get to know some of the pilots
permanently stationed there. Among the
members of the Zerstörerstaffel was a certain
Oberfeldwebel Theodor 'Theo' Weißenberger,
who would later go on to achieve an incredible
string of successes. Weißenberger didn't just fly
with his head – he was a virtuoso, the complete
master of his aircraft and a natural flyer. What
he could make a machine do in the air very few
were able to emulate. Although he was then
flying the twin-engined Me 110, an altogether
slower and much more cumbersome aircraft
than the nimble Me 109, he had already
amassed twenty-three victories against the
Russians, most of them fighters. Among the
units based at Kirkenes was a long-range
reconnaissance Staffel, the Stukas of StG 5 and
the squadron to which Weißenberger
belonged, 13.(Z)/JG 5, the so-called
'Dackelstaffel'. One of the Zerstörer unit's crew
members had brought a dachshund, or
'Dackel', with him to Kirkenes. Almost
immediately upon its arrival in the Arctic the
Staffel had shot down a Lockheed Hudson
maritime reconnaissance aircraft, and their
Dackel mascot was promptly rechristened
'Lockheed'. Since that time the Staffel's aircraft
had sported a unit badge showing a
dachshund with a Russian Rata aircraft
clamped in its jaws, and 13.(Z)/JG 5 became
known to us all simply as the 'Dackelstaffel'.

Oberleutnant Karl
Fritz Schlossstein,
Staffelkapitän of
13.(Z)/JG 5

'Lockheed' a Rata eating dachshund was the Staffel badge of 13.(Z)/JG 5

Theodor Weißenberger initially flew with the Zerstörer

An Me 110 tailfin scoreboard

The custom of having squadron or personal mascots, particularly dogs, dated back to the First World War and was a tradition that was carried into our Luftwaffe. Most such dogs were pets brought from home, not just for company but also to provide their owners with at least a small reminder of their earlier civilian lives. These animals were soon so smart that they could identify each aircraft by its engine noise alone and knew exactly when it was their master who was coming in to land. There were also cases of dogs suddenly becoming listless, trembling all over or howling piteously when their owners were away flying a mission. Then one could be fairly certain that something untoward must have happened and that the dog's master had either been wounded or would not be returning at all. The animal would of course immediately be adopted by one of the other pilots who would try to comfort it as best as he could. But some dogs pined so much for their missing master that they would refuse to eat, or ran away to search for him.

During my free time I continued to explore my surroundings, enjoying the wild beauty of nature. September had brought with it a lot of rain, and the air was fresh and clear. The days were becoming shorter, and at night it was at long last possible to sleep again.

7. Staffel's mascot 'Biene' (above) and (below) her puppy, my dog 'Mischka'

9 Burning ice

At the beginning of September 1942, once 9./JG 5 had been brought up to full operational establishment, we were transferred from Kirkenes back to Petsamo. The officer appointed to be our Staffelkapitän, Hauptmann Gerhard Wengel, was a straightforward type whose only concern was the flying abilities of those serving under him. In addition to Scharmacher and myself, the new Staffel was further strengthened by Richard Luy, Feldwebel Oskar Timm and Unteroffiziere Link and Friedrich Rennemann. Leutnant Günther Fuhrmann and Unteroffiziere Klaus Betz and Hans Thomann, who were fresh from fighter training school, were likewise assigned to 9. Staffel. In mid-September I received some sad news: Unteroffizier August Braun, my friend

Helping to strengthen 9. Staffel were Oskar Timm (right) and Unteroffizier Link (above)

from 7. Staffel, had been shot down over enemy territory and was officially posted missing. Braun came from Saarbrücken and in the past we had often sat together and chatted about the good old times in the Saarland. Losing Braun, it was as if my links with home had been severed.

Finally, and not before time, our rather war-weary Me 109E-7s were replaced by Me 109F-4s. However, by now the 'Friedrich' itself had, in turn, already been superseded by the new 'Gustavs' currently entering service in the homeland. Because of this continuing practice of supplying us with mainly second-rate equipment from the Reich, some cynics had dubbed our units up in Norway and northern Finland the 'Luftwaffe's bargain basement'. None of the 109Fs sent to us were factory-fresh – they had all seen previous service. Most came from JG 54, some with that Geschwader's famous 'Green Heart' badge still on their fuselage sides, and a few even bearing visible signs of battle damage. Nonetheless, the Friedrich was, in my opinion, a very attractive fighter aircraft, if not indeed the best Me 109 variant ever produced. It had not yet acquired all the lumps and bumps that were to disfigure its successor and earn the Gustav the nickname 'Beule' ('Bump'). It was powered by a 1,350hp Daimler-Benz DB 601E engine and, because of its rounded wingtips, it could turn and bank much more sharply than the Me 109E. Its turning circle was also appreciably smaller, and it was not so quick to stall as the more angular Emil. Another improvement was in the armament. The Me 109F retained the two fuselage-mounted 7.92mm machine-guns of the E version, but the accuracy of aim of the single 20mm MG 151/20 cannon firing through the propeller hub was much greater than the spread effect of the Emil's two wing-mounted 20mm MG FF cannon. In my spare time I practised with a dismantled KG 13 control column grip. I wanted to be able to flick off the safety cover on top of the grip and fire the two machine-guns without, at the same time, automatically pressing my thumb on the button of the engine-mounted cannon as well. It proved extraordinarily difficult not to fire all three weapons at once. But after a time I managed to master the 'piano-playing' dexterity this required, which was to save me a lot of ammunition in future combat.

I had probably been given one of the best Friedrichs of the bunch. During one check flight Feldwebel Josef 'Jupp' Kunz of 8. Staffel and I took the opportunity to put our Friedrichs through their paces, and I soon discovered that my machine was faster than his. But as I also knew that our superior officers were in the habit of grabbing the best and fastest Messerschmitts for themselves, I immediately eased off the gas. After landing, I made a point of shouting across to him: 'Jupp, I couldn't keep up with you. That's some machine you've got there!' The result was that one of the officers laid claim to Jupp Kunz's Friedrich and I was able to hang on to my much better bird.

Gruppen-
kommandeur Scholz
over Petsamo, still
in the 'Emil' …

... before the
arrival of the later
'Friedrichs' and
'Gustavs' with their
rounded wingtips
and more powerful
engines

Servicing the
Daimler-Benz
engine

Josef Kunz, whose personal watchword at that time was 'We're all just small fry', remains a close friend to this day and I still visit him as often as I can. Some pilots, like my wingman Scharmacher, for example, needed a little longer than others to get used to the more powerful Friedrich. Although Scharmacher was the most dependable No 2 I could possibly have wished for, it took quite some time before he fully mastered the Me 109F.

In October winter began to make itself felt, and for us this meant a total readjustment to some very hard and unfamiliar weather conditions. Up there between November and January it was the period of Polar night with darkness lasting nearly twenty-four hours each and every day. Only around noon did a dull gleam appear briefly along the horizon, otherwise everything was cloaked in darkness. It was hard enough to keep one's bearings in the Far North at the best of times, but in this darkness every flight became a nightmare. In order to be able to find our way about at all we had to fly fairly low and orientation was only possible if the moonlight reflecting off the snow revealed some distinctive feature or other in the terrain below. When returning from a mission we would often have only a vague notion of where the airfield was and if we were near it. At Petsamo there was some approach lighting and a primitive form of runway illumination, but this was only switched on if we reported our return over the radio. When pilots were too far away to see either 'Salvation Mountain' or the lights of Petsamo, they could, in emergencies, be guided back to base by searchlight or the firing of flares.

From the left, August Lübking, myself practising with his trigger finger on the control grip, and Horst Stephan

Josef 'Jupp' Kunz

Kunz's 'Black 9'. His motto was 'We're all just small fry'

At the end of 1942 we were made fully aware for the first time that the balance of strength between ourselves and the Russians had shifted. After the Allied landings in Algeria and Morocco, the larger part of Luftflotte 5's Stukas, bombers and torpedo aircraft were withdrawn for transfer to the Mediterranean theatre. In addition, it was also clear that the Russians were sending more and more of their own improved fighter types, the likes of the LaGG-3 and Yak-1, to the Arctic front. The Yaks, in particular, were the equal of our Messerschmitts and made life very difficult for us. When, on 12 November, the Ju 88s of I./KG 30, the only Kampfgruppe remaining in the area, were sent to attack shipping in Murmansk harbour, we provided an escort of four Me 109s. Staffelkapitän Wengel entrusted me with command of the Schwarm. I enjoyed the feel of playing Staffelkapitän for once and of being able to decide the tactics to be employed. But during the mission we only encountered a few Curtiss P-40 Kittyhawks at 4,000 metres, one of which I managed to bring down.

At Petsamo too a number of changes were taking place. Part of II./JG 5 was transferred to Alakurtti, and other elements to Rovaniemi. My erstwhile 7. Staffel was divided between Kirkenes and Nautsi, leaving just 8. and 9./JG 5 at Petsamo. Together with Oberfeldwebel Franz Dörr and Feldwebel Josef Kaiser, the latter hailing from Vienna and known simply as 'Beppi' on account of

his strong Austrian dialect, another pilot soon numbered among my circle of very close friends. This was Unteroffizier Jakob Norz of 8. Staffel, a typically sturdy and self-assured Bavarian farmer. Because of my mushroom-gathering activities I was well in with the head cook, Jupp Heinrichs, who would sometimes see that a steak came my way. This I would then cook on the iron stove in the middle of our tent – note that this was the Arctic, the onset of winter 1942, and we were still living in those lousy, cold Finnish tents! The aroma of grilled steak naturally attracted quite a crowd, and among them on one occasion was the aforementioned Unteroffizier Norz. Although at twenty-two we were both the same age, his quiet and composed manner gave him an air of much greater maturity.

While on the subject of food, we were relatively well provided for at Petsamo during this time. The men would sometimes catch a ptarmigan, which they would take to the kitchen. This northern bird, the size of a small chicken, had very tough flesh, but it added a touch of variety to our otherwise somewhat monotonous menu. And as I knew the recipes for one or two mushroom dishes, the dried mushrooms now came in very handy. Occasionally we would also take the Kübelwagen and pay a visit to one of the nearby coastal artillery batteries. Here we would swap our special pilot's rations, mainly biscuits, liquorice allsorts and Choca-Cola, for freshly caught fish.

| Josef 'Beppi' Kaiser

| Jakob 'Jockel' Norz

In a letter to my mother I had mentioned that many of my comrades were suffering from scurvy due to the lack of vitamins in our diet. Concerned for my health, she had promptly bought all the lemons she could find and sent them to me up on the Arctic Ocean. Because it was forbidden to send parcels or packages to the front, the postmistress in Oberbexbach had given her a tip: she should wrap each lemon separately in strong paper and tie the twisted ends of the paper together with string. This produced a chain that – provided it was no more than twelve lemons long – was, for some inexplicable reason, classed as a letter; and letters could be sent. When the lemons arrived after a six-week journey by land and sea, their skins were so hard that I had to use a hacksaw to cut them in half. The juice was then scooped out with a spoon and trickled over the fish obtained from the coastal artillery. Salmon, catfish or cod with lemon soon became a popular delicacy with us.

Because of the constant darkness and icy temperatures, flying was reduced to a minimum. As the Russians were no doubt labouring under the same navigational and orientation difficulties as ourselves, there was little danger of air attacks on our field during this period. Our permanent quarters were also finally completed at around this time, so I was at last able to move out of the rancid Finnish tent into a three-man barracks hut. One room was occupied by Oberleutnant Wulf-Dietrich Widowitz, an officer newly posted in to 9. Staffel, the other two being assigned to a Feldwebel and myself. The one good thing about this dark season of the year was that we now had a lot of free time. In the mess barracks, which we had christened the 'Cloud hut', my portable gramophone was in almost constant use as more and more of my comrades began to share my musical tastes. With 'Tiger Rag' blaring out into the Stygian blackness of the Polar night, anybody passing

Fresh catfish, a
welcome addition
to the cookhouse

by could have been forgiven for thinking he
was not on the shores of the Arctic Ocean at
all, but somewhere in Harlem. And this
impression would only have been reinforced
had he entered the 'Cloud hut', for there he
would have seen dimly illuminated figures
drinking, smoking and playing cards, tables
littered with all sorts of bottles and glasses,
ashtrays filled to overflowing and, in the
middle of it all, my gramophone and several
piles of records – a scene straight out of a
smoke-filled, pre-war jazz club.

Every week we visited the sauna situated
on a hill overlooking the Petsamo Joki not far
from the airfield. Here the locals showed us
how to enjoy a really hot Finnish sauna.
When we could hardly bear the heat any
more, we rushed outside, slid down the icy
embankment and plunged into a hole
previously hacked in the thick layer of ice
covering the surface of the river. As the
temperatures sank lower, sometimes to 30
degrees below, heating our quarters became
a real problem. Although each room in the
barracks hut had its own stove, they were not
very effective in such extremes of cold. In
order not to freeze during the night, I had

New buildings
under construction
on Petsamo airfield

devised my own way of making up my bed. On the base I first spread out a thick layer of newspapers. On top of this came two woollen blankets, a straw palliasse, then two more blankets. To cover myself I used another five or six woollen blankets. Despite this I often woke up in the middle of the night freezing cold and with my teeth chattering. Even so, I still preferred the winter to the constant daylight and the loss of sleep caused by the summer's midnight sun. The slightest breeze might turn everything to ice, the Polar winds might drive my comrades into the mess or their barracks, but I enjoyed walking through the quiet cold landscape. Thickly bundled up in greatcoat and woollen scarf, I always returned from such outings greatly refreshed. Occasionally I was rewarded by one of nature's most spectacular displays – the Northern Lights.

During these weeks the groundcrews had it far less easy than we did. Because the fragile air of peace and calm could be shattered at any moment, the airfield had to be kept operational at all times. Several tractors, each dragging three heavy iron rollers behind it, were constantly trundling up and down the runway keeping the snow pressed flat and hard for possible emergency scrambles. To prevent the engines of our fighters from freezing solid, catalytic heaters were used to feed warm air through flexible hoses into the lower section of the engine nacelles. Prior to start-up the engine oil, made viscous by the extreme cold, would also be thinned with aviation fuel. But once the engine had caught, the pilot then had to take off within three minutes or risk piston seizure.

Off-duty hours in 'Little Harlem', with Franz Dörr

Nature's spectacle: the Northern Lights over Petsamo

On 1 December 1942 I was promoted to Feldwebel. Any joy I felt was short-lived, however; the following day our Staffel was ordered to carry out a reconnaissance sweep of the Varlovo area, during the course of which Leutnant Guido Erber was shot down by Flak. He managed to escape from his blazing machine, but was subsequently posted missing.

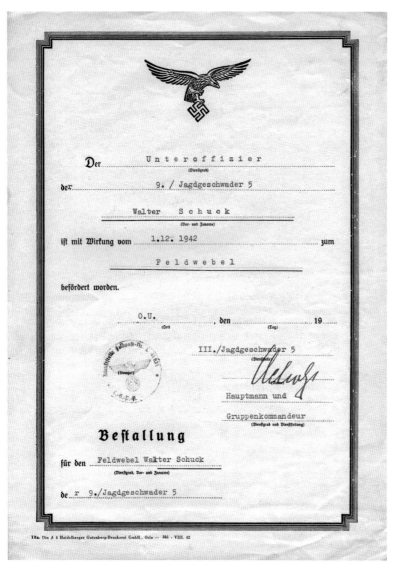

Promotion to Feldwebel

The Arctic winter tightens its grip

Catalytic stoves are lit ready to warm up the engines

Prior to take-off in temperatures of around 30 degrees below

Towards the end of December 1942, which brought a slight improvement in visibility, at least for an hour or two each day, the Russian bombers resumed their activities and started attacking our airfields again. As a counter-move, our Stukas of I./StG 5 took off on 26 December to raid Murmansk harbour. Together with my friend Beppi Kaiser and four other pilots, I was assigned to fly escort for the dive-bombers on this mission. Near Murmansk we became involved in a vicious struggle with a far superior force of Russian LaGG-3s and Hurricanes. This enabled the Stukas to carry out their attack unmolested and get back home without loss. In the heat and confusion of battle, I was unable to see whether my comrades claimed any victories, but at a height of 1,300 metres I managed to shoot down a LaGG-3, which was later confirmed. When we returned to base Feldwebel Josef Kaiser was no longer with us. We hoped that Beppi had either parachuted or force-landed and would make his way back to us somehow. These hopes were not to be fulfilled until many weeks later, and in those intervening weeks Beppi had been through some most unusual experiences indeed, more of which later.

Battleground Murmansk: LaGG-3 fighters curving in to attack

The following day, 27 December, started off badly. On this date almost the entire III./JG 5 had been ordered to escort a raid on Murmansk. The attacking force consisted of Ju 88 bombers coming in from Banak/Alta and the Stukas based at Kirkenes. While III. Gruppe was taking off in separate waves, two of the Me 109s collided on the runway; I heard later

that one of the pilots had to be pulled from his aircraft and taken to hospital with serious injuries. We divided up into individual Schwärme and approached the target area by coming in over the Kola Inlet, then heading south for Murmansk. My Schwarm's task was to clear the airspace over Murmansk for the Stukas following on our heels. All along the approach route the Russians had lined the banks of the Kola with a network of some seventy Flak batteries stretching southwards from the coast down to the town and beyond.

We had hardly turned in over the mouth of the inlet before being met by vicious anti-aircraft fire. Seeing that one of the Ju 87s had taken a direct hit in the fuselage and that large sections of the cockpit canopy had been blown off, I closed up alongside it. We were flying at a height of about 2,000 metres and I wanted to check whether the crew would be able to turn round and nurse the crippled machine back to base. The gunner lay slumped over his machine-gun and was clearly already dead. The pilot motioned for me to give him a little more room as he now intended to bale out. He climbed out of the cockpit, but must either have fouled or pulled his ripcord too quickly, for the parachute lines got tangled up with the tailplane of his machine. The Stuka continued to fly straight and level for a short while, dragging the unfortunate pilot behind it. Then it went into a shallow diving turn. Still fully conscious, the pilot was flailing wildly with his arms and legs in a desperate attempt to free himself. Meanwhile I was racking my brains for a way of helping the poor wretch, but there was absolutely nothing I could do. My first thought, to position my wing underneath him and carefully ease him on to it, I dismissed immediately; even if this risky manoeuvre were to succeed, in these low temperatures he would quickly be frozen stiff and slide off. Never before in my life had I felt so totally helpless. When, after what seemed an eternity, the machine finally exploded into the ground below, I was filled with anger and a sense of horror. I swore savagely over the R/T, but it didn't help. Then I could hold back no longer. I howled like a baby.

Continuing on towards Murmansk, we encountered some Kittyhawks at an altitude of some 3,500 metres and I shot one of them down. It was my fifteenth victory, but I still couldn't get that unfortunate Stuka pilot out of my head. When I opened fire on an opponent, it was the machine alone that was the enemy; it was the machine that had to be

| Kola Inlet

A Me110 of 13.(Z)/JG 5 above the Kola Inlet
heading to the Barents sea

Fighter escort over the Kola Inlet, with Ehrler (left) and Müller

'finished off'. I didn't have a picture in my mind's eye of the enemy pilot as my sworn foe, nor did I give much thought to what was happening to the pilots and crews in the aircraft that I was raking with my guns. On the other side of the coin, however, I was deeply moved every time one of my own comrades was shot down, failed to escape from his burning aircraft or died of wounds suffered in an emergency landing.

For us at Petsamo the morning of 31 December 1942 began at cockpit readiness, and when outposts reported the approach of Pe-2 and Ilyushin DB-3 bombers we took off into the darkness led by Oberleutnant Widowitz. Lines of tracer climbing into the sky from our Flak positions along the Litza front guided us towards the Russian bombers. As soon as they spotted us they tried to escape by diving to ground level – but it was too late. In my first pass I hammered a burst into one of the fleeing Pe-2s, which went down like a brick from a height of only 50 metres. Then I chased at low-level after its partner, setting this one's starboard engine on fire. Once the flames spread to the wing, the second Pe-2 also careened into the ground. At about the

same time Oberleutnant Widowitz brought down a DB-3 and Unteroffizier Oskar Günthroth claimed a Curtiss P-40. By now the rest of the Russians had disappeared and we returned to base without loss.

After re-arming and refuelling we took off again almost immediately, this time to escort Stukas and Ju 88s in an attack on the Russian anti-aircraft positions bordering the Kola Inlet. For this mission, too, we split up into Schwärme, with our four aircraft detailed to protect a Kette of three Ju 87s. After we had reached an altitude of 3,000 metres, my wingman and Oberfeldwebel Franz Dörr climbed higher still to take on the role of top cover. About halfway between the front line and Murmansk a bunch of Airacobras and Kittyhawks suddenly appeared on the scene. They were quickly joined by more and more Russian fighters and a ferocious scrap ensued. Up at 4,500 metres Franz Dörr swept a Curtiss P-40 from the sky, while I clamped myself on to the tail of another Kittyhawk that was busy chasing one of our Stukas, and sent it down in flames. This was the first time that I had scored three victories in a single day. But this action cost us Unteroffizier Dietrich Gathmann, another of my old comrades from 7. Staffel. I found out later that he had been able to bale out after his machine was hit by Flak, but as the whole thing had taken place over enemy territory, he no doubt ended up in Russian captivity.

The year 1943 carried on where 1942 had left off, with us escorting bombers to Murmansk and the Russians continuing to attack our supply convoys. Because of the dearth or total lack of road and rail connections in the region, all our supplies had to be delivered by tugs or barges. An operation against Murmansk on 8 January 1943 resulted in the loss of Unteroffizier Friedrich Rennemann. On 10 January Oberleutnant Widowitz and I, accompanied by our wingmen, took off for Kirkenes to intercept an enemy formation reported to be approaching one of our convoys. The attacking force was made up of Pe-2 bombers and heavily armoured Ilyushin Il-2 'Sturmovik' ground-assault aircraft. The Sturmovik's thick armour plating enclosed the whole of the machine's forward fuselage and protected the pilot and gunner, the engine and fuel tank. Its armament consisted of cannon and heavy machine-guns. Because it was so strongly armoured, the Sturmovik was also known to us as the 'Cement bomber' or 'Iron Gustav', for it could withstand even direct hits from our 20mm cannon.

Despite the poor visibility we found the enemy flying at a height of 300 metres. They were strung out in a long line-astern formation with a large gap between each machine and the next. This was most unusual, as Russian pilots normally flew packed tightly together. This time they would have to be picked off one by one. The enemy's fighter escort, which I identified as Kittyhawks and Hurricanes, were hovering some 1,200 metres above the bombers. Fahnenjunker-Feldwebel Anton Schöppler and I climbed to 2,000 metres to act as top cover. As the Russian bombers descended ever lower, readying themselves to carry out their attack on the convoy, Oberleutnant Widowitz and Oberfeldwebel Helmut Kischnick also pointed the noses of their Messerschmitts downwards and swooped on the Il-2s from above. In the meantime Schöppler and I had to keep the escorting fighters occupied. This resulted in quite a dogfight and I quickly realised that today we were up against a bunch of well-trained and experienced opponents.

Now my own long years of training paid off. When attacked from behind in the past, I had always pulled back hard on the stick to take full advantage of the Me 109E's superior rate of climb. But in the Me 109F I could now turn much more sharply, and had developed a special evasive manoeuvre all of my own: if an enemy fighter was on my tail, I would again start by climbing steeply, but would then execute a half roll and at the same time tramp hard on the rudder. While the machine was still yawing through 180 degrees on its back, I would complete the roll by use of the ailerons, dive sharply into another 180-degree turn and, with the excess speed first built up in the dive, quickly regain height and suddenly be sitting right behind the astonished enemy pilot. Even my wingman Scharmacher, who otherwise always stuck to me as if nailed there, was never able to follow me through this aerobatic figure, which he christened 'Walter's nasty surprise'.

An Ilyushin Il-2 making a low-level pass

During the opening rounds of the dogfight we had lost a little height. But at 1,500 metres I was able to turn inside a Kittyhawk and get in a good burst at it. It looked at first as if the pilot wanted to make an emergency landing, but just before hitting the ground the Kittyhawk unexpectedly reared up again, only to falter and slam into the rocks below. Then Oberfeldwebel Kischnick reported shooting down one of the Il-2s. Our actions had already driven the bombers further and further away from their intended targets, and now they turned tail and attempted to flee the scene altogether. Abandoning our top-cover role, Schöppler and I descended at full speed. I had just opened fire on a low flying Il-2 and seen my hits registering on its radiator when Schöppler gave a warning shout: 'Achtung Walter, Indians on your tail!' I skidded quickly to one side and the Russian's bullets went wide. Now I instructed Schöppler to finish off the damaged Ilyushin. When the Russian fighter saw what was happening, he broke off his attack on me and went chasing off after Schöppler. But the Il-2's fate was already sealed: although its engine was by now blazing fiercely, the pilot managed to pull off a forced landing. After this we returned safely to base.

On the morning of 24 January we escorted a formation of Ju 88s along their northern route to the Rybachi Peninsula. Shortly before the bombers reached their objective, a gaggle of Kittyhawks appeared at a height of 2,000 metres. As my wingman and I were flying some 500 metres above our bombers, we were ideally positioned to bounce the enemy fighters and I claimed two of them in the space of just four minutes.

One evening Feldwebel Heinrich Bartels of 8. Staffel came into my room. The Austrian-born Bartels preferred to be known as Heinz, but we all called him 'Heiner'. He displayed a winning combination of caution and boldness in the air and I liked him a lot. He had been awarded the Knight's Cross in November 1942, and now here he was accompanied by

his wingman Kurt Dylewski, who had a guitar tucked under his arm. Bartels was well known for getting into all sorts of scrapes and, as it was also common knowledge that he liked a drink of two, I immediately realised that this wasn't just a social call. He was aware that I always kept a certain amount of alcoholic refreshment in my room and got straight down to business. Without so much as a by your leave, he opened my locker and took a bottle of cognac from it. I was already in bed and didn't feel at all like celebrating.

'Heiner, I'm tired. Help yourself by all means, but leave me out of it,' I implored him, giving an exaggerated yawn for added effect.

But he wasn't to be put off. 'Nothing doing – we're going to crack open a bottle. You'll be getting your Knight's Cross soon and we'll drink to that,' he announced in his strong Upper Austrian accent. His determined attitude told me that he wasn't going to take no for an answer, so I resigned myself to my fate. He took three water glasses from a shelf and put his Knight's Cross around my neck. Then he dangled the Knight's Cross in one of the glasses, poured cognac over it and raised the unusual mixture to my mouth. After he had filled the other two tumblers to the brim as well, I had to clink glasses and join him and his Katschmarek, or wingman, in a toast.

A downed Il-2 'Sturmovik'

The award certificate of the Combat Flight Clasp in Gold

Heinrich ('Heinz' or 'Heiner') Bartels

Heinrich Bartels is presented with the Knight's Cross by General Holle

I was already pretty befuddled by the time I had emptied the first full glass of cognac, but Bartels insisted upon my having a second one, and then a third. Each time he repeated the process of pouring the spirit over the Knight's Cross suspended in the glass and soon the medal's ribbon was smelling like a distillery. When the first bottle was finished he took another from my locker, quickly emptied that and helped himself to yet another. After the third tumbler of neat brandy I was so far gone that, with the best will in the world, I couldn't join them in another drop. The whole thing lasted barely an hour. But throughout the whole time Bartel's wingman, Dylewski, was strumming madly away on his guitar and warbling 'Und sein Reichskatschmaaa-rek, and sein Reichskatschmaaa-rek, und sein Reichs …' Presumably Unteroffizier Dylewski couldn't think of any words to follow 'And his Reich's wingman', whatever that might mean. At last the pair seemed to have had enough, and when they departed Bartels left his Knight's Cross with me. He had two and this was his everyday one, he declared, so I should hang on to it until I got my own. As I lay in bed desperately trying to stop the room from revolving, I couldn't get Dylewski's stupid ditty out of my head, 'Und sein Reichskatschmaaa-rek'.

Next day I heard that Bartels had got up to several more tricks during the night that would ultimately result in his being posted away from the Arctic Ocean front and appearing before a court-martial. After leaving my quarters he had first attempted to start up a truck parked in front of the other ranks' barracks. He didn't get far, however. The driver of the vehicle had taken the precaution of removing the ignition key. So every time Bartels tried the self-starter the truck simply jolted forward. But he didn't give up until the vehicle got stuck fast in a pile of snow. Woken by the commotion, the driver had leapt out of bed, pulled on his felt boots and dashed outside. There the drunken Bartels was half dragged, half falling out of the driver's cab to be given a swift uppercut full on the chin. When the driver realised who had been on the receiving end of his punch, he shot back into his barracks, quickly climbed back into bed and pretended to be asleep. But Bartels, who was no shrinking violet, chased after him, switched on the light in the hut and started searching for his assailant. He still had enough of his wits about him to concentrate his search under the two-tiered bunks, looking for a pair of felt boots that were still wet. When he found a pair that still had some snow clinging to them, he pulled the man out of the lower bunk and returned the uppercut. Unfortunately, he'd got the wrong one: the real culprit was in the upper bunk and, not surprisingly, keeping as quiet as a mouse.

Bartels's 'Black 13' at Petsamo

After this Bartels and his Katschmarek continued on their way, leaving the Staffel area and marching across to the field's civilian quarters. One of the barracks here housed the Lapp women who carried out cleaning duties and other such chores around the base. Bartels went into the dormitory that accommodated about twenty women. By this time of night they were naturally all sound asleep. He lifted the blanket at the foot of each bed, wrinkling his nose in distaste every time he did so, saying, 'Ugh, disgusting. Perfectly foul. What an awful stink of cheese. Ripe cheese, really ripe old cheese.'

The Lapp women weren't quite so bothered about the sort of cleanliness normally associated with the fairer sex. Perhaps they had a different concept of personal hygiene, or maybe they smelled so strongly because they so often had to camp out in the open when the reindeer needed attending to. After making the rounds of the women's sleeping quarters Bartels was still not ready to call it a night, for he next went to the stable where the pack mules were kept. He untied one of the animals and led it to the hut of the senior NCO, a Hauptfeldwebel, with whom he didn't get on at all – he and the Chiefy were constantly at loggerheads. Having been a butcher in civilian life, Bartels knew how to handle the obstinate beast. As the story goes, he pulled the mule into the Chiefy's room, positioned it with its backside above the sleeping Hauptfeldwebel, and dug his elbow into a certain spot on the animal's flank until it could contain itself no longer and emptied its bladder all over the bed.

The Staffel badge of 8./JG 5 depicts the Edelweiß emblem of the mountain troops, here with the Lapp boot on the Finnish cross shield of III. Gruppe

81

Word of the night's events quickly spread all over the base and the Gruppenkommandeur had no alternative but to report Bartels to the higher authorities. Shortly afterwards he was removed from the Arctic Ocean front and, after disciplinary proceedings had been taken against him, transferred to JG 27 in the Mediterranean theatre. There he continued to add to his score of enemy aircraft destroyed and was quickly back in favour. It was perhaps typical of his style that he should contribute to his own demise. At the end of 1944 Bartels was posted to 15./JG 27 in Defence of the Reich, by which time his number of victories was standing at ninety-eight. Bartels and his current wingman had both already been granted Christmas leave, but Bartels chose not to go – he wanted to celebrate the festive season instead by 'clocking up the hundred'. On 23 December 1944, above the tiny community of Villip, south of Bonn, he shot down his ninety-ninth opponent, a P-47 Thunderbolt. But then fate finally overtook him.

'Yellow 13' brought Bartels no luck: part of the wreckage of the tailfin of his Me 109G-10

Early in February 1943, after the Stukas of I./StG 5 had been sent to other flashpoints on the eastern front, we were tasked with taking over their role. Together with the Focke-Wulf fighter-bombers, we were now also expected to attack Russian shipping in northern coastal waters. I did not relish these type of missions at all, but my neighbour in the next room,

Oberleutnant Widowitz, considered himself a past master of such operations. It was under his leadership that we were to take off early in the morning of 26 February on an anti-shipping strike, each of our machines with a 250kg bomb under its belly. My wingman Schöppler and I lifted off first at about 8.00am, followed by Widowitz and his No 2. For today's mission Widowitz had selected as his wingman Unteroffizier August Lübking, who was to play an important role in my later flying career. Off the south-west coast of the Rybachi Peninsula we discovered a Russian warship, which we attacked with our bombs, although not one of us scored a hit. After making several firing passes at the vessel, also without inflicting any significant damage, Widowitz ordered us to head for home.

I simply couldn't bear the thought of returning to base empty-handed, having done nothing more than bomb 'holes in the water', so I pretended not to have heard Widowitz's command and instead gave my wingman the signal to head south-east in the direction of the Kola Inlet. Meanwhile Widowitz and Lübking had set off on the usual route back to Petsamo, flying south-west across Motovski Bay. They didn't notice that my Rotte was no longer with them until they were attacked by a squadron of Curtiss P-40s. Fighting for their lives, Widowitz shot down two of the Kittyhawks before they were able to make their escape by diving steeply away. The dive down to sea level paid unexpected dividends for August Lübking, for he spotted two Beriev MBR-2 flying boats skimming the waves close inshore and despatched both of them. I only learned all this later after landing. In the meantime, just as we were crossing the mouth of the Kola Inlet, a solitary Pe-2 suddenly popped up in front of me at an altitude of 2,000 metres. It was just what I needed to make up for what I felt was the disgrace of the abortive Jabo (fighter-bomber) mission. I bored in, hit one of the bomber's engines and sent it down on fire into the sea. When Schöppler and I landed back at Petsamo, my mechanic Wevers approached me with a worried expression on his face. He told me that Widowitz had returned just before us and had immediately dashed off to see the Staffelkapitän, incandescent with rage.

I went across to the ops room to give my report on the mission and my kill. Hauptmann Wengel and Widowitz were already there waiting for me. As well as these two there were a number of other pilots in the room who were trying hard not to look interested, but who were obviously agog to see what was

going to happen next. Widowitz couldn't control himself any longer. He had gone bright red in the face and his voice was hoarse.

'Schuck! Have you any idea at all of the position you put me in? You simply hared off without a word and I could have been shot down! Your job was to stay in position and give me top cover!'

Then something quite unexpected happened. Apparently not satisfied with the effect his words were having, he took out his service pistol, pointed it at me and yelled: 'I swear to you, if anything of this kind happens again I'll have you up in front of a court-martial or shoot you here on the spot!'

I looked across at Hauptmann Wengel, who seemed to be completely taken aback by this outburst. 'Oberleutnant Widowitz, get a hold of yourself,' he admonished.

But by now Widowitz had lost it altogether. He was waving his pistol about as if he wanted to mow down everyone present. As the

Staffelkapitän Wulf-Dietrich Widowitz (centre), Amend (far left) and Lübking (far right). I am third from left

My trusty mechanic Karl Wevers (left)

83

situation appeared to have got totally out of hand, I drew my own pistol. Pointing it at Widowitz, I said quietly but firmly: 'Herr Oberleutnant, shall we see who shoots first?'

Widowitz glared at me angrily; he hadn't been prepared for this kind of response. Then Wengel intervened again: 'Stop it, the pair of you, stop it right now!' he roared.

Widowitz threw his pistol on to the desk and stormed out of the ops room, swearing loudly. 'I'll talk to you later – now disappear,' Hauptmann Wengel said.

Adolf Galland (far left) stands next to Gerhard Wengel

There was no disciplinary follow-up to the altercation between Widowitz and myself. True, I hadn't accompanied him back to base and I regretted that he and Lübking had run into trouble. On the other hand, he should have kept control of himself and that business with the pistol was not exactly in the best of taste. Hauptmann Wengel put the fracas down to nerves already stretched to breaking point by the increasing pressure of combat, and advised us to forget the whole thing as quickly as possible. But my opinion of Oberleutnant Widowitz had taken quite a knock and was now decidedly ambivalent. I liked him for his normally free and easy manner, and nobody could tell a corny Bonifatius Kiesewetter joke better than he could. I also respected him for the many search-and-rescue missions he undertook, criss-crossing the dangerous skies above the tundra in the Fieseler Storch looking for downed comrades. But his constant boasting got on my nerves. He loved to brag about his adventurous life to any

newcomer. On one occasion in the mess, when he was in the middle of a particularly exaggerated flight of fancy, I tapped loudly on a lampshade in front of all present. This was our way of saying, 'He's having us on.' Naturally, that didn't exactly help to improve relations between Widowitz and myself.

Shortly after the pistol incident Hauptmann Wengel was sent on leave. This was somewhat surprising for he had already been on leave immediately prior to his posting to us. Widowitz was appointed Staffelkapitän of 9./JG 5 in his stead, bragging that he had his fiancée to thank for this happy occurrence. Apparently she was a Luftwaffe female auxiliary serving in the signals branch in Oslo and it was rumoured that her father, an Oberstleutnant in the signals service, had put the screws on the appointments department. Gerhard Wengel never returned to us on the Arctic front. He was killed in action over Sofia on 10 January 1944. Bulgarian aviation historians, or perhaps his erstwhile comrades there, have erected a granite block at the crash site. It bears an inscription reading: 'To the memory of Hauptmann Gerhard Wengel, German pilot, killed in air combat on 10.01.1944 in the defence of Sofia.'

By the end of February 1943 the news I was hearing on the radio was starting to make me uneasy. It was strictly forbidden to listen in to BBC London, but this station did at least broadcast some decent music. The news reports, however, were pretty shattering: the defeat of our 6. Armee at Stalingrad, Rommel's reversal at El Alamein and the increasingly heavy bombing of our towns and cities in the Reich.

On 28 February we were alerted by forward air observers that Russian fighter-bombers were heading for our field at Petsamo. Widowitz and I took off with our wingmen and climbed to about 5,000 metres. We spotted the enemy Jabos below us, six Curtiss P-40 Kittyhawks together with eight or so Airacobras, and dived down to attack them. When they saw the approaching danger the enemy also promptly headed earthwards. The long-drawn-out diving pursuit, with us firing at the Kittyhawks the whole time, brought us back down almost over our own airfield's dispersal areas. At this moment the field's Flak defences opened up, letting fly with all barrels at whatever was in the air above their heads regardless of whether it was friend or foe. The Kittyhawks released their bombs, creating a hellish inferno of explosions, fires and smoke. Between the Flak and the ricochets flying in all directions, a confused tangle of aircraft was now desperately twisting and turning. When I emerged from a cloud a black smoke at 600 metres I suddenly found myself right behind a Kittyhawk. A quick burst of fire sufficed to send it spiralling into the ground where it exploded on impact. After 20 minutes of hard fighting the enemy finally withdrew, which was just as well as we were by then down to our last few rounds of ammunition.

The next day the Russians came again, this time a bunch of armoured Il-2 Sturmovik ground-assault machines escorted by even more fighters. The field's Flak gunners brought down a Kittyhawk, and Jockel Norz claimed one of the ground-hugging Ilyushins. The raid cost us several dead or wounded among the ground personnel and Flak crews. None of the buildings had been damaged, the Russians having concentrated solely on the many dummy aircraft dispersed about the field.

Shortly after midday on 2 March 1943 I surprised a twin-engined Boston as it came in to land at Afrikanda, an airfield on the shores of Lake Imandra, a large body of water on the Kola Peninsula south of Murmansk. Produced by the American manufacturer Douglas, the Boston was delivered in large numbers to the Russians, who used it extensively as an attack and torpedo-bomber, as well as for reconnaissance, transport and courier duties. This, my first Boston, took my overall total to twenty-five.

With the Russian raids on our airfields growing ever stronger and more frequent, we were finally re-equipped with the new Me 109G-2. We had to watch enviously as the first machines to be delivered again went to the Experten of 6./JG 5. But soon our 9. Staffel also received its long awaited 'Gustavs', which gave us the technical edge over the enemy in the Arctic once more. Theo Weißenberger, the earlier star of the Me 110 Zerstörer at Kirkenes, had since transitioned to single-seaters and had been transferred to the Expertenstaffel back in September 1942. After a mission on 12 March he told us: 'I was briefed to fly to Murmashi with Leutnant Hans Döbrich and three other pilots. Our intention was to destroy any machines we found on the ground there, and then go on to carry out a freie Jagd – unrestricted sweep. But about 20km south-east of Murmashi we found six or seven Kittyhawks waiting for us. Hans managed to knock one of them down and I got two, then a whole pack of Airacobras suddenly pounced upon us. Thanks to the superiority of our Gustavs we were able to add three P-39s to our bag before quickly making ourselves scarce. Unfortunately Dietrich Weinitschke was hit by one of the Airacobras, but was able to bale out. As this was close to the Russian airfield we couldn't send the Storch to pick him up. Poor old Dietrich is sure to be in captivity by now – I only hope he isn't wounded.'

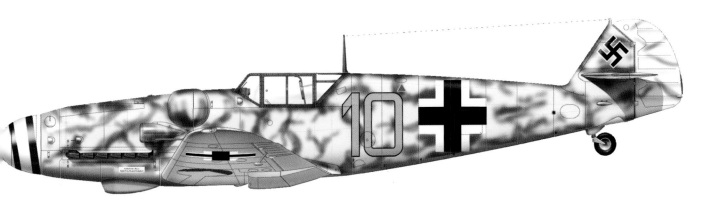

Me109 G-6 in winter camouflage similar to that flown by Walter Schuck. *Richard Caruana*

On 14 March I was detailed to escort a Storch setting off to rescue the crew of a Junkers Ju 88 that had force-landed behind enemy lines. When we reached the site at about 17.00 hours there was no one to be seen; the Russians must have got there before us. An ancient Polikarpov U-2 biplane was still circling over the area and this I shot down. On 19 March I was credited with two Kittyhawks, apparently claimed at 6,000 metres above the Rybachi Peninsula, but for the life of me I can't remember a single detail of this mission. The two fighters had raised my score to twenty-eight, however, for which I was awarded the Luftwaffe Honour Goblet on 23 March 1943.

On the evening of 25 March Obergefreiter Britz and I were at alarm readiness. When a report came in that Russian aircraft had crossed the front line and were heading towards Petsamo, we were given the order to scramble. We scoured the entire area for a sign

that was retiring south-eastwards at low level in the direction of Murmansk. Britz was a new boy and I wanted to help him gain his first victory, so I closed up alongside him, indicating that he should attack the Ilyushin. It took him an age to get into the correct firing position, and when he was finally ready he began loosing off long bursts of fire at the Il-2's fuselage. I saw that his rounds were bouncing harmlessly off the armoured hide of the Sturmovik and that the ricochets were a greater danger to us than to our opponent. I called to him over the R/T: 'Move over to one side – I'll show you how it's done!'

I then eased my Me 109 directly behind the Il-2, which was now flying barely metres above the ground. The Sturmovik's weak spot was the radiator beneath the belly. This could be retracted into the fuselage for protection, but never for more than two or three minutes at a time, otherwise there was the risk of the

A teletype from Kommodore JG 5 congratulating me on the award of the Honour Goblet

The Luftwaffe Honour Goblet for outstanding performance in air combat

of the enemy machines but without success, then returned to base. Both Messerschmitts were pushed back into their dispersal points and immediately refuelled. Suddenly a whole pack of Il-2s dived on the field from out of nowhere. My wingman and I dashed to our aircraft and began to roll. As I was lifting off I saw one of the Ju 88s of KG 30 parked on the field go up in flames. We chased after an Il-2

engine's overheating. Fleeing at full throttle, the Russian soon had to lower his radiator again. And when he did I was ready and waiting. I had him centred in my gun sight and let him have both barrels of my 7.92mm machine-guns. The salvo tore the whole radiator to pieces, the Il-2 started to trail a thick banner of smoke and exploded into the ground. On this occasion the Il-2s' escorting fighters had turned up much too late. All they could do was perform a damage limitation exercise by shepherding the rest of the Sturmoviks safely home. But one of the fighters had seen me shooting down the Ilyushin and dived to attack us. After a brief skirmish I sent him down too from a height of 50 metres.

minutes a whole covey of enemy machines appeared and entered the landing pattern. I smuggled myself into the circuit with them, latched onto the tail of a Kittyhawk and opened fire. There was a sudden blinding flash as the fighter nose-dived into the runway. I quickly got behind another of the enemy. He also smashed into the ground after a single burst of fire from my guns.

By this time the field's Flak defences had woken up to the situation and were shooting wildly and indiscriminately up into the darkening sky with everything they had. Only a few metres off the ground, far too low to be worried by the enemy's anti-aircraft fire, I roared along the runway. At its end I climbed into a

Meanwhile, the chase had taken us close to the airfield at Murmashi, south-west of Murmansk. It was getting darker by the minute and soon the returning Sturmoviks and their escorting fighters would have to come in to land. As Britz was out of ammunition after his unsuccessful attack on the Il-2, I instructed him to circle at 1,000 metres while I went down to keep an eye open for any homecoming aircraft. My hunch proved correct; within a very few

steep 180-degree turn and flew back in the opposite direction. Just at that moment another machine was touching down. While the pilot was still trying to swerve around the burning remains of the two previous crashes I caught him fair and square to leave a third wreck littering the runway. Having now emptied my guns as well, I joined up with Britz and we set course for base. Behind us we left a scene of carnage; blazing aircraft, exploding ammunition

A 'freie Jagd' in the Murmansk area

and long tongues of blue flame from the escaping fuel that was burning fiercely on the runway all added an eerie glow to a night sky that was already lit up by the fiery patterns of bright red and white tracer still being hosed up in all directions by the Flak gunners.

As we neared Petsamo the runway lights were switched on to guide us in. Some time later the Herzberg radio station based at Petsamo broadcast a translation of an intercepted Russian report: as the runway at Murmashi was blocked by crashed aircraft, those machines still in the air were unable to land. Some pilots even had to bale out due to lack of fuel. These successes were not credited to me, however. From 1,000 metres up, Britz was unable to confirm that the destruction was entirely the result of my actions, and there remained the possibility that one or more of the enemy machines may have been brought down by their own Flak.

During a later operation against Murmashi airfield flown on 3 April my wingman Britz went missing. Nothing more was ever heard of him and his ultimate fate remains unknown to this day. Twenty-four hours later the Russians returned the compliment with a savage attack on Petsamo. Our 7. and 9. Staffeln became involved in a bitter fight with the low-flying Sturmoviks and their escorting fighters, during the course of which Leutnant Wolfgang Rost claimed an Il-2 and I shot down a couple of Kittyhawks.

10 Costly Murmansk

At the beginning of spring 1943 the thaw set in and greatly hampered all flying activity at Petsamo. On some days several Me 109s would come to grief while attempting to take off. The main runway, part of its surface consisting of reindeer-moss, turned slushy and the narrow tyres of our fighters sank so deeply into the ground that undercarriage damage was a very real threat. After a number of take-off accidents in March and April, it was decided that only the special 'thaw period runway' should be used. This was the track made up of wooden planks that lay parallel to the main runway and was kept operational throughout the winter by the constant use of a rotary snowplough. But even this trackway had its drawbacks. Time and time again the Messerschmitts, always susceptible to crosswinds, would be caught by a sudden gust and sent slithering into the 3-metre-high walls of snow that lined each side of it.

During this time the name Theo Weißenberger began to crop up with increasing frequency. It was said that Weißenberger, who had been an outstanding glider pilot, had transferred his flying skills to the Me 109. Some of our pilots flew their machines with their muscles, others with their heads. But not one of them could make his aircraft perform with the same smooth, deadly elegance as Theo Weißenberger. In the late afternoon of 13 April 1943 he returned from a mission to the north-east of Murmansk where, in the space of just eleven minutes, he had shot down six Russian fighters: two Kittyhawks and four Airacobras. This had been his sixty-third operational mission since his transfer from the Zerstörer to 6. Staffel, and in those sixty-three missions he had claimed fifty-four victories.

An Me 109 behind a protective wall of snow at Petsamo in the winter of 1943

Leutnant Theo Weißenberger

Behind the 'Revi 16' reflector gunsight

I often flew
Messerschmitt Bf
109 F-4 'Yellow 9'

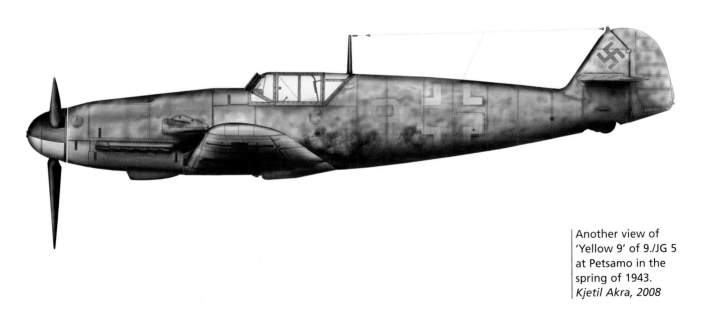

Another view of
'Yellow 9' of 9./JG 5
at Petsamo in the
spring of 1943.
Kjetil Akra, 2008

91

As the days grew longer we all began to fly more missions again. Late in the afternoon of 14 April 1943 I took off with four other pilots of 9./JG 5 to escort a force of Fw 190 fighter-bombers ordered to attack the airfield of Varlamovo, not far from Murmansk. As our intended target was hidden under a thick blanket of cloud, we turned our attention instead to nearby Vaenga, where we were greeted by a heavy Flak barrage and a number of enemy fighters. While the Jabos dived on the field from a height of 4,000 metres, we tackled the waiting Airacobras and Hurricanes. Unteroffizier Günthroth brought down an Airacobra and I managed to get the better of two of the Hurricanes.

The end of winter has softened the surface of the field

Weißenberger taxies out of his blast pen on to the thaw weather wooden trackway

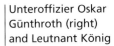
Unteroffizier Oskar Günthroth (right) and Leutnant König

Our clashes with enemy fighters were growing ever tougher. It was clear that the Russians were making all-out efforts to remedy the shortcomings of their earlier pilot training programmes. In mid-April our air reconnaissance reported the presence of a previously unknown type of fighter on an airfield close to Murmansk. We later discovered that this was a new indigenous Russian design, the Yak-7. But of far greater import to the future course of the air war in the Far North was the fact that, at the beginning of April 1943, the Russians had set up two radar stations in the Murmansk region. At the time we knew nothing of their existence, but their presence was to bring about fundamental changes in the enemy's tactics. They didn't just cause us a lot of headaches – they also became fatal traps for many of our pilots.

The Messerschmitts of 6. Staffel were armed with 20mm cannon in underwing gondolas

A Rotte of Me 109s

6./JG 5's fifth scoreboard, commencing with victory No 567, a P-40 shot down by Oblt Ehrler near Murmansk on 13 April 1943

Abſchußtafel der 6. Staffel/J.G 5

Nr. 5

Lfd.Nr.	Datum	Staats-Ang.	Typ	Abschuss durch	Ort
567.	13.IV.43	U.d.S.S.R	Curtiss P-40	Oblt. Ehrler	40 km nord-ost Murmansk
568.	"	"	"	Ofw. Brunner	40 km nördlich Murmansk
569.	"	"	Airacobra	Oblt. Ehrler	40 km südlich Murmansk
570.	19.IV.43	"	"	Oblt. Ehrler	40 km nord-ost Murmansk
571.	"	"	"	Oblt. Ehrler	40 km südlich Murmansk
572.	"	"	Curtiss P-40	Ofw. Brunner	40 km südlich Murmansk
573.	"	"	Airacobra	Ltn. Weißenberger	40 km nord-ost Murmansk
574.	"	"	Curtiss P-40	Oblt. Ehrler	40 km nördlich Murmansk
575.	"	"	Airacobra	Fw. Fahldieck	40 km nördlich Kola
576.	"	"	Kittyhawk	Ofw. Brunner	40 km nördlich Kola
577.	22.IV.43	"	Curtiss P-40	Ltn. Weißenberger	40 km nördlich Murmansk
578.	"	"	Mustang	Ofw. Brunner	40 km südlich Murmansk
579.	"	"	"	Oblt. Ehrler	40 km südlich Kola
580.	"	"	Curtiss P-40	Oblt. Ehrler	40 km süd-ost Kola
581.	"	"	"	Ofw. Brunner	40 km südlich Murmansk
582.	"	"	Jak-1	Ltn. Weißenberger	40 km süd-ost Murmansk
583.	"	"	"	Ltn. Weißenberger	40 km nördlich Kola

'Yellow 9' undergoing maintenance

On 19 April II. and III./JG 5 took off to provide the escort for Fw 190 Jabos, again being despatched to attack the enemy airfield at Varlamovo. However, after two or three aircraft of III./JG 5 were damaged in take-off accidents it began to seem as if the whole operation was ill-fated. As our formation neared the target area Russian fighters were ready and waiting for us. In the ensuing dogfight two of our pilots were brought down, and two others limped back to Petsamo with their machines badly damaged. One of the pilots shot down had been able to bale out and made his way back to us, while the second remained missing. This was one of the leading aces of the Expertenstaffel, the Knight's Cross-holder Oberfeldwebel Rudi Müller. At the time of his loss the cheerful and friendly Müller, a favourite with the entire Geschwader, had amassed a total of ninety-four confirmed victories. Rarely would there be so much speculation, at least among us at Petsamo, about the eventual fate of any pilot than that following the disappearance of Rudi Müller. It was known for a fact that he had been able to put his Me 109 'Yellow 3' down on its belly on the surface of a frozen lake not far from Murmansk. It was also established that he had strapped on the short skis that formed part of the emergency pack carried by every Me 109 operating on the Arctic Ocean front and had set off in the direction of the front line. The athletic Müller covered some 20km across country before the Russians caught him and sent him to one of their notorious prisoner-of-war camps.

We had already heard some stories of what went on in these camps, but we didn't learn the whole truth until much later: wounded prisoners received hardly any treatment, living and sanitary conditions were degrading, and hunger, sleep deprivation, endless interrogations, threats and even beatings were the normal order of the day. The era of the Red Baron, when the 'Knights of the Air' respected each other and their downed opponents were treated with honour, was well and truly a thing of the past. I didn't even want to imagine how the Russians would behave towards a highly decorated pilot like Rudi Müller, especially as he had his scoreboard of kills proudly displayed on the rudder of his machine for the enemy to see.

Oberfeldwebel
Rudi Müller

'Yellow 3' has Rudi Müller's personal emblem below the cockpit …

... and his scoreboard on the rudder

Three 'Experten' of 6. Staffel: from the left, Theo Weißenberger, Heinrich Ehrler and Rudi Müller

Opposite: The 'Expertenstaffel': a cutting from the air fleet's own magazine 'Luftflotte Nord'

Asse unserer Jagdflieger
an der Eismeerfront

Alle Aufnahmen: Kriegsberichter Hirschfelder

Pilots of 6./JG 5:
from the left,
Döbrich,
Weißenberger,
Ehrler, Müller and
Brunner

Pilots of 6./JG 5: from the left, Döbrich, Weißenberger, Ehrler, Müller and Brunner

At all events, it was said that the Russians had worked on Rudi Müller for so long that he finally revealed the full details of all our coming operations. This rumour gained credence as the Russians suddenly seemed to know in advance the routes we were taking to our various targets, even if we had taken the precaution of flying some sort of diversionary measure beforehand. This information was, of course, being provided by the enemy's radar stations that had just begun operating, but of which we were still entirely unaware, so may all those who questioned Rudi Müller's loyalty at the time be thoroughly ashamed of themselves. Another story going the rounds was that the Russians had brainwashed Müller and turned him so completely that he served them as a flying instructor until well into his old age. But all these rumours can confidently be dismissed as utter rubbish. Even if the full details of just what happened to him may now never be known, the research undertaken by the Red Cross organisation probably comes closest to the truth: in the 1960s the German Red Cross informed Rudi Müller's mother that her son had 'died' in a Russian prisoner-of-war camp on 21 October 1943.

At the end of April 1943 our airfield suffered a surprise Russian air raid. The Il-2 Sturmoviks' bombs hit a maintenance hangar, which burned to the ground. A few hours later our Staffel was ordered to escort Ju 88 bombers to Murmansk. The Expertenstaffel had taken off before us in order to carry out a

freie Jagd sweep and clear the airspace prior to our arrival. But again the Russians were warned by radar of our coming. Feldwebel Erwin Fahldieck, Rudi Müller's erstwhile wingman in 6. Staffel, was shot down in his 'Yellow 2' over Murmansk. He was seen to bale out and we presumed the pair met up again in captivity.

At first light on 7 May both 8. and 9. Staffeln received orders to escort a mixed force of Ju 88s, Me 110s and Fw 190 Jabos that would be taking off at intervals to attack Murmansk. The wingman assigned to me for this mission was Heinrich Friedrich 'Heinfried' Wiegand and our specific job was to provide cover for the Focke-Wulfs led by Hauptmann Strakeljahn. As the Jabos were faster than both the Ju 88s and Me 110s, we were among the last to take off, and while we were still climbing away the machines of 6. Staffel, which had set out well before us, were already on their way back from the target area.

It was during this operation that another leading ace of the Expertenstaffel, Oberfeldwebel Albert Brunner, claimed his last victory. Brunner was one of the most daring of 6./JG 5's pilots. Although he had only been on the Arctic front for a year, he had in that time flown 135 operational missions, been shot down himself three times, and had claimed a total of fifty-three confirmed victories. On this day he was being shadowed on his return flight by an unseen enemy. Vectored on to the unsuspecting Brunner by one of the Russian radar stations, an

Oberfeldwebel
Albert Brunner

Airacobra crept up on his tail and opened fire. He managed to bale out, but his machine was already too low; there was insufficient time for the parachute to open and he plunged to his death. Albert Brunner was awarded a posthumous Knight's Cross.

Brunner's tragic end must have taken place just before Wiegand and I appeared on the scene with the Fw 190 Jabos. The Airacobras were flying slightly off to our right at a height of about 1,200 metres and, with Wiegand covering me, I turned in to the attack. In order to give Strakeljahn's Jabos a clear run at the target, it was imperative that we got the Airacobras involved in a fight. As I knew that the Me 109 was easily able to outmanoeuvre the heavier Airacobra in the climb, I pulled the stick back and opened the throttle to the full. As we roared upwards I saw the Airacobras forming a defensive circle 300 metres below us. Although the Airacobra could usually more than hold its own against the Me 109 in a dogfight, it had poor stalling characteristics and could all too easily go into a flat spin. I therefore went back down again and played the enemy's game by inserting myself into the defensive circle. With the help of the trim wheel I reefed my Messerschmitt into ever tighter and steeper turns. This enabled me to avoid the fire from the Airacobra behind me, while at the same time allowing me to get my sights on the machine flying ahead of me. In addition, I was aware of the fact that the 37mm cannon projecting from

the nose of the Airacobra was apt to jam if subjected to high g forces. I stayed with the Russian formation while they flew one defensive circle after the other. Then suddenly it seemed as if the belly of an Airacobra flying just above my cockpit was starting to descend on me. In reality, of course, it was I who was getting closer and closer to the Russian. I let him creep ahead of me slightly and opened fire. I saw my rounds disappear into the Airacobra's fuselage and dived away. Mortally hit, the enemy fighter was already on its way down and I left it to its fate.

After I had landed back at Petsamo, the MPs brought in a Russian pilot they had picked up. He had come down by parachute and the German officer accompanying him, who spoke a little Russian, introduced him to me as the opponent I had shot down a little earlier. As I had not yet had breakfast, I invited the pair of them to join me. The Russian sneeringly accepted the proffered breakfast egg, white bread and ground coffee. No doubt his propaganda people had told him that we were on the point of starvation, so he refused to believe that we could afford to indulge in this kind of luxury. Nor could I convince him that the meal was not a special ration served to me only because I had shot down a Russian aircraft. When I informed him that he was my thirty-fifth victory he shook his head in disbelief. Later we took him into the 'Cloud hut' and showed him the Staffel's scoreboard, but this clearly made no great impression on him either. Despite everything we did, the Russian regarded the meal, our conversation and the scoreboard as a total charade that we had staged solely for his benefit. When the MPs came to collect him again we didn't part as brother flyers, and certainly not as friends. But at least he must have realised that we bore him no animosity.

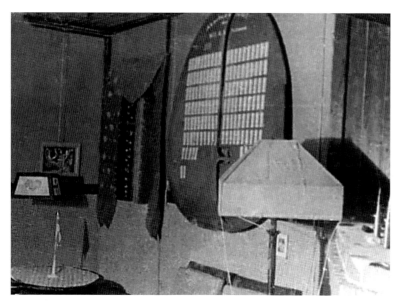

The unit scoreboard of 9./JG 5 on the tailfin and rudder of a Pe-2 in the 'Cloud hut'

On 8 May the adjutant of III./JG 5, Leutnant Rolf-Viktor Sadewasser, was shot down by Russian fighters near Murmansk and remains officially missing to this day. It was about this time too that we had a visit from a war correspondent by the name of Dietrich, who had been commissioned to write an article for a Luftwaffe magazine describing our day-to-day life up on the Arctic Ocean. When he expressed a need to go to the toilet we showed him where our lavatory was; between the barrack huts, the mess

and an open field, a trench some 2 metres deep had been dug, and this was where we answered the call of nature. A rough wooden bench with two round holes sawn in it had been placed above the trench to make life easier and allow us to 'jettison bombs' more comfortably. The entire construction was enclosed in a small wooden hut. During the cold months from October to May the excrement froze solid and when, after a time, it had built up into a pyramid nearly to the top of the trench, the whole lot would be knocked over with a shovel. Because it got so bitterly cold in the little hut during the long winter months we would take the torn-up sheets of newspaper provided for wiping purposes, set light to them and toss them into the trench. The burning paper not only warmed our backsides a little, but also went some way towards masking the foul stench of the accumulated faeces.

We passed on this tip about the newspaper before sending the war correspondent on his way to do his business. It wasn't long before an airman came rushing into the mess in a state of some agitation: 'The whole shithouse has gone up in flames!' he yelled.

We grabbed a fire hose and rushed to the spot, only to find a thoroughly unnerved war correspondent, trousers still round his knees, standing in front of the furiously blazing wooden hut. After we had made a few futile attempts to put the fire out and the hut had burned to the ground, the correspondent told us what had happened. Because he was feeling the cold, he had followed our suggestion and lit some pieces of newspaper. But as there was so much paper already in the heap piled high in the trench beneath him, his contribution was all that was needed to set the whole lot on fire.

My attempts at fire-fighting fail, and the toilet hut burns to the ground

For nearly two years now our troops had been trying, without success, to take the strategically important port of Murmansk. Even though we were inflicting severe losses on the enemy, it seemed as if we were fighting against a seven-headed hydra. Every time we thought we had finally destroyed enough of the enemy's aircraft, ships and equipment to bring him to his knees, an apparently inexhaustible supply of fresh war material would turn up. We had only a very sketchy idea of what was going on in the other theatres of war. In Petsamo our thoughts revolved mostly around the next operation or our chances of surviving the next encounter with the enemy. Furthermore, it seemed as if the supplies from our ally Finland, so essential and so urgently needed, had suddenly dried up. During a German-Finnish military conference back in March 1943 the Commander-in-Chief of Finland's armed forces, Marshal Carl Gustav Emil Baron von Mannerheim, had stated categorically: 'We have already lost too many people and will no longer take part in hostilities.' At the same time the Finnish Government had opened negotiations with the Allies with the object of obtaining good terms once the Finns had withdrawn from the war.

The Reich's leadership had learned of the Finns' activities and knew that something had to be done, and done very quickly, to keep Finland on Germany's side in the fight against Russia. In the summer of 1943 Hitler's Foreign Minister, Joachim von Ribbentrop, assured the Finns that the Soviet Union had been comprehensively defeated. In the light of the war situation at the time, this pronouncement was not just highly questionable, it belonged – especially after the fall of Stalingrad – in the realms of fantasy. But Germany's leaders realised the need to show the Finns some immediate signs of military success. In our region this task fell to the ground troops of the 20th Mountain Army and the air units of Luftflotte 5. Up there the Soviets' Achilles heel was the supply lines to their forwardmost troops holding the Rybachi Peninsula. All weapons, munitions, supplies and reinforcements for these forces had to be transported by water across the Motovski Bay. As our troops were tied down on the fighting fronts, Luftflotte 5 was given the task of disrupting the Russians' seaborne supply routes from the air. The actual tactical targets were a whole fleet of smallish ships, motorboats, tugs and launches. If we could sever their supply lines, the Russian troops on the Rybachi Peninsula would be isolated and cut off from their logistics. Our air attacks were therefore concentrated on the port of Eina, known today as Zina, situated in a bay on the southern side of the peninsula. Now that it was summer and light for twenty-four hours a day, our ground

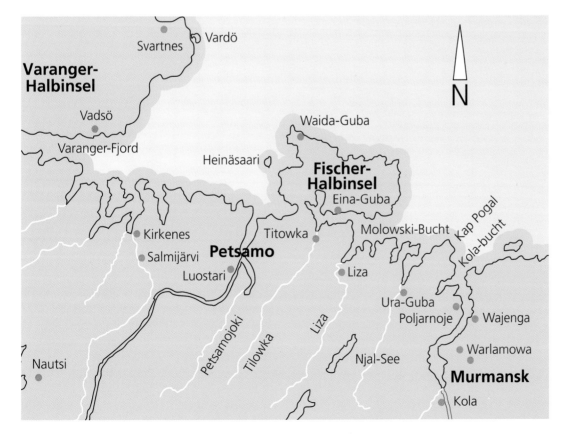

The area of air operations around the Rybachi (Fisherman's) Peninsula

Focke-Wulf Fw 190 fighter-bombers of JG 5 bearing the Eismeer badge

troops on the opposite, mainland shore of Motovski Bay could keep Eina under constant surveillance and immediately report all enemy movements. In response to these reports our Jabos could take off from Petsamo and be over Eina in a matter of minutes.

On the evening of 22 May 1943 our 7., 8. and 9. Staffeln were briefed to escort Hauptmann Strakeljahn's Jabos in an attack on Russian tugs and torpedo-boats. The enemy vessels were hugging the southern shore of the Rybachi Peninsula, heading west into Motka Bay and making for the tiny port of Ozerko on its far side. While our Jabos dived on their targets through a broken curtain of cloud, we began mixing it with the Airacobras, Hurricanes and Kittyhawks that were meant to be protecting the ships. I saw a group of four Hurricanes split into two pairs, the first of which then turned in towards us. When one of

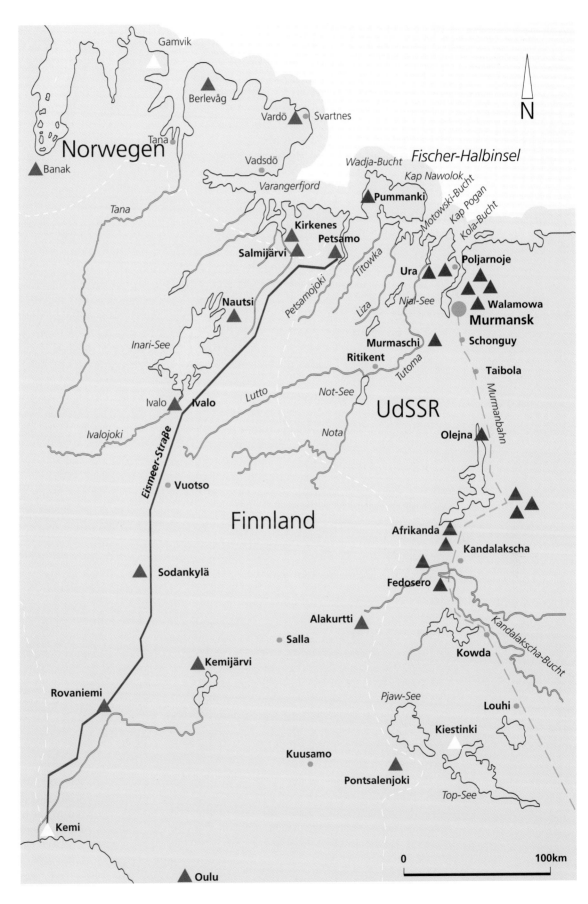

Far Northern theatre: blue triangles indicate Luftwaffe airfields, while those of our opponents are in red. *Eric Mombeek*

the Hurricanes attempted to carry out a head-on attack at me, I skidded smartly out of the way into a sharp 180-degree left turn that brought me back on to my opponent's tail and seconds later he went down to disappear into the waters of Motka Bay. Now more and more Russian fighters were arriving on the scene and we became involved in a wild free-for-all with machines continuously disappearing in and out of the clouds. By the time the confused melée was finally over we had shot down three of the enemy, two of them having fallen to my guns.

As the fighter-bombers had not inflicted any serious damage to the enemy ships, we returned to base and immediately started preparing for a follow-up mission. An hour after the first attack 8. and 9. Staffeln took off again, refuelled and re-armed, to escort the Focke-Wulf Jabos back to the same target. This time our force consisted of about ten Me 109 fighters and four Fw 190 Jabos. We crossed the Motovski Bat with the fighter-bombers keeping to a height of 1,000 metres, eight of our Me 109s flying a little above them, and with my Rotte acting as top cover. Over the south coast of the Rybachi Peninsula, close to Eina Bay, we saw six to eight Hurricanes patrolling above the ships. While my wingman and I maintained our height, the two Schwärme of Messerschmitts below us launched themselves at the Hurricanes. At that moment a gaggle of Airacobras and Kittyhawks broke out of the clouds with the obvious intention of bouncing our fighters. Giving a warning shout over the R/T, I led my wingman down to join in the fray. During the savage fight that followed, Oberleutnant Widowitz and his No 2, August Lübking, each hacked down a Kittyhawk, and I sent an Airacobra into the sea a few minutes earlier. When one of the Russians spotted two Messerschmitts diving straight for him, he panicked and peeled left, almost colliding with his wingman. He also lost contact with his leader and within a moment an Me 109 was sitting on his tail. The shells from the Me's cannon sawed through the Russian machine, which shortly afterwards went down in flames to crash into a mountain close to Eina Bay. This Russian had probably fallen victim to our Jockel Norz.

After their initial clash with us, the Airacobras had tried to re-form and began to climb upwards in a tight spiral. But one of the Russian pilots must have failed to get the message for he single-handedly continued to attack the Messerschmitts below us. I soon put a stop to his activities, and when his Airacobra hit the water it gave me my thirty-ninth confirmed victory. By the end of the day we had claimed no fewer than fourteen kills. But I was so exhausted from the battles that I didn't even have the energy to find out whether the Jabos' second mission had been any more successful than the first.

Although some good results were achieved during these missions, which were being flown several times daily against the Russian supply ships, it proved impossible to stop the flow of supplies to the enemy's forward positions altogether. This meant that the preconditions demanded by our ground troops prior to any attempted breakthrough had not been met, and the result was that General Dietl, the GOC of the 20th Mountain Army, was unwilling to respond to his superiors' demands for a ground offensive. But such matters of strategy were no concern of ours as we got on with our day-to-day lives at Petsamo. And as our losses at this time were not yet unbearably high, neither did we give much serious thought to our chances of survival.

Even though there was a distinct lack of feminine company up in our part of the world, there were the occasional goings-on between operations. The Lapp women exuded a rather strong aroma, which afforded them a kind of built-in self-protection. We were therefore more interested in the female members of Finland's armed forces. These women were regular soldiers of the Finnish Army and were frequently employed by us on signals and communications duties, as interpreters, or secretaries and writers in our ops rooms. In Finland they were popularly known as 'Lottas', after the heroine of an epic poem. And although this word may have had certain other connotations to German ears, it in no way implied that Finland's female soldiers were of doubtful virtue. Quite the opposite, in fact – the vast majority were thoroughly respectable and well-behaved women. And if they did allow themselves to be approached by a German, it would only be one of higher rank.

Instead, therefore, we whiled away a lot of our time with music. By now, however, my records were all so scratched that it was difficult to make out the tunes, let alone the words. Those that had completely had it were sorted out and taken to the edge of the airfield where they were thrown around like so many flying saucers. In my room in the evenings I used to enjoy tuning in to those foreign radio stations that broadcast the hotter kind of music programmes. Up here at the edge of the world it disturbed nobody. And no one would have dreamed of expressing the ridiculous notion that listening to foreign stations was 'undermining military morale' or made one some sort of dissident. Radio Stockholm, for example, often had some excellent music. I particularly liked the voice of a singer named Alice Babs, whose rendition of 'Swing it, Maestros, Swing' I simply couldn't get out of my head.

One night my neighbour in the adjoining room, Staffelkapitän Widowitz, was entertaining one of the much-sought-after Lottas. With several missions under my belt, the day had been a particularly exhausting one and I desperately needed to get some sleep. But the unmistakable sounds of love-making coming from the room next door kept me awake. It must be pointed out that the walls between the rooms were by no means solid structures; in fact, they were no thicker than cardboard. Suddenly I heard Widowitz yell 'Abschuss!' This was the word we used to signify a kill, and a moment later there was a loud bang and something smacked into the wooden outer wall of the hut above my head – my love-crazed neighbour had fired a round from his pistol through the partition wall! I threw myself to the floor as further bullets came whizzing into my room, each one accompanied by the shout of 'Abschuss!' Really teed off by now, I grabbed my own pistol and sent a shot back through the thin wall at ceiling light level. When my bullet shattered the lamp next door my neighbour abruptly stopped shooting. Then all I heard was a frightened female voice whisper something about 'the light' and Oberleutnant Widowitz swearing. The next morning I was told to report to Gruppenkommandeur Scholz's deputy, Hauptmann Lüder. Widowitz had informed on me, accusing me of having fired into his room. But the subsequent examination of both our quarters indicated that six shots had come from his room and the bullets were found still lodged in the wall above my bed. As it was no longer possible to establish who had opened fire first, and as no one had been injured, the whole affair was quietly swept under the carpet.

On 24 June 1943 I was awarded the German Cross in Gold for my thirty-nine victories to date and sent home on leave. I climbed into a Me 109 and set off for Bodø, where I was to get the machine refuelled before delivering it to Oslo. It was in Bodø that I met for the first time the then nineteen-year old Leutnant Ernst Scheufele, with whom I have remained close friends ever since. Scheufele, who was to achieve eighteen victories and be appointed Staffelkapitän of 14./ JG 4 in Defence of the Reich before the war's end, is today President of the Eismeerjäger, or Arctic Ocean Fighter Pilots' Association, the official title of JG 5's ex-members' association. I'll let him describe our first meeting in his own words.

**IM NAMEN DES FÜHRERS
UND OBERSTEN BEFEHLSHABERS
DER WEHRMACHT**
VERLEIHE ICH
DEM

FELDWEBEL

WALTER   SCHUCK

DAS DEUTSCHE KREUZ
IN GOLD

HAUPTQUARTIER. DEN   24. JUNI 1943

**DER REICHSMINISTER
DER LUFTFAHRT
UND OBERBEFEHLSHABER
DER LUFTWAFFE**

REICHSMARSCHALL

DIE ERFOLGTE VERLEIHUNG
WIRD BEGLAUBIGT.

GENERALOBERST

The certificate accompanying the award of the German Cross in Gold, signed by Reichsmarschall Göring

The German Cross in Gold

'While II. and III. Gruppen of Jagdgeschwader 5 had contact with the enemy on an almost daily basis from their airfields at Kirkenes, Petsamo and Salmijärvi up on the Arctic Ocean, we of IV. and I. Gruppen based along Norway's western coast at Bodø, Trondheim, Herdla and Stavanger had nothing to do but provide aerial cover for our Navy's big ships, such as the *Tirpitz*, *Köln* and *Prinz Eugen*. News of the successes being achieved by the likes of Müller, Carganico and Weißenberger got through to us and aroused not only our awe and respect, but also a certain amount of envy. What's the good of a fighter pilot with no victories? From Hauptmann Rudolf Lüder, the new Kapitän of our 12. Staffel in Bodø who, immediately prior to his appointment, had been Major Scholz's adjutant in III. Gruppe, we also heard about such up-and-coming pilots as Schuck, Beyer and Schumacher, all of whom could already lay claim to more than thirty

Leutnant Ernst Scheufele

kills. Then, one day towards the end of June 1943, an unknown Me 109 landed at Bodø and from it climbed a slightly built, boyish-looking lad with the German Cross in Gold on his chest, who introduced himself as Walter Schuck. He had already achieved what all of us could still only dream of: he was well on his way to becoming a top fighter pilot and role model. But there were no grand airs about him, he was relaxed and friendly. We looked upon him as somebody from another world, especially that evening when he described his most recent successes to us in vivid detail. We would dearly have liked to have him stay with us a little longer, but you don't detain a man who is heading home on leave. We subsequently followed his continuing successes in the pages of our air fleet magazine, 'Luftflotte Nord'.'

After handing over my machine in Oslo, I caught the ferry for Denmark. While waiting for my rail connection to Germany I had a little time to take in the hustle and bustle of Frederikshavn's weekly market. One of the fishmongers was selling small wooden casks of fifty salted herrings steeped in brine. I bought two casks before boarding my train to Berlin. There I visited the girl I had made friends with during that long-ago children's holiday when we had been sent to the Baltic seaside resort of Ahlbeck. I presented her mother with one of the casks of herrings. Such fish were hard to come by in the capital at this time and they obviously made a very welcome gift. From Berlin I then set off again by train for Bexbach, where I planned to spend a few restful days with my family. The other cask of herrings, which was intended for home, I put on the luggage rack above my seat. I fell asleep at the start of the long journey and didn't notice that the bottom of the cask had developed a slight leak; the steady drip of fish brine slowly saturated my entire uniform. Put off by the strong smell, my fellow passengers gave me an increasingly wide berth until I soon had the whole compartment to myself. When I got home and my mother hugged me, she wrinkled her nose and said, 'You stink like an old fishing smack. Since when have you been in the Navy?'

I spent the rest of my leave at Bad Schachen on the shores of Lake Constance, where a room had been reserved for me in an elegantly appointed convalescent home. The actual purpose of such homes was to provide front-line personnel with a well-earned change of scenery far from the war to help them recharge their batteries. Good food and fine wines, comfortably furnished rooms, music, sporting activities, games, glorious surroundings and charming young ladies ensured that the 'weary

heroes' were able to forget the war, at least for a little while. But was it chance, or did someone want to put me to the test? One morning a most attractive lady – I would guess her age to have been between twenty-five and twenty-eight – joined me at the breakfast table. She immediately began to chat to me in a very pleasant manner, explaining that she had just arrived from Switzerland and wanted to spend a few relaxing days here before travelling on to Berlin. After we had exchanged some idle pleasantries we arranged to meet that evening, and so on and so on… I must admit that I was really smitten and would dearly have liked to continue the flirtation. She was such a joy to be with and we found ourselves laughing together a lot. But now and again she would ask some rather odd questions: she wanted to know which unit I belonged to, what decorations I had won, whether I could soon expect to be wearing something around my neck – an oblique query as to my chances of winning the Knight's Cross. In other words, all those kind of questions that you wouldn't necessarily ask someone you had only just met. And the deeper meaning behind her cryptic words, 'Walter, you've still got to smile, even when you are being shot down,' still has me stumped to this day. Anyway, the whole thing struck me as very peculiar, and I was frankly sorry to end our little affair. Perhaps I did her an injustice and she wasn't some sort of informer at all. But in those days the only people you could really trust were your closest family and your comrades.

Leutnant Ernst Scheufele

11 Battle of the supply lines

Hauptmann Ehrler is awarded the Oak Leaves and becomes Kommandeur of III./JG 5

When I returned from leave to Petsamo there had been a number of changes. Unteroffizier Oskar Günthroth, one of our keenest pilots, had failed to return from a mission over the Rybachi Peninsula on 9 July 1943. Shortly after that Staffelkapitän Oberleutnant Widowitz had crashed while flying one of the unit's light communications aircraft, a Gotha Go 145. The wreckage, together with the bodies of Widowitz and his chief mechanic, who had been in the back seat of the Gotha, was found in the mountains. Hauptmann Hans Hermann Schmidt, known to everyone simply as H. H. Schmidt, was Widowitz's successor at the head of the Staffel, while Major Günther Scholz had been appointed Geschwaderkommodore of Jagdgeschwader 5. His place as Gruppenkommandeur of III./JG 5 had in turn been taken by Hauptmann Heinrich Ehrler, hitherto the Kapitän of 6. Staffel. On 2 August 1943, with his score standing at 112, Ehrler was awarded the Oak Leaves to the Knight's Cross of the Iron Cross.

But the most welcome news of all was that Josef 'Beppi' Kaiser, my Austrian friend from 8. Staffel who had been shot down over Russian territory back in December 1942, had returned and was risen from the dead, so to speak. The story of his adventures could fill a whole book; after he had been brought down he was captured by the Russians, and to his utter amazement was interrogated by a commissar who was a Russian Jew and an old friend of his brother. Before the war this brother had been the President of the Young Communists' League in Vienna. Kaiser always carried one of his brother's letters with him, and this was now to stand him in good stead. The commissar presented him with two alternatives; he could either cooperate with the Soviets or be put to work in the forests. When Beppi said he would prefer the former, he was sent for special training where he was taught how to operate a radio and use codes. Upon completing his training in the summer of 1943 he was told that he was to be dropped by parachute behind the German lines, his mission being to inform the Russians by radio of all German movements on Salmijärvi airfield and along the Arctic Ocean highway. One evening he was taken out to a Russian airbase. There, together with a Feldwebel of the mountain troops who had been put through the same process, he was bundled into the bomb bay of a Pe-2 and a couple of parachutes were tossed in after them.

Unlike Beppi, the mountain NCO was a giant of a man and the two chutes had been adjusted beforehand so that both fitted properly. But in all the confusion the pair got them mixed up. The Russian machine lifted off and, after about half an hour's flying time, reached the area of Nautsi where the two, each equipped with a radio and some rations, were ordered to jump. While Kaiser nearly slipped out of his loose parachute harness, his companion was trussed up so tightly that he was unable to cushion his landing and hit the ground with such force that he broke a leg. Kaiser administered first aid, then marched off in the direction of the Arctic Ocean highway, where he waited until a convoy of German trucks appeared. He waved the column down, quickly told the soldiers the whole story and appealed for help. Suspected of being saboteurs, Kaiser and the mountain NCO were arrested and brought in for questioning. The fact that it took nearly another four weeks before we were informed of the safe return of one of our pilots, and that he stood accused of being an enemy agent to boot, filled us with righteous indignation. Eventually, however, the MPs were convinced that Kaiser had never had the slightest intention of collaborating with the Russians and had set out to hoodwink them from the start.

When Beppi was finally released and turned up back at Petsamo we were overjoyed to see him again. It was from him that we also learned more of the circumstances surrounding Rudi Müller's capture and subsequent treatment. Kaiser was critical of the rules laid down by our leaders regarding behaviour in the event of capture. If these were followed, he said, it could only result in the harshest of treatment being meted out in the Russians' prisoner-of-war camps. In his opinion it was far better to play along with the enemy than offer stubborn resistance. Staffelkapitän H. H. Schmidt listened to Kaiser with interest. When he himself later went into Russian captivity he was able to make good use of Kaiser's advice.

While I was on leave in Germany most of our Me 109F-4s had been replaced by the newer Me 109G-2. There are still those who maintain that the Gustav was much too heavy to take full advantage of the improvements embodied in its design. In actual fact the G-2 was only some 200kg heavier than the F-4. To offset this, its Daimler-Benz DB 605A engine produced 1,475hp, and with water-methanol injection would even deliver 1,800hp for short periods.

On 18 August 1943 the Focke-Wulf Jabos again flew several missions against Russian ships attempting to deliver supplies to their troops on the Rybachi Peninsula. This time our

From the left, Stoll, König, Gayko, H. H. Schmidt, myself, unknown, Timm and Amend

After 'cooperating' with the Russians, Josef Kaiser never flew ops with us again on the Arctic Ocean front

escorting fighters clashed with a mixed bag of La-5s, Airacobras, Hurricanes and Kittyhawks over Eina Bay. In an effort to keep our machines tied to the ground, Russian bombers had simultaneously tried to mount a raid on Petsamo. But they were intercepted by the Expertenstaffel, with Hauptmann Heinrich Ehrler managing to bring down three of the attackers. On the afternoon of that same day Stab III./JG 5, together with 8. and 9. Staffeln, more than twenty Me 109s in all, took off to escort Fw 190s on another anti-shipping strike. On this occasion the target was a small group of Russian supply vessels spotted heading northwards up the eastern coast of the peninsula. We split up into three separate formations of varying sizes, planning to attack the ships from different directions. It was the job of my group of Me 109s to protect the Fw 190 Jabos; while the Focke-Wulfs dived on the ships, scoring hits on most of them, we attacked the vessels' air umbrella of escorting Hurricanes and Airacobras. As soon as they saw that we had the advantage in numbers, the Russians quickly formed a defensive circle, but I knew how to deal with this manoeuvre by

now and clamped myself onto the tail of the leading Russian machine. After taking a moment to adjust my angle, I opened fire and the Hurricane went down.

With the leader gone the defensive circle was split apart and the remaining fighters scattered panic-stricken in all directions. I chased after one of the Airacobras and was soon able to claim it as my second victim of the day. Before launching my next attack I decided to gain a little more altitude and climbed upwards through a thick bank of clouds lying directly overhead. Just at this moment some Kittyhawks appeared. In his excitement one of the newcomers perhaps forgot our invariable tactic of keeping at least one Rotte in position as top cover. But for whatever reason, this particular Kittyhawk unluckily chose to follow me up into the clouds. When he emerged the Messerschmitt of Major Scholz pounced on him from above and shot him down. After my third pass at another Russian, unsuccessful this time, the sky was suddenly emptied of the enemy; Oberleutnant Horst Berger and Hans-Bodo Diepen of 8. Staffel had despatched our last two opponents. With a combined total of ten enemy aircraft destroyed, my former 7. Staffel was the most successful of the day. Three of their victories had been claimed by my old friend Franz Dörr, now promoted to Leutnant.

On the evening of 3 September Russian Hurricanes carried out a surprise low-level attack on our airfield. Causing no damage, they disappeared just as quickly as they had come. Six of us set off after the Hurricanes and caught up with them before they reached the front lines. My first victim crashed shortly after 19.00 hours. Still at low level, Leutnant Horst Stephan and I then chased two of the Hurricanes that had become separated from their formation. At a height of between 40 and 50 metres, and within the space of a minute, we each claimed one of the stragglers.

Prior to every mission a briefing was held, the only exceptions being when we were ordered off on emergency scrambles. But even on these occasions there had usually been enough time beforehand to decide who was to fly with whom, who would lead each Rotte and Schwarm, and who would be in overall command. Back in my days with 7. Staffel it was normally the case that Franz Dörr and his wingman would provide top cover at altitudes of some 6,000 to 8,000 metres. The Schwärme making up the main part of the formation would fly correspondingly lower, at about 4,000 to 6,000 metres, ready to engage

Hauptmann Günther Scholz is promoted to Major and appointed Kommodore of JG 5

the enemy. And if the enemy were Russian fighters, we could be fairly certain that they would be flying at an altitude of some 2,000 metres. Torpedo-bombers, on the other hand, would approach at heights of only 50 to 100 metres above the waves. After entering the water the torpedoes would either run in a straight line or describe an ever-widening circle in the vicinity of the target vessels.

The Russians also employed parachute-torpedoes. These weapons were mostly carried by US-supplied Bostons, which would launch them against convoys from heights ranging from 300 metres to a maximum of 500 metres. Upon splash-down the parachute was released and the torpedo would zig-zag through the water. Russian torpedo-bombers would usually attack our convoys coming in from around the North Cape in the Vardø or Vadsø regions off the eastern and south-eastern tips of the Varanger Peninsula. On most occasions, however, we were able to intercept them en route to their targets, either off the Rybachi Peninsula, over Motovski Bay or between the Varanger Peninsula and the North Cape. Then they would hastily jettison their torpedoes or turn back to base as soon as they saw others of their number already on fire and attempting to escape. Usually a single burst into one of the Boston's engines was enough to ensure that the machine wouldn't make it home. The flames from the burning engine would quickly spread to the fabric-covered control surfaces and the lack of lift meant that the aircraft would be unable stay in the air for any length of time.

The personal emblem carried on Scholz's Me 109

Leutnant Franz Dörr. 'Yellow 4' wears both the Staffel badge of 9./JG5 and the Gruppe shield

Many victories could not be confirmed by wingmen or other pilots flying the same mission simply because the remains of an aircraft shot down at sea were immediately swallowed up by the swell. The waves in this region were more often than not higher than a house. Other typical indications of an aircraft going into the water, patches of oil for example, were also dispersed by the heavy swell within a very short space of time. It can generally be assumed that Artic Ocean pilots shot down appreciably more enemy aircraft than were reported at debriefings. During some missions enemy aircraft could be claimed as destroyed, but wingmen or other pilots were unable to confirm the kill because they themselves were engaged with the enemy, either intent on attacking an opponent or fully occupied trying to keep him at bay.

There were also instances of duplicate claiming. These came about when an enemy machine was shot down at high altitude and the kill was both witnessed and confirmed by the wingman. But if, on its way down, the victim chanced for a few seconds to level out again before hitting the ground and another pilot attacked it, delivering the coup de grâce, then he too would claim its destruction. During post-op debriefings only those claims corroborated by a witness were accepted. Then there would be seven forms to complete including, for example, the combat report, the aerial witnesses' report or reports, the claimant's own verification of time and location, altitude, identity of the enemy, weapons and type of ammunition used, number of rounds expended, etc. These would then be taken to the Gruppe's command post where the Kommandeur would check them and append his own written report. The next stage was to send all the documents via courier aircraft to the General Staff in Oslo. Here they would undergo further scrutiny before being forwarded to the Reichsluftfahrtministerium, or Air Ministry, in Berlin. And only after approval by the RLM would the original claim be officially recognised as a confirmed victory.

Since the previous winter the aggression displayed by the Russian Air Force on the Arctic Front had increased enormously. There was evidence that the number of enemy attack aircraft, bombers, torpedo-bombers and ground-assault machines had doubled. The earlier types used by the Russians for offensive operations, such as the Il-4, Hampdens and Pe-2s, had given way to Il-2 Sturmoviks and the twin-engined Bostons. Protected by Yak and Airacobra escort fighters, the Boston bombers and torpedo-bombers, together with Il-2 Sturmoviks armed not only with bombs but now also with rocket projectiles, were seriously harassing our convoys and tankers rounding the North Cape. Close fighter cover for our coastal convoys had become a necessity during the recent summer months. Prior to that they had simply been escorted by the floatplanes, which were also employed on anti-submarine duties, and, from time to time, by a few Me 110 Zerstörer. Now most of the Zerstörer had to fly additional convoy escort missions, which meant that the number of other operations they could mount, for example attacks on the Kirov railway line running south from Murmansk, was reduced dramatically. But the Me 110s on their own could no longer protect our convoys from Russian air attack. Since the early summer we had been encountering Yak-1 and Yak-7 fighters with ever-increasing frequency and soon we were to make the acquaintance of the new Yak-9 fighters, which were at least the equal of our Me 109s. I am still firmly of the opinion today that it was the introduction of these Yaks that heralded the end of our air supremacy on the Arctic Ocean front.

On the afternoon of 12 September six machines of our Staffel took off for a freie Jagd sweep along the north-eastern coastline of the Kola Peninsula. As always, one Rotte remained high as top cover to guard against surprise attack, while the remaining Schwarm of four machines hunted at a lower level for worthwhile targets. As there was not a thing to be seen in the sky and the needles of our fuel gauges were indicating that it would soon be time to head back, we resigned ourselves to returning to base empty-handed. But just as we were about to alter course onto a south-westerly heading my wingman Hermann Amend and I spotted eight Kittyhawks skimming the waves above the coastal shallows between the shore and open water. They appeared to be completely unsuspecting, for they were keeping perfect formation and showing no signs of agitation or alarm, neither scrabbling for height nor going into a defensive circle. Amend and I dived on the Kittyhawks and shot down six of them. You could almost feel sorry for them as, one after the other, they smashed into the water 20 metres below.

On 14 September the Navy tried to utilise the adverse weather conditions to slip one of our supply convoys across Varanger Fjord into Kirkenes harbour. Although there was a layer of unbroken cloud over the water and thick fog enveloped the coast, our ships were discovered by the Russians. With an improvement in the weather, the cloud base over the fjord now having risen to some 1,000 metres, the whole of III./JG 5 was scrambled at around 18.00 hours to defend the convoy. Before we could intervene, however, a number of Sturmoviks had managed to sneak up on it. While they flew directly into the barrage fire thrown up by the ships' Flak gunners, we turned our attention to their numerous escorting fighters, which had split up into several separate groups. Catching sight of some Airacobras at 1,200 metres, I set off in pursuit. I soon overhauled them and, with my wingman Amend faithfully guarding my back, prepared to launch an attack.

The Airacobra leader neatly avoided my pass and took up the challenge. Our two machines whirled and swooped through the air like two battling birds of prey. Despite the unholy confusion I succeeded in bringing down two of the Airacobras within three minutes of each other. When we then dived down to tackle the Sturmoviks I found I had a pair of Hurricanes clinging to my tail. Leaving Amend to 'sort them out', I opened fire on a Sturmovik that had just emerged from the curtain of Flak surrounding the convoy. Although the Il-2's rear gunner was putting up a desperate defence and firing at me like mad, the machine's fate was already sealed. At an altitude of 500 metres my rounds hit the Sturmovik's radiator. A white stream of liquid vapour immediately poured from the aircraft, which moments later crashed in a shower of spray, taking its two-man crew with it. The chase had brought me down almost to sea level and I had drawn several enemy fighters down with me. Three minutes after claiming the Il-2 I was sitting squarely behind an Airacobra. When it too went into the waters of the fjord from a height of only a few metres it gave me my fiftieth victory. At the end of the day's fighting we had scored thirty-one kills, divided between sixteen pilots from the various Staffeln. Among those who had been successful were my friends Franz Dörr, Helmut Klante and Jockel Norz. Amazingly for a battle of such savage intensity we had suffered just one casualty; 7. Staffel's Oberfeldwebel Erich Beulich being reported missing.

There were also occasional cases of confirmed kills not being officially allowed, such as that on 18 September when we escorted several Me 110s in an attack on Murmashi airfield. The Russians put up Kittyhawks to intercept us and I managed to bag two of them,

yet although both kills were established beyond doubt by eyewitnesses, I was only credited with one of them.

On Monday 20 September I had my first encounter with torpedo-carrying Bostons. It was around 14.00 hours that a Schwarm from 9. Staffel, led by Staffelkapitän Hauptmann H. H. Schmidt, took off for Kongs Fjord in northern Norway, which lay some 150km to the north-west of Petsamo. Our job was to escort yet another of our supply convoys coming in from around the North Cape. Six machines of 5./JG 5 and four Me 110 Zerstörer of 13.(Z)/JG 5 were also taking part in the operation, and because of the distance involved we were flying with belly tanks. The weather was typical for the time of year: the cloud base was little more than 300 metres, but visibility above it extended for several kilometres. When we arrived over the reported position of the ships and descended through the clouds we immediately spotted a large number of enemy aircraft. There were about twelve to fifteen Bostons, escorted by some

Even a General can make mistakes: I claimed my fiftieth victory on 14 September 1943 and was not made up to Oberfeldwebel until 1 October. Seen here are the handwritten congratulations sent by Generaloberst Stumpff, GOC Luftflotte 5, on the occasion of my fiftieth victory, but addressed incorrectly to 'Oberfeldwebel' (it should have been 'Feldwebel' and dated 14 September)

twenty-five fighters, heading for the convoy at low level from a south-easterly direction. The Bostons, which were flying at a height of about 50 metres, split up into several groups in order to force us to do the same, thus preventing us from concentrating our fire upon them. While some of the Bostons turned away to starboard with the clear intention of attacking from the north, others continued on their course; hugging the grey wave-tops as they made straight for the ships.

However, before they had time to release their torpedoes we were upon them. While my wingman, on this occasion Unteroffizier Hubertus Schubert, guarded my back, I singled out one of the bombers flying on the right of the group. Closing to within a distance of 200 metres, I opened fire with both machine-guns and my cannon and saw my hits registering on the enemy's starboard wing and engine, which immediately started to burn. When I was only 50 metres behind him the right wing suddenly folded downwards, struck the surface of the water and was violently torn off. The next instant the clock on my instrument panel was showing 15.21 hours, and the Boston somersaulted and smashed into the water on its back. I then pulled my machine up and prepared to launch an attack on another pair of Bostons that had by now released their torpedoes.

Perhaps at this point it might be interesting to give a couple of examples of the typical sort of combat reports written by aerial witnesses in the immediate aftermath of an action such as this. Here, therefore, are extracts from the reports of Hauptmann Schmidt and my wingman Schubert detailing my next two kills:

'After shooting down a Douglas Boston during the course of the action at 15.21 hrs, Feldwebel Walter Schuck was then able to attack a second Douglas Boston at low level from the right rear quarter and set its starboard engine on fire while closing in from a distance of 150 metres to 30 metres. After a second attack from the left rear quarter the port engine, hit by all weapons from a range of about 50 metres, issued black smoke and the enemy aircraft hit the water at 15.24 hrs some 26 kilometres north of Kongs Fjord (Grid square 27/East NT 3.9. D). I clearly observed and witnessed the destruction of the aircraft. Schmidt, Hauptmann and Staffelkapitän.'

After shooting down the Boston I turned round to see an Airacobra attached to Schubert's tail. His report explains what happened next:

'After observing the first shooting down of a Douglas Boston by my Rotte leader (Fw Walter Schuck), I was attacked from behind by an Airacobra. But Fw Schuck noticed this attack at once and so had enough time to get into firing position behind the Airacobra. The enemy aircraft thereupon immediately turned away to the north-east at low level, during which manoeuvre he was shot down by my Rotte leader by a short burst from all weapons at a range closing from 80 to 20 metres. Enemy crashed into the sea at 15.26 hrs about 30km NNE of Kongs Fjord (Grid square 27/East NU 1.3 D). At the time of the shooting down I was positioned approx 80 metres to the right rear of "Yellow 1" (Feldwebel Walter Schuck). Hubertus Schubert.'

From out of the clouds, a Rotte of Me 109s prepares to attack

In the meantime our aircraft had wiped out almost all the Bostons, but Leutnant Manfred Stahlschmidt of the Stab of II. Gruppe had also been shot down and killed. Our fuel was now too low to allow us to chase after the fleeing escort fighters. During the return flight we made a refuelling stop at the airfield of Svartnes on the north-east coast of the Varanger Peninsula before landing back at Petsamo shortly after 17.00 hours.

Nothing much happened for the next two days as heavy rain showers kept us anchored to the ground. When the weather improved on 23 September a force of Fw 190 fighter-bombers, Me 110 Zerstörer and Ju 88 bombers was despatched at around midday to attack a hydro-electric power station to the south of Murmansk. Our 6., 8. and 9. Staffeln were assigned to protect the force against enemy fighters. Fanned out in a wide formation above the low-lying clouds, we were able to surprise the several groups of Russian fighters that came barrelling up through them. Oberfeldwebel Norz opened the attack against a gaggle of Kittyhawks that were still clawing for height. They were able to avoid his first pass, but Norz quickly reefed round into a second and shot down their leader. Then Oberfeldwebel Rudi Linz, one of the rising stars of 8. Staffel, and Jockel Norz began to play 'hide and seek' with their opponents, flitting in and out of the clouds before bringing the game to a speedy conclusion with two kills apiece. The fiercest

battles were fought over Tuloma to the south-west of Murmansk, where we tangled with a whole bunch of Kittyhawks and Airacobras at heights of between 600 and 200 metres. By the time it was all over I had managed to score four victories: three against Kittyhawks and one against an Airacobra.

As our tactic of providing the fighter-bombers and Ju 88s with an exceptionally large fighter escort had proved so successful, a similar operation was ordered for the following day. This time the target was to be Polyarnoe, a port and enemy naval base near the entrance to the Kola Inlet. By 07.00 hours next morning most of III./JG 5's pilots were at cockpit readiness, and when the Ju 88 bombers passed overhead half an hour later we took off together with the Focke-Wulfs that were stationed with us at Petsamo. Our Me 109s, more than twenty in all, escorted the bombers and Jabos south-eastwards. Before long we had crossed the front lines along the River Litza with our Messerschmitts flying at an altitude of 4,500 metres and our charges 1,500 metres below us. Midway between the Litza and Murmansk we parted company with the Ju 88s and Focke-Wulfs; while the bombers swung on to a north-easterly heading, we maintained our course to the south-east heading straight for the clutch of Russian airfields at Murmashi, Songui and Arktika. The plan was to attract the Russian fighters' attention on to ourselves and keep them away from the bombers.

Rudi Linz, the up-and-coming ace of 8. Staffel

In the background, from the left, are Heinrich von Podewils, Franz Dörr and Rudi Linz

However, the enemy was already in the air – large numbers of Hurricanes, Kittyhawks, Airacobras and LaGG-3s were waiting for us at heights from 100 up to 2,000 metres. We flew a wide turn to the left, putting our Messerschmitts between the enemy and the sun, then the wild dogfight began. It was the superiority of our Me 109 Gustavs over the enemy fighters that determined the outcome of the battle. We emerged from it having scored a total of twenty-nine kills without loss to ourselves. Oberfeldwebels Rudi Linz and Jockel Norz, Leutnant Schumann and I returned to base with two confirmed victories each.

Two days later, on 26 September, Leutnant Friedrich Schumann was posted missing. He had shot down an Airacobra over Motovski Bay, but all trace of him was lost after that. Then, early on the morning of the 27th, a force of Pe-2s and Il-2 Sturmoviks, escorted by LaGGs, Airacobras and Kittyhawks, attacked our base at Petsamo, shooting up a Fieseler Storch and one of the Focke-Wulf Fw 58 Weihe aircraft of the air-sea rescue service. 7. Staffel was ordered to scramble and set off after the raiders. Catching up with them, my erstwhile Staffel comrade Feldwebel Helmut Klante brought down a Kittyhawk and two Sturmoviks.

A Focke-Wulf Fw 58 Weihe of the air-sea rescue service

By now my score on the Arctic Ocean front had risen to fifty-nine and on 1 October I was promoted to the rank of Oberfeldwebel, or Flight Sergeant.

At noon on 13 October more than twenty Me 109s of II. and III./JG 5 took off to protect a convoy laden with supplies that was approaching Kirkenes. While the Sturmoviks and Bostons were boring in against our ships almost at sea level, Oberleutnant Weyl, Feldwebel Lehner and Unteroffizier Klaus waded into the higher-flying Airacobra escort. This enabled Theo Weißenberger to break through to the torpedo-bombers and bring down five of them – three Il-2s and two Bostons – all from a height of just 50 metres above the sea. Shortly afterwards a group of Petlyakov Pe-2 dive-bombers, also with a fighter escort, appeared at an altitude of 1,000 metres. The machines of 5. Staffel rose to meet this new threat and were just able to prevent the Il-2s from releasing their bombs over the target.

At this time I was with 9. Staffel on the far side of Varanger Fjord in the Kiberg-Vadsø area where another wave of torpedo-aircraft was preparing to attack a second convoy following close on the heels of the first. I manoeuvred into firing position behind one of the Bostons flying on the far right of the enemy formation just as it was about to release its torpedo. A few brief, initial bursts of fire were enough to set the starboard engine well and truly ablaze; one more and the engine exploded into fragments, sending the bomber down into the sea. A Kittyhawk rushing to the Boston's aid joined it moments later when I shot that down too. After our Staffeln had all landed back at Petsamo we had another notable success to celebrate: altogether we had destroyed fourteen enemy aircraft.

But whether an operation was a success or not depended on many factors. Apart from the obvious ones, such as for example the serviceability of our aircraft, the numbers available, distance to the target area, and at what height and in what strength the enemy engaged us, the most important prerequisite for a successful mission was to have as accurate a weather forecast as possible. Even though weather-reconnaissance aircraft were constantly in the air feeding a stream of data back to the meteorologists, our 'weather frogs', as we called them, faced huge problems in providing us with even tolerably accurate forecasts as the weather conditions, particularly up here, were forever changing. After a time, however, I found myself able to

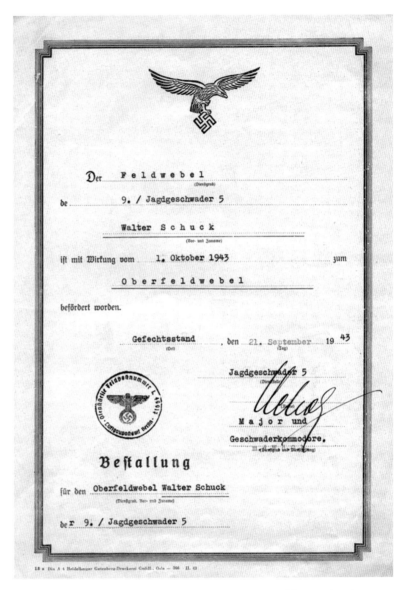

Promotion to Oberfeldwebel

| Over Lake Urd, west of Murmansk

'Northern Knight', a painting by Robert Bailey, showing Russian Boston torpedo-bombers attacking a German supply convoy

tell from the heights and types of clouds we were flying through – cumulus, stratus, cirro-stratus and the like – whether the forecast we had been given would apply as far as the target area, or whether a sudden change in conditions was on the cards. As my predictions, which I immediately passed on to my comrades, often proved right, a number of planned operations were diverted to alternative targets. After word had got round about my 'weather nose', Staffelkapitän H. H. Schmidt had a special flying certificate made out for me: 'Pilot Ofw Schuck Walter is authorised, irrespective of the current written weather report, to decide on his own initiative whether any flight he is ordered to undertake is possible for him to carry out in the weather conditions then prevailing.'

The onset of another Polar winter, with flying activity severely curtailed by the long twenty-four-hour nights, meant that a number of our pilots were allowed to go on leave, and I was one of the lucky ones. This time, though, I had to make the hazardous journey by road and rail. The former involved climbing on the back of a truck, which was to take me and several of my comrades to the nearest railway station at Rovaniemi, 280 miles away. I knew this stretch was going to be no picnic in the icy temperatures, so had taken the precaution of bringing along twelve of the large paper sacks in which sugar was delivered to our cookhouse. Much to the amusement of the

others I put three of these sacks inside each other, climbed into them, pulled a fourth – in which I had cut eye-holes – over my head, and covered myself with the rest. Halfway between Petsamo and Rovaniemi we pulled into a large depot where we were to spend the night. By this time my fellow passengers were almost frozen solid and no longer laughing. Before setting off next morning they begged me for some of my paper sacks. I handed them out, but was careful to keep enough for myself.

At Rovaniemi I boarded a train that would take me to Helsinki. More and more troops clambered aboard at every stop of the long journey down to the capital. Soon the train was full of Finnish soldiers, some of them no longer entirely sober. One of them, a huge fellow, was already quite drunk and proving particularly unpleasant. He was staggering from compartment to compartment demanding liquor. When he got to me all he said hoarsely was, 'Alcohol!' I fended him off with a gesture indicating that I didn't have any with me. But he wasn't to be put off. Constantly muttering 'Alcohol, schnapps' to himself, he began rummaging in my kitbag. Then, with a triumphant expression on his face, he pulled a bottle from among my things and read the label aloud in broken German: 'Dralle's birch-water hair lotion'. Babbling a few unintelligible words in Finnish, he opened the bottle, lifted it to his lips and drained the contents in one go. I fully expected him to explode. But nothing of the sort happened. 'Thanks,' he grinned widely before staggering off, eyes glazed, to the next compartment.

From Helsinki I crossed the Gulf of Finland by ferry to Tallinn in Estonia and there caught a train to Berlin. As I was so tired I didn't pay much attention to the passing landscape. The train made a number of stops in open country and at each halt farmers would appear offering geese for sale. I bought two of the birds and put them in the last of my paper sacks. In Berlin I presented the geese to the mother of my childhood girl friend, who had since got married. Although some districts of the city were displaying evidence of the English night-bombing raids, it hadn't yet suffered the appalling devastation that would later be visited upon it. Besides, I was on leave and my thoughts were on anything but the war. I celebrated Christmas 1943 at home with my family in Oberbexbach; my parents and my two sisters were there, and my younger brother Heinz had also been given leave from the front and had managed to get home as well. Everything was just as it had been in the days before the war, or at least one could be forgiven for thinking that there wasn't a war on at all.

Christmas leave at home in Oberbexbach

12 Yaks, Bostons and the Knight's Cross

When I returned to Petsamo in January 1944 the Polar winter still held the area tightly in its grip. My friend and wingman Kurt Scharmacher was no longer there. Because of his severe rheumatism he had been sent for treatment to clinics in both Germany and France, but, as I learned later, they were unable to do anything to alleviate his condition. Scharmacher's position as my regular wingman was now taken by Leutnant Horst Stephan. Unlike many other wingmen who, in the fever of the chase, dashed off to try their own luck only to fall quick and easy prey to the enemy, Stephan was more cautious and stuck rigidly to that most important of all basic rules for survival: 'Keep close'.

By this time II. Gruppe of Jagdgeschwader 5 had been transferred to another sector of the eastern front, which meant that our III./JG 5 was the only Jagdgruppe remaining on the Arctic Ocean. Despite the relatively sporadic air activity of the winter months, the occasional minor actions had already shown that the easy times were over. During the early weeks of January JG 5 had been able to claim only a few successes and had lost several pilots, including four members of my former 7. Staffel, in the process. 9. Staffel had been hit particularly hard by the loss of our highly respected Staffelkapitän H. H. Schmidt. He had taken off on a special mission to the Rybachi Peninsula to try to discover whether the Russians were building submarine pens on its western coast. As he could see no signs of construction work on his first pass, he decided to risk a second in order to get a closer look. His machine was promptly hit by Flak. After making an emergency landing he remained in his aircraft to await rescue, but because heavy snowfalls had set in it was three days before we could send out a search aircraft. All it found was H. H. Schmidt's abandoned fighter; he had been captured by the Russians and taken to a prison camp. When we met up again after the war he told me of the events that had followed his emergency landing and of his time in the camp.

On 28 January 1944 another large Allied convoy laden with war material put into Kola Inlet prior to unloading at Murmansk. The following day at around noon, having waited for the dull grey glow that passed for daylight up in this part of the world at this time of year to creep above the horizon, we took off for Murmansk. Flying in three groups of six aircraft each, we were being led by the Kapitän of 8. Staffel, Hauptmann Heinrich Ehrler. While still short of Murmansk, having not yet encountered any enemy fighters, we swung south-east to avoid the heavy concentration of Flak defences ringing the harbour area. Ehrler's original intention had

Hptm.H.Schmidt   Fw.W.Schuck

"Wenn ich über Walter Schuck, mit dem ich von Juli –Dez.1943 zusammen war, etwas sagen soll: er hatte die besten Augen, Adleraugen! – eine wesentliche Grundlage seiner Erfolge !"

been for us first to fly in individual groups to the area south of Murmansk, where we would then close up into a single force to attack the Russian airfields of Murmashi and Songui situated there. But his plans came apart at the seams due to the differences in formation flying as practised by 8. and 9. Staffeln. While Ehrler and his lead group turned to the right, the formation outside him on the far right flank disappeared into high cloud and lost contact. In the meantime the machines on the left, which had a greater distance to cover in the turn, lagged behind.

Quick to spot our confusion, a number of Yak-7s that had scrambled from Songui charged in to attack us. Although we managed to parry this first assault to some effect, the Staffelführer of our 9. Staffel, Leutnant Klaus Walter, was shot down. Then a second group of Yak-7s dived on us from a height of 4,000 metres and I turned to engage them head-on. For the next twenty minutes or more a grim battle was fought out, with our Me 109s somehow or other always being kept on the defensive. By the time we disengaged and returned to base, Hauptmann Ehrler and Unteroffizier Rudolf Stoll had each claimed a Yak and I had been able to bag a couple. But two of our own pilots had gone down. One of them was fortunate enough to make it back to the German lines on foot, but Staffelführer Leutnant Klaus Walter remained missing, having been last seen descending by parachute south of the Russian airfield at Arktika. Our 9. Staffel had thus lost yet another Staffelführer; Walter's place now being taken by Leutnant Wolfgang Rost.

It was also around this time that I too had to take to my parachute. It happened when I suffered engine failure while carrying out an air test in one of our newly delivered Me 109G-6s. Landing heavily, I strained the ligaments in my legs and sustained haemorrhages in both knees. Far worse was to come, however, for I spent the journey to the field hospital at Luostari south of Petsamo stuffed into a sleeping bag lined with reindeer fur that was absolutely crawling with lice. This meant that on arrival I first had to be de-loused, as did every item of the uniform I was wearing. As the latter was a longer process, my uniform was taken from me and the nursing staff, having no way of knowing that I was an Oberfeldwebel, put me into an airmen's ward. The nurses had probably heard mention of an Ober... something or other, and, perhaps because of my youthful appearance, had entered my rank as Obergefreiter – Leading Aircraftman – on the medical admission form. I

didn't bother to point out the mistake; I just wanted to get out of there as quickly as possible.

Every morning the ward sister, a domineering, heavily built woman – we called her the 'Dragon' – would fling open the door to the ward, whereupon the inmates, fellow-sufferers all, would have to lie to attention in their beds and chorus a cheery 'Guten Morgen, Frau Oberschwester'. As I didn't join in this ritual, but continued instead quietly to read my newspaper, she gave my bed a hefty kick with her stout shoes.

'The Herr Obergefreiter is a fine little dandy indeed. He wants to show us that he can read already!' she said in a sneering tone of voice, angrily tearing the pages from my hands.

'You'll regret that one day,' I responded calmly.

At the time I hadn't a clue as to how I could bring that about, nor did I know that the day of reckoning would come quite so quickly. For the rest of my stay in hospital I was well and truly in the Dragon's bad books on account of my supposed insubordination and was therefore delighted when, after a thoroughly disagreeable time, I was finally allowed to return to my Staffel. A few weeks later three of the nurses from Luostari, the Dragon among them, turned up at Petsamo airfield. They had been given leave and had heard that one of our courier aircraft would shortly be taking off for Königsberg. When they went to flying control to ask politely whether the pilot of the Ju 52 could possibly take them along, I got wind of the matter. As I knew the pilot, an Unteroffizier, fairly well, I took him to one side and explained just how badly our men in hospital were treated by this particular nurse and how she abused her authority by terrorising her patients. I then said I had a favour to ask of him.

'Put the fat one in the emergency seat right at the back of the machine and dance a few Flak waltzes during the flight.' In other words, perform some violent evasion manoeuvres and throw the aircraft about a bit.

The Unteroffizier nodded. In fact, the idea of really putting the Dragon through the hoops obviously appealed to him so much that he almost overdid it. When he got back he told me with a broad grin on his face that the Valkyrie had spewed horizontally in all directions. And as the machine didn't stink of only puke afterwards, he suspected she had done a little something in her pants as well. At any rate, after landing at Königsberg he saw her waddling off to the washrooms with her legs held unnaturally wide apart.

121

While on the subject, now might be as good a time as any to answer the often-asked question as to whether we didn't sometimes fill our trousers during a really tough fight in the air. The honest reply to that is, yes, most of us certainly had our trousers full on some occasions – but only in the sense that this was the expression we used to describe being shit-scared! As to the literal meaning of the phrase, our fighter missions were usually too short to pose any problems in that direction and besides, except for when we were ordered up on emergency scrambles, there was always time before take-off to perform any necessary bodily functions. That's not to say, however, that there weren't instances of pilots returning from an operation with their trousers somewhat fuller than when they started. Speaking personally, the excitement of battle didn't have its full effect on me until after I had landed, when I would sometimes feel a distinct pressure on my bladder. On such occasions there wouldn't be time to make it to the toilets. After climbing out of my machine I would dash round behind it, support myself with one hand on the elevator and do what came naturally all over the tail wheel.

The poor visibility hadn't improved much by the end of February 1944. During this month Oberfeldwebel Gerhard Reinhold, Leutnant Ernst Scheufele and Oberleutnant Theo Weißenberger were the most successful pilots of their respective Staffeln. On 29 February 1944, the last day of the leap-year month,

Leutnant Rost collided in mid-air with his wingman during a dogfight near Murmansk, and parachuted straight into Russian captivity. This meant that, since my arrival on the Arctic Ocean front less than two years before, I had lost five Staffelkapitäne or Staffelführer to various causes.

With the spring of 1944 the days became longer and the level of air activity escalated accordingly. On 3 March III./JG 5 was able to claim four victories, three going to 8. Staffel's Leutnant Bernhard von Hermann alone. On 12 March three of our new Me 109G-6s were written off in landing accidents, with a pilot of the Stabsschwärm being injured. The following day 8. Staffel flew a successful mission over the Rybachi Peninsula, which netted Hauptmann Ehrler three kills and Jockel Norz two. In addition, Leutnant Bernhard von Hermann also claimed one, as did my friend Oberfeldwebel Josef 'Jupp' Kunz.

Shortly after mid-morning on 17 March all available machines of III. Gruppe took off to protect one of our convoys making its way down the east coast of the Varanger Peninsula between Vardø and Kiberg. By the time we arrived over the ships at around noon they had already been subjected to one attack by enemy fighter-bombers. It wasn't long before we sighted another group of Russian aircraft approaching, a very mixed bunch indeed. As they got closer we counted more than thirty Yaks, Bostons, Il-2s, Kittyhawks and Airacobras. Taking full advantage of the hazy conditions,

Jockel Norz (front) and 'Jupp' Kunz on a reindeer sledge

Hauptmann Ehrler's Staffel dived on a gaggle of enemy escort fighters and soon one of the Yak-9s, hit by Ehrler's cannon, came tumbling out of the clouds. Meanwhile Ehrler's wingman, Bernhard von Hermann, was chasing another of the Yaks. The Russian pilot tried to escape by spiralling steeply upwards but the moment he reappeared out of the cloud tops, Bernhard von Hermann nailed him. Then Ehrler came down to join me and the other pilots of 9. Staffel in tackling the Bostons. The torpedo-bombers were on the point of climbing back up from wave-top height when Ehrler's first pass set the outer left-hand machine ablaze. When it hit the water I was already positioned behind the third Boston from the left. My fire resulted in a thick gout of smoke pouring from the machine and I watched as it too went in.

My next attack on another of the Bostons didn't quite come off, so I gained a little altitude before swooping down on it again. Although one of its engines was already burning, the enemy machine was trying to escape out to sea. I set off after it and quickly finished it off. In the meantime Oberleutnant Georg Bayer, Oberfeldwebel Jockel Norz and Unteroffizier Fritz Hain were mixing it with the escorting Airacobras.

In his obvious panic, one of the Airacobra pilots pointed the nose of his fighter steeply upwards. Norz had no difficulty in picking off the enemy machine as it hung in the air like a ripe plum. Now another group of Airacobras joined in the attack on Norz and his wingman

Berger. But as they dived on the pair, Unteroffizier Fritz Hain slid into position behind the last Airacobra in the line. His fire separated part of its tail unit, sending the enemy fighter down vertically into the sea from a height of 100 metres. All our Me 109s were by this time embroiled in a ferocious fight with the Russians, during which I succeeded in shooting down a pair of Yak-7s. It was only after about half an hour that the furious melée began to subside when not just we, but no doubt our opponents too, were all but out of ammunition.

We flew back to base where our Messerschmitts were immediately re-armed and refuelled. As another Russian attack on the convoy could be expected at any moment, we took off again straightaway. The enemy had already launched another torpedo strike against the ships crawling southwards along the coast of the Varanger Peninsula before we reappeared. I was one of a formation of eight Me 109s being led by Hauptmann Ehrler and we saw the enemy aircraft just turning for home. We chased after them and caught up with them to the south-east of the Rybachi Peninsula, but we couldn't penetrate the strong fighter screen to get at the torpedo-bombers. I did, however, manage to bring down three of the escorting Kittyhawks. As this took my total for the two missions to seven, my comrades named me Petsamo's 'Hero of the Day'.

'Jupp' Kunz is congratulated by Jockel Norz on his latest victory

Fleeting fame: 'The homeland is proud of you' reads this teletype, in the name of my parents and siblings, but sent by the local party official (Ortsgruppenleiter) and town mayor

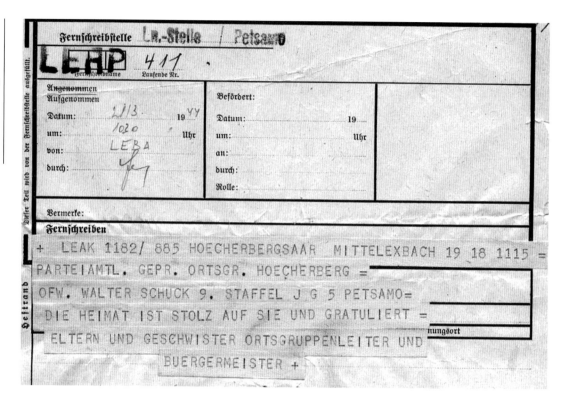

Servicing 'Black 14'

From the left, Ulla, myself, Jockel Norz and Bernhard von Hermann

Jockel Norz (left) after the award of the Knight's Cross

That same day, 17 March 1944, also proved very successful for Jockel Norz. In the course of several missions he destroyed five of the enemy, raising his overall score to seventy, for which he was awarded the Knight's Cross shortly afterwards.

But our victories of that day were dearly bought: we lost two highly experienced pilots and very good comrades. Leutnant Bernhard von Hermann was forced to bale out and was taken prisoner, and Feldwebel Werner Hakenjos was shot down and killed.

Shot down on 17 March 1944: Leutnant Bernhard von Hermann

Despite the impressive number of kills we were achieving, more had been expected of us; we should have provided better protection for our own convoys and we should have inflicted more damage on the enemy's ships. The earlier mistake of withdrawing one unit after the other from our area of operations for transfer elsewhere was now cruelly exposed for what it was – a major strategic blunder. It had robbed the Arctic theatre of the concentration of striking power we so urgently needed. For it was only up here that supplies of Allied war materials were arriving in such quantities, and it was vital that they be destroyed before the Russians could transport them to other sectors of the eastern front for use against our hard-pressed forces. But it was simply impossible for those few Gruppen still remaining to us, all flying missions under the most appalling conditions, to meet the many offensive and defensive demands being made upon them. A typical example was 23 March, when Russian torpedo-bombers again attacked one of our incoming convoys. Our Staffeln were unable to prevent a lot of our own essential supplies from being sent to the bottom and claimed just one victory in recompense – I shot down a Yak-9.

On 1 April a Ju 88 of the long-range reconnaissance Gruppe sighted another of the large Allied convoys, laden with all kinds of war material for the Russians, approaching from the direction of Iceland. The machine's crew also reported that the convoy's escort included two aircraft carriers, whose decks were crowded with fighters. It was on this date that I claimed two victories east of the Rybachi Peninsula, both of them P-40 Kittyhawks.

On the afternoon of 2 April Franz Dörr and I spotted a number of low-flying Yak-9s in the same area. Diving down on them, it didn't take us long to despatch several of the enemy machines; I got three of the Yaks in the space of seven minutes. Far out to sea, meanwhile, the convoy's escorting carrier fighters had shot down three of our four-engine Fw 200s, a flying-boat, and two Ju 88 reconnaissance aircraft. Then, on 3 April, using as a diversion the convoy that was now just two days' sailing away from the Kola Inlet, a strike force of some forty Fairey Barracuda bombers from two fleet carriers off northern Norway attacked our battleship *Tirpitz*, anchored in Alta Fjord. When the bombers withdrew they left more than 120 of the *Tirpitz*'s crew dead and 316 wounded.

As our recce machines were being prevented from getting close to the Allied convoy because of its strong defensive screen, III./JG 5 was ordered to fly to Murmansk to find out whether it had already put it into harbour there. While I was being briefed for the job by Ehrler that morning, strong winds were blowing in from the sea. The spring thaw had turned the main runway into a quagmire again and consequently we were having to use the planked trackway. I pointed out to Ehrler the risk of our machines being blown into the walls of snow still piled high on either side of the track should we be buffeted by a fierce gust during our take-off run, and suggested waiting for conditions to improve. But Ehrler brushed my objections aside. So my wingman and I started the engines of our Messerschmitts and taxied along the planks to the take-off point. At first all went well, but the moment the tail lifted off the ground I could feel the wind taking control of my machine. A few seconds later it sheered off to the right and dug

A pilot waggles his wings to indicate a victory to the waiting groundcrew

A long-range reconnaissance Ju 88 takes off past a winter-camouflaged Me 109 that has come to grief beside the runway

The *Tirpitz* still anchored under cover in Alta Fjord

itself into a heap of snow. As I had suspected that something of the sort might happen, I was prepared for the impact and escaped with just a few bruises. About 50 metres behind me my wingman's machine had ended up the same way.

When we reported back to the ops room Ehrler greeted us by saying, 'You pair of nitwits! Do I have to do everything myself?' Whereupon he stomped out, trailed by his wingman, having decided to fly the mission in our stead. Presumably he wanted to prove that he hadn't sent us off to do the impossible. Shortly afterwards the canopy of Ehrler's Me 109 was slammed shut and we all watched with interest as the Gruppenkommandeur's machine began to pick up speed along the wooden trackway. Again, all seemed to be going smoothly, but then a gust of wind caught Ehrler's machine and slammed it sideways straight into the wall of snow. When he came back into the ops room he whispered to me in passing, 'I'm a bit of a nitwit myself.'

Early in the afternoon a Hauptmann and a Hauptfeldwebel from the mountain troops holding the line along the Litza front turned up at Petsamo asking for our help. They explained why their postal clerk hadn't been to collect their mail from us for such a long time. All their post, coming either via the liaison staff in Oslo or direct from the Reich, was delivered to us in Petsamo for safekeeping and would normally be picked up by their clerk at regular intervals. The thaw had already set in along the Litza, however, making the tracks across the tundra impassable in places. This meant that delivery of the growing piles of mail by an overland route was out of the question for the foreseeable future. As I had always been curious about the sort of conditions our comrades on the ground had to

put up with at the front, I volunteered for the job of postman, saying I would make the deliveries 'by air mail' in the Fieseler Storch. The two mountain soldiers showed me the exact location of their forward positions on the grid map and suggested that, because of the inhospitable nature of the surrounding terrain, I should have the Storch fitted with skis and land on the frozen surface of the lake right next to their lines. Then they also asked if I could perhaps bring a few loaves of freshly baked ration bread with me, as they had been existing on just tinned bread for weeks. I therefore loaded the Fieseler Storch with a whole heap of mail, two dozen loaves and all sorts of tinned meats and sausage that our chief cook Jupp Heinrichs had dug out of his storeroom for me. As I intended to stay overnight, I added a few personal items to the already fully packed Storch before taking off on the approximately 80km flight to the front.

I informed the mountain troops by radio of my imminent arrival and they sent up a flare to indicate the lake on which they had recommended I land. As I approached, however, I saw that the ice around the edges of the lake had already melted and that it was rimmed by a thin strip of water. I therefore went round again and came in at a higher speed. This enabled me to skip the skis of the Storch over the narrow channel of water and slide up the slight incline surrounding the lake. A group of soldiers came hurrying across. I asked them to cut down a few bushes and branches and place these under the skis of my machine so that they didn't freeze solid to the boggy ground overnight. The troops set to with a will and I gave no further thought to the morning's take-off and return flight to Petsamo.

Paratroopers of the 20th Mountain Army, with a Fieseler Fi 156 Storch in the foreground

A ski-equipped Fieseler Storch above the tundra

Not surprisingly, the mountain troops fell upon the supplies I had brought them. A bottle of French liqueur was soon making the rounds, its square shape giving a strong clue as to the kind of heads those indulging in more than a few glasses of the stuff would be waking up with in the morning. After a lousily cold night I had to admit that our quarters at Petsamo were the height of luxury when compared to those of the unfortunate mountain troops. Because of the cold I gave myself 'a lick and a promise' instead of my usual good wash, declined the offer of breakfast and looked forward to soon being back home.

The soldiers pushed the Storch down the slope, across the strip of shallow water and out onto the solid ice of the lake. After saying my farewells, I pressed the button in the cockpit to ignite two of the four cartridges that were attached to either side of each ski to assist me in my take-off. But only one cartridge fired, which resulted in the Storch promptly performing several crazy pirouettes across the ice. The watching soldiers were highly amused by my antics, but I quickly made it clear to them that if they didn't help me in my next attempt to get off by giving me a really good push, they'd be in for a much harder job: the aircraft would have to be bodily lifted up and the undersides of the skis rubbed clean again. This did the trick. I gave full throttle, fired the remaining charges, and with three soldiers putting their full weight behind each of the left and right bracing struts, the Storch began to gain speed and lifted cleanly off the ice.

On the flight back I realised that the right-hand ski had somehow been damaged during the cartridge-assisted take-off; it was only hanging on by a single bolt and was spinning in the airstream like a sideways-mounted propeller. If the ski happened to be reversed when I landed, with the upward curve at the tip pointing downwards, the right undercarriage leg would buckle and be torn off, and a crash would be inevitable. I radioed ahead to Petsamo to inform them of my predicament and, as I made my approach, I could see the fire crews racing across the field. A large crowd of spectators had already gathered around the perimeter to witness the expected pile-up. But I came in fairly low, throttled the machine right back to idle and put her down the moment the dangling ski reappeared with its tip facing forward and upward.

The gods of war were not in the least concerned about minor episodes of this nature, however, and on 7 April the next air battle flared up over yet another of our convoys, inbound from the North Cape, as it skirted the Varanger Peninsula on the last leg of its voyage to Kirkenes. As I headed towards the ships early that morning in the company of seven other pilots of 9. Staffel, two formations of enemy aircraft appeared out of the mist. In a matter of minutes we found ourselves involved in a fight against superior numbers of Kittyhawks, Yak-9s, Airacobras and Sturmoviks. I sent one Curtiss P-40 down from an altitude of 800 metres and a second not long afterwards from 300 metres. Then I despatched a third Kittyhawk and an Il-2 at little more than wave-top height. A few hours later – we had in the meantime returned to base to re-arm and refuel – we were back over the convoy again. This time I shot down a pair of low-flying Airacobras within the space of three minutes. The six enemy aircraft I had destroyed on this day had taken my overall number of victories to eighty-four.

Trotz 16facher Uebermacht

Deutsche Jagdfliegerrotte schoß 10 Sowjet-flugzeuge ab

An der Eismeerfront griffen im Abschnitt der Fischerhalbinsel sowjetische Schlacht- und Jagd-flugzeuge ein deutsches Geleit an. In die erste Angriffswelle von 12 Schlacht- und 20 Jagdflug-zeugen stieß eine Rotte deutscher Messerschmitt-Jäger. Trotz sechzehnfacher Uebermacht schossen die deutschen Jagdflieger zwei sowjetische Schlacht-flugzeuge und drei Jäger ab. Bei einem zweiten Anflug wurden erneut fünf feindliche Maschinen zum Absturz gebracht.

Die deutsche Jagdfliegerrotte (eine Rotte besteht bekanntlich aus zwei Flugzeugen) vernichtete also bei der Abwehr der sowjetischen Angriffe auf das deutsche Geleit zehn feindliche Flugzeuge, von denen der junge saarländische Oberfeldwebel Schuck allein sechs abschoß und damit seinen 84. Luftsieg errang.

On the Saturday evening before Easter Sunday – 8 April 1944 – I was watching a film in the barracks with a few other pilots of II./JG 5. Suddenly there was an announcement over the loudspeakers: 'Oberfeldwebel Schuck to the telephone!' When I picked up the receiver in the flight office a female telephone operator said: 'Herr Oberfeldwebel, please hold the line for a moment. I am putting you through to Herr General Kammhuber immediately.'

The next thing I heard was the high-pitched voice of the GOC Luftflotte 5: 'General Kammhuber here. My dear Schuck, I am especially pleased to be able to be the first to inform you that the Führer has awarded you the Knight's Cross. I would also like to add my own sincere appreciation and heartiest congratulations!'

Although I had never particularly hungered after decorations, I could hardly get the words out to thank Kammhuber properly – there was such a huge lump in my throat. The Knight's Cross! That was surely something only for the likes of such aces as Weißenberger, Ehrler, Rudi Müller or Heinrich Bartels. I made my way back to the main building in a state of some excitement. I had decided to keep the news to myself for the time being, but that simply wasn't possible. When I re-entered the room where the film was being shown, all heads turned in my direction and everyone wanted to know who had phoned me. So much for keeping quiet – I had to tell them all about the call and the decoration. Instant jubilation all round! Major Ehrler gave me a bear-hug and the others, in genuine joy and pleasure, began slapping me on the shoulder and simply wouldn't stop. Then the record player was brought into action and JG 5's unofficial anthem 'Carry me back to old Virginny' rang through the 'Cloud hut'. It turned into a long night.

A cutting from the *Berliner Morgenpost* newspaper of April 1944, describing the action of 7 April when I got six kills, taking my total to eighty-four

A congratulatory teletype from Secretary of State for Air Erhard Milch on the award of the Knight's Cross

IM NAMEN
DES DEUTSCHEN VOLKES
VERLEIHE ICH
DEM OBERFELDWEBEL
WALTER SCHUCK
DAS RITTERKREUZ
DES EISERNEN KREUZES

FÜHRERHAUPTQUARTIER
DEN 8 . APRIL 1944
DER FÜHRER
UND OBERSTE BEFEHLSHABER
DER WEHRMACHT

The Knight's Cross award certificate signed by Hitler

The following day our Staffel was transferred down to Pontsalenjoki. Since the drama surrounding the loss of Schumacher, Philipp and Helms back in August 1942, the one-time primeval forest airstrip had been somewhat enlarged and improved. But there was still a certain amount of chaos and confusion when we came in to land as the field could be approached from both left and right, and we were unsure which circuit to join. General Julius Schulz, the officer in command of all Luftwaffe units in Finland, had flown across from Rovaniemi in a Ju 52 for the Knight's Cross award ceremony. He was accompanied by several of his staff officers and by Hauptmann Jung who, like me, came from the Saarland. I must still have been looking pretty rough from the previous evening's celebrations in Petsamo, for after the presentation Hauptmann Jung went up to General Schulz with a look of concern on his face.

'Herr General,' he said, 'it certainly won't have escaped your attention that this man is showing signs of complete combat exhaustion. I urgently recommend that he be sent home on leave immediately before he gets shot down and we lose him.'

As Jung told me later, the General acceded to his request. I was to fly back with him and the other officers to Rovaniemi where leave papers would be made out for me. I was still feeling, and showing, the after-effects of the previous night's party, but, I thought to myself, at least my suffering has turned out worthwhile for once.

The atmosphere that prevailed at Pontsalenjoki was a far cry from what I had become used to at Petsamo. I was no longer accustomed to all the military niceties that had to be observed on the base. The station commander did not appear to appreciate our presence at all. Perhaps our arrival was associated in his mind with all the bigwigs that were turning up to disrupt his otherwise peaceful daily routine. At the meal that followed the presentation he was most punctilious in the seating arrangements and in making sure that everyone was served

A teletype from local air command HQ Kirkenes to III./JG 5 informing them that a crate of champagne is on its way to Ofw Schuck to mark his winning the Knight's Cross

Hauptmann Waldemar Jung from Saarbrücken (centre)

according to the rules of military hierarchy. General Schulz was ushered to the centre table and I, as 'guest of honour', was allowed to sit on his left. The staff officers were then shown to their places in strict order of rank and seniority. The General, station commander and staff officers were served first with sausage, fresh white bread and butter. As I had to wait somewhat longer for my meal, I presumed I was to be given something extra special today. I leaned back in my chair in expectation; I had all the time in the world, and besides, it would probably take a little while to grill a chicken or prepare a nice juicy steak. When a mess waiter then put a plate of ration bread and jam in front of me the look of bewilderment on my face must have been quite something to behold.

Left: General Julius Schulz

The official Knight's Cross photo for the press

After the meal General Schulz insisted that the best cognac available be brought out to drink to my Knight's Cross. The station commander was at great pains to show just how well stocked his mess bar was. In contrast to the previous evening's festivities, however, I held back on the alcohol this time. The same couldn't be said for the station commander; while he was drinking himself senseless, some of his men, who couldn't stand him either, were preparing to blow up his quarters. He had had an open fireplace illegally installed in his room – a breach of safety regulations for which he had already been reprimanded by General Schulz. Anyway, an airman had tied several stick grenades together and climbed onto the roof of the commander's hut. He then lowered the bundle of grenades down the chimney into the fireplace at the end of a long cord, slid down off the roof and detonated the whole lot from a safe distance. While we were flying back to Rovaniemi in the Ju 52 later that same night General Schulz asked me whether I had heard the explosion.

'I believe the station commander's fireplace blew up,' I replied innocently.

General Schulz turned to a Major travelling with us. 'Take a note. I have already told the man once to have that fireplace removed. If he disobeys my orders again he will face disciplinary action!'

To get away home at long last I travelled by train to Helsinki the next day. There I boarded a Finnair machine bound for Berlin on which Hauptmann Jung had reserved a seat for me.

13 Russian roulette

My unexpected leave simply flew by, but then the war beckoned again. By the time I set off by rail back to my unit I had already overstayed my leave by two days. I had to change in Berlin to catch the train for Tallinn, Estonia. At the Berlin station military police – commonly knows to us 'chained dogs' on account of the metal gorget chest plates they wore suspended from a chain around their necks – were checking the papers of all military personnel passing through. One of the MPs was examining every single paybook, leave pass and travel warrant. When he got to me and looked at my leave papers, he immediately spotted the two unauthorised days. In order to get some sleep during the train journey, and not to have to keep answering the inevitable 'hows, whens and what fors' from my fellow passengers, I had stuffed all my decorations in my jacket pocket. I didn't want suddenly to produce the Knight's Cross now to get the MPs off my back. If the worst came to the worst and I was taken into custody, I could always use it as a 'magic wand', hopefully to talk myself out of trouble. For the time being the MP simply ordered me to step to one side and wait on the platform until all the troops being checked had been given back their papers.

But in this large terminus hundreds of soldiers, sailors and airmen were clambering aboard trains heading off in all directions. They were hanging like bunches of grapes in the open windows shouting for the military police to get a move on and return their passes before their particular train departed. As the MP marched up and down the platform calling out the names of those whose papers he had finished checking, he was clearly beginning to sweat buckets. The troops were getting more and more impatient and starting to call him all

sorts of unprintable names. Then a few jumped from the train and surrounded him angrily demanding their passes back. The MP stretched up his arm, holding all the documents aloft so that no one could make a grab for them. In the resulting chaos one of the soldiers knocked his arm and the entire sheaf of papers was scattered on the platform. Everybody, including myself, made a dive for them, each scrabbling about for his own papers. By pure chance I found mine fairly quickly and promptly climbed into the train.

I dashed along the corridors until I came across a compartment where a number of men were dozing in their seats. Burrowing in amongst them, I pulled someone else's greatcoat over me as if I wanted to get some shut-eye too. It wasn't long before I heard the MPs hurrying through the train, shouting to each other about someone 'overstaying his leave'. One of them pulled open the door to my compartment, only rapidly to disappear again as the train gave a jolt and started to move. There may not have been time for them to make a note of my name, but they must have telephoned ahead requesting that a search be carried out at the train's next stop, for when we arrived in Königsberg later that afternoon another group of MPs started examining everyone's papers all over again. Luck was still with me – before they got to my compartment it was time for the train to pull out. But I knew they wouldn't give up and that more MPs would continue the search for me the next time the train stopped.

We continued on through the Baltic States during the night before reaching the Estonian capital, Tallinn, the following morning. As I had expected, the MPs were already at the station checking papers, but this time I was better prepared for the situation. I slipped between two trains standing on neighbouring tracks and spotted a Luftwaffe truck parked on the other side of the station. The driver was sitting at the wheel and I managed to persuade him to take me with him to the nearby airfield. As we drove out of town it was with no little relief that I watched the station disappear from sight behind us. Still my luck had not deserted me. At Tallinn airfield I discovered that a Ju 52 loaded with stores would soon be taking off for Pori in Finland. After a short chat with the crew they agreed to take me along and I spent the next few hours in the aircraft's freight hold jammed between crates of spare parts and piles of ammunition boxes. On arrival at Pori I was pointed towards a Me 109 that was waiting to be ferried up to Petsamo. The next morning, with a long-range tank slung beneath the Messerschmitt's belly, I flew to Rovaniemi where I refuelled before completing the journey back to my Staffel at Petsamo.

From May 1944 onwards yet more savage battles were to flare up around our convoys. We fought all the harder because it was a matter of ensuring that our own supplies got through to Petsamo. But with each attack the Russians launched against our ships, the greater their strength grew. On 11 May a large force of torpedo-bombers mounted a strike against one of our convoys and we became embroiled with their fighter escort. And although we succeeded in shooting down fourteen of their number, five falling to Ehrler alone, we ourselves lost two pilots, with many more Me 109s returning to base severely damaged. On 13 and 14 May the Russians carried out heavy raids on our ships lying in Kirkenes harbour. It was estimated that more than 200 enemy aircraft were involved in these attacks, but our successes were minimal. Only a few of the raiders were brought down by the harbour's Flak defences and our fighters, Oberfeldwebel Rudi Linz claiming one of the Russian machines. On 16 May the whole of III./JG 5 was scrambled to intercept the approaching enemy. Several hard-fought encounters took place and by the evening we had been able to account for twenty-one of the attackers. Oberleutnant Fritz Dörr, recently appointed as Kapitän of 7. Staffel, was the highest scorer of the day with six victories. But we had lost three more of our own aircraft, and a pilot of my 9. Staffel had been wounded.

On 25 May another German convoy had rounded the North Cape and was off Berlevåg, the northernmost tip of the Varanger Peninsula, heading towards Kongs Fjord. It was bringing us some urgently needed supplies and had to be got safely into Kirkenes harbour at all costs. Because of the long distances involved, and in order to be on station above the convoy when the enemy attacked, the Stab and all three Staffeln of III./JG 5 were temporarily transferred up to Vardø. There we were immediately placed on readiness to await the first signs of any enemy air activity from our signals intelligence service, from intercepted radio traffic, or from any sighting or sound of Russian aircraft from our spotter posts.

At about 20.30 hours – it was still broad daylight – the alarm was raised. Following the report that a large enemy formation was approaching Berlevåg, more than twenty of our fighters were scrambled to protect our ships against the impending Russian attack. Hardly had we taken up our positions at various altitudes above the convoy when the enemy appeared – a force of Boston torpedo-bombers with a considerable number of escorting fighters, some forty machines in all. As soon as they saw our strong aerial umbrella the Bostons began trying to launch their torpedoes from heights that were clearly too great to be effective. I scythed through a gaggle of Kittyhawks to get at the Bostons, lined myself up on the tail of one of the bombers flying out on the flank of the group and shot it down. Alongside me, Oberfeldwebel August Lübking claimed another of the Bostons. A few Kittyhawks who wanted to get in on the act thought better of it less than a minute later after Lübking and I had each sent one down. Breaking off from the fighters, I returned to the torpedo-bombers.

Throughout the short but vicious engagement I had just one thought in my mind – to protect our ships. The moment I saw that I had hit the enemy aircraft centred in my gunsight, I immediately turned to attack the next. There was no time to worry about whether my opponent had gone into the sea or, if it had, whether any of the other pilots had witnessed it and were able to confirm it as a kill. The important thing was to keep the enemy away from the convoy. We not only achieved our aim, but also inflicted an overwhelming defeat on the Russians in the process. In just twenty minutes our fighters had destroyed more than thirty of the enemy; in other words we had wiped out almost the entire attacking force. When we landed back at Vardø everybody was in a jubilant mood. My six victories, four Bostons and two Kittyhawks, had taken my overall score to ninety. Oberfeldwebel Rudi Linz had got five, Major Ehrler and Oberleutnant Franz Dörr four each. Even some of the younger pilots, not normally among the top scorers, had had a successful day: Feldwebel Heinz Arnold returned with three kills under his belt, while Oberfeldwebel August Lübking and Feldwebel Helmut Neumann had been credited with two apiece. In addition, the very talented newcomer Unteroffizier Rudolf Artner, whom I liked having at my side as a wingman, had been able to claim an Airacobra.

But it was clear to us that the Russians wouldn't let up until they had sent our supplies to the bottom. Under no circumstances were they going to allow the convoy to reach its port of destination, Kirkenes. In order to be ready for any new attack by the enemy we didn't go to bed, but remained at readiness close to our machines out on the field. I was just on the point of nodding off in my deckchair when the next order to scramble was given at about 4 o'clock in the morning. Once again we were able to reach our ships in time. By now the convoy had crossed the entrance to Kongs Fjord and was continuing on its slow but steady progress towards Vardø. This time the Russians, groups of Sturmoviks and Bostons escorted by at least thirty Airacobras and Kittyhawks, were coming in low and from various directions. A ferocious series of engagements erupted at little more than sea level, with the attackers trying to get through to the convoy and the ships' Flak gunners, in their turn, keeping up a constant barrage against any approaching aircraft. Although grimly fought, the battle again lasted only half an hour, and by its end we were able to celebrate yet another large 'bag'. With a total of thirty-eight enemy aircraft destroyed, we had given the Russians an even bigger hiding than the one delivered just a few hours earlier. The most successful pilots again included Major Heinrich Ehrler, Oberleutnant Franz Dörr and Oberfeldwebel Rudi Linz with five victories each. My contribution to the proceedings consisted of one Il-2 and three Kittyhawks.

It was during one of these convoy actions – unfortunately I can no longer recall the exact date – that I saw a Boston, already damaged and on fire, launch a torpedo at one of our freighters. I deliberately flew my Me 109 low over the vessel so that the crew could plainly identify me as a German fighter from the crosses on my wings and fuselage. Then I reefed the machine around in a tight turn and flew back to the torpedo that was still cutting through the water directly towards its target

and loosed off a few rounds at it. Alerted to the approaching danger, the ship was able to alter course in time and so avoid the torpedo.

The enemy's dogged air attacks on our lines of supply had a direct impact on us at Petsamo. The good times, when we enjoyed plentiful rations, were now a thing of the past, and in order to ensure the arrival of at least a minimum of the most urgently needed spare parts, ammunition and fuel we had to fly even more missions. The results were not always outstanding. On 12 June, for instance, Leutnant Werner Gayko and Feldwebel August Lübking were able to claim just an Airacobra each and I managed to down a single Kittyhawk. Because the Petsamo-Liinakhamari harbour basin did not have sufficient depth, the coastal convoys could not deliver supplies

Unteroffizier Rudi Artner and, on the right, Martin Ullmann, later of 12./JG 5

Congratulations on my 100th victory

to us direct, but first had to unload them on to shallow-draught tugs and barges at Kirkenes for onward shipment. One such group of small vessels loaded with vital spare parts was making its way along the final 80km leg from Kirkenes to Liinakhamari during the night of 14/15 June. The first Russian attack on the little convoy was launched by bomb-carrying Kittyhawks accompanied by Airacobras. But the vessels' escorting motor torpedo boats laid a thick smoke-screen around the slow-moving group and, instead of sinking our ships, the attackers found themselves on the receiving end when we waded into them. I shot down two of the Kittyhawks in as many minutes. We were lucky this time; all our supply vessels put in to Liinakhamari undamaged.

That evening the Russians tried again, sending in their Sturmoviks, escorted by a mixed force of Yaks, Airacobras and Kittyhawks, to attack the ships berthed in Liinakhamari harbour. While 7. Staffel under Oberleutnant Dörr concentrated on the Il-2s, 9. Staffel tackled the enemy Yaks and Kittyhawks. Between 19.11 and 19.15 hours I reported four kills over the R/T all were Kittyhawks. They were victories Nos 98 to 101 for me.

The two missions of 15 June 1944 were hailed as a great victory. Not only had we successfully defended the convoy and shot down eighteen of the enemy, another Eismeerjäger had clocked up his century! The mood of euphoria back at base was captured by a war correspondent named Laubenthal who happened to be present. He interviewed me, extolling me as the 'youngest ace' to have 101 victories to his credit. The interview was recorded on the then new medium of magnetic tape and I was completely taken aback when it was replayed to me and I heard my own recorded voice for the first time. For me, however, the biggest reason for celebrating was the fact that our essential supplies had got through safely.

But the Russians were allowing us no respite. That same evening one of their high-altitude reconnaissance aircraft, a Spitfire PR IV supplied by England, took aerial photographs of Liinakhamari harbour. On 16 June they discovered another of our convoys consisting of

Teletypes of congratulation on my 101 victories from Generaloberst Dietl (left) and General der Flieger Kammhuber (opposite)

War correspondent Laubenthal interviewing me about my 100th victory

several ships escorted by a small number of patrol boats. It was becoming clear that their attacks on our convoys were being planned and carried out mainly on the basis of information brought back by these Spitfire reconnaissance machines. On that day I happened to be on duty in the fighter control room, where my job was to evaluate the incoming reports of enemy air activity and decide on the strength of them whether or not our fighters should be scrambled. On this occasion, although the listening post set up on 'Salvation Mountain' had reported the presence of a Spitfire approaching Petsamo, I did not give the order for an emergency scramble. The Leutnant in charge of the post later visited the Petsamo control room and was most surprised that I hadn't sent up our fighters. He asked me almost accusingly, 'Why didn't you scramble when that Spitfire came over?'

I explained to him, 'We have been forbidden to because of the shortage of fuel. If we go up chasing Spitfires it's a matter of pure luck whether we catch them or not. The Spitfire flies at altitudes of between 6,000 and 7,000 metres and is carrying only a lightweight camera – otherwise it's unarmed. That means it can do 600kmph. By comparison, at those heights our Messerschmitts can manage 500kmph maximum. So it's not that easy for us simply to chase after them and bring them down. Besides, we've discovered that a reconnaissance machine will immediately

break off its mission and turn back the moment it spots the clouds of dust our fighters kick up when they take off.'

Then I added, 'I've noticed, however, that the Spitfires always fly one of the following routes: route number one takes them out over the Kola Inlet, around the Rybachi Peninsula to Kirkenes, and from there to Salmijärvi, Petsamo and back home again.'

Something new – hearing my own voice on tape

The following day, 17 June 1944, was destined to become one of the most thrilling of my entire operational career. During the night a Russian reconnaissance aircraft had discovered another of our coastal convoys skirting the Varanger Peninsula bound for Kirkenes. The Russians alerted every available unit for a major effort against the convoy. At around 7 o'clock in the morning our 7., 8. and 9. Staffeln took off to intercept the enemy between Kirkenes and the southern and eastern coastlines of the Varanger Peninsula. Less than an hour later we were confronted by the largest force of Russian aircraft we had ever seen; heading towards our Messerschmitts at an altitude of 1,000 metres was a veritable armada of well over 100 Sturmoviks, Bostons, Kittyhawks and Airacobras. We engaged the forward screen of Kittyhawks east of Vardø and I quickly shot down two of them. With more and more Me 109s arriving on the scene, Gayko, Linz and I next turned our attention to a group of Sturmoviks that was sneaking in towards the convoy at low level. The leading Il-2 was hacked to pieces by shells from Rudi Linz's cannon.

In order to get into a better firing position behind the Sturmoviks, I led my Schwarm around them in a curve to the right. At that moment another formation of Il-2s, escorted by numerous fighters, came charging into view. The Airacobras were clearly getting ready to

He listened with interest as I traced each individual leg of the flight with my finger on the fighter grid map hanging up in the control room. I continued: 'The second route starts from Murmashi, flies direct to Salmijärvi, Kirkenes, Petsamo, then back again. The third option is for the recce pilot to fly first to Petsamo, on to Salmijärvi and Kirkenes, then make out to sea for the return trip. If we're to shoot him down, it can only be done if he takes the first route I've described. And the fighter controller here has to be informed well in time. But all we need to be told is, "Aircraft noise over the Litza, route number 1".'

He promised immediately to raise the alarm the next time a Spitfire set out along this northern route.

A fighter control room with loudspeaker and enemy aircraft recognition charts

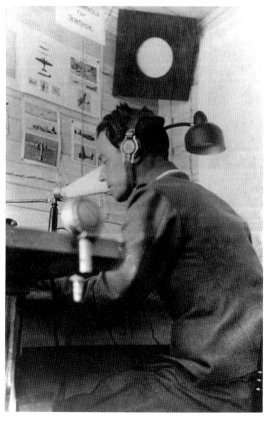

bounce us, but I spoiled their plan with a warning yell to the others: 'Climb!' While the Russians in their heavier fighters were still struggling to follow us skywards I quickly turned my Me 109 onto its back, yanked the stick into my stomach and dived at full throttle towards one of the Sturmoviks. My rounds smashed into its cockpit. As it started to go down I banked sharply away, then levelled off to slide into position behind another Il-2. In order to gain a little extra speed the pilot of the Sturmovik put his nose down to go lower still, but then suddenly pulled up again. And that was his undoing, for it exposed his most vulnerable parts: I sent a short burst of fire into his radiator, the Ilyushin started to burn and went down, pouring large quantities of smoke. In the meantime Oberfeldwebel August Lübking had despatched another of the Sturmoviks.

However, despite our best efforts the enemy's sheer weight of numbers was beginning to tell against us. We couldn't bring them all down. Even as we went after yet more of the Sturmoviks, another group managed to slip past and carry out a lightning attack on our ships. Then it was the turn of the Bostons, which came in a little higher to release their parachute-torpedoes. And still the fight wasn't over. I next accounted for a Kittyhawk and a Boston before nearly being caught napping by a second formation of Bostons escorted by yet more Airacobras. Even as Franz Dörr. Rudi Linz,

Gayko and I became aware of this new danger, the Bostons' gunners began firing wildly in our direction. Fiery pearls of tracer arced through the sky towards us, whizzing dangerously close past our cockpits. I tramped hard on the rudder pedals and skidded the Messerschmitt out of the enemy's line of fire. Then I selected one of the Bostons flying far out on the flank of the formation, triggered a series of quick bursts at its starboard engine and watched it go down with its wing ablaze.

When we got back to Petsamo I was completely worn out. I lowered myself from my machine and walked wordlessly past a subdued knot of mechanics. I had a feeling that this wasn't going to be the end of it. And I was proved correct, for that same evening the Russians sent over several waves of bombers to attack the ships of the convoy now tied up in Kirkenes harbour. These new raids were again almost certainly the result of enemy high-altitude reconnaissance.

Oberfeldwebel August Lübking, Unteroffizier Heinrich Wiegand and I took off to intercept the incoming bombers. When we clashed with the first group of attackers I flew straight through the middle of them, quickly claiming one of the escorting Airacobras. Then we fell upon the six Sturmoviks and shot down the entire formation. Later it was confirmed that Lübking had got one, Wiegand two, and that I had accounted for

From the left,
Gayko, Thome,
unknown,
Heinfried Wiegand
and myself

141

the other three. Returning to Petsamo for a second time, I was aware that I had just set a new day's record for victories on the Arctic Ocean front. It was now getting on for 22.00 hours and I was, if anything, even more exhausted than before. But I wanted to indicate in some way to the waiting ground staff that something special had been achieved today, not least because it was due solely to the untiring yet unsung efforts of the 'black men', our groundcrews, that I always had a perfectly maintained machine upon which I could not only rely in the tightest of corners, but upon which I could depend while continuing to add to my successes. The usual way for a Luftwaffe fighter pilot returning from an op to demonstrate that he had scored a kill was to fly low over his home field waggling his wings. But I wanted to do something a little different on this occasion. A series of rolls – that would fit the bill, I thought. And so as I came in over Petsamo I gained a little height and performed four neat rolls before touching down.

'Another four!' the ground crews yelled in jubilation. 'That's eleven in all that Schuck's knocked down today!'

But I was dead on my feet. I headed for my quarters to get some desperately needed sleep.

A few hours later I was roused none too gently. The control room was reporting excitedly: 'Aircraft noise over the Litza, Number 1!' I threw on my clothes and dashed outside. On the way I shouted to Leutnant Gayko: 'Emergency scramble! Come on Werner, but radio silence please!'

We climbed into our cockpits and moments later our Messerschmitts were roaring down the dusty runway. After lifting off we started climbing towards the heavens with our throttles rammed to the gate. Gayko was lagging slightly behind and I quickly realised that he wasn't familiar with the trick of leaving the flaps fractionally extended when climbing. Seven degrees of flap gave the Me 109 its optimum angle of ascent, and at that setting you could climb really steeply without fear of stalling. I climbed higher and higher, keeping an eye on the Spitfire's condensation trail the whole time. A glance at the altimeter: 3,000 metres. The Russian pilot didn't seem to be aware of our approach yet. I could feel the tension mounting within me as I put on my oxygen mask.

In order to take his pictures the Russian was flying a complete circle high and wide above Kirkenes. Then he turned towards Salmijärvi, still at an altitude of 6,000 metres. Reversing course, I turned through 180 degrees and carried on climbing. There was a crackling in my headphones, and although we had agreed on absolute radio silence, Gayko's voice piped up: 'Hey, that really is a Spitfire. And the Russian's flying it with British roundels!'

Despite the cold I was beginning to sweat with excitement. 'Ivan still hasn't spotted us yet,' I responded.

Loading the MG 131 machine-guns

'Well, he's certainly not in any hurry, is he? We'll soon have him,' Gayko said.

But I was concerned that my quarry might slip through my fingers at the last moment. 'If he looks round now, he'll push off like a flash and we'll be left with damn all,' I murmured half to myself.

'He won't do that,' I heard my wingman answer. And Gayko was right.

Leutnant Werner Gayko

Without the work of the 'black men' no victories would have been possible

By now the Russian was calmly describing another full circle, this time over Petsamo. When it was completed he pointed the nose of his machine eastwards preparing to set off home. The longer he remained on course for Murmansk, the more I was closing in on him. Another quick look at the altimeter – 9,000 metres. At last I had the advantage of height, an advantage that could be traded for extra speed when I commenced my dive on the Spitfire.

'When are you finally going to start shooting?' Gayko asked impatiently, for by this time, the dive successfully carried out unseen, I was sitting snugly behind the Russian in the perfect position to open fire.

'I want to take a better look at him. I've never been this close to a Spitfire before.'

I remained some 30 metres behind the Spitfire's tail, then events began to unfold almost automatically. When I pressed the gun buttons it was almost as if I was aiming at a target on the shooting range. Even so, it seemed an age before my rounds bored into the Spitfire's engine and fuselage. When large pieces of metal started flying off and came whirling through the air dangerously close to my own machine, I was forced to break away. At about 5,000 metres a small white dot detached itself from the doomed aircraft – the pilot had managed to bale out. By the time the remains of the Spitfire smashed into the tundra far below, we were already heading back to base. It later transpired that it had taken me just five shells from the MG 151/20 cannon and thirty rounds of MG 131 machine-gun ammunition to score my latest kill.

At Petsamo the pilots and groundcrews had been exchanging bets on my chances – the mechanics were convinced to a man that I would be successful, but the pilots wagered against it. 'He hasn't a hope in hell of pulling it off,' they countered.

While they were all still staring skywards the station commander turned up to ask what was going on. 'What's all the fuss about?'

'The recce Spitfire's in the air,' the men replied.

'So? What am I supposed to do about it?' he asked, shrugging his shoulders.

'Schuck and Gayko have gone up after it!'

The station commander rushed to the scissors telescope to get a close look at the chase. He was no doubt thinking to himself that if this accursed reconnaissance machine were finally brought down, the Russians would no longer be able to find our supply convoys quite so quickly. The mechanics told me later that the station commander had let out a loud whoop of joy when he saw the Spitfire tumbling earthwards.

A large crowd was waiting for us when we landed. I was treated like some sort of hero and everybody was clapping me on the shoulder. The station commander, who had quickly broken out his supply of schnapps and cigarettes, grabbed me in a bear-hug and didn't want to let go. I was

A flyer's motto of the times: 'Watch out, wooden-eye' – ie. keep a sharp lookout for enemy aircraft. The words at the bottom read: 'There she is already, old Mrs Spitfire'

naturally delighted to have got the annoying and nerve-wracking recce machine off our backs at long last. But I took even greater pleasure in collecting all the alcohol off those pilots who had lost their bets, and distributing it among the men of the groundcrews.

Later I even got a call from General Kammhuber, who wanted to find out for himself what had been happening. 'Schuck, what have you been up to, chasing after that Spitfire? You know it's forbidden to take off after individual reconnaissance aircraft because of the shortage of aviation fuel,' he said.

'Herr General,' I replied, 'we simply received a report of enemy aircraft over the Litza, whereupon we scrambled to investigate.'

'Very well, if that's the case everything is in order then,' retorted Kammhuber, and I almost could picture him in my mind's eye giving a conspiratorial wink at the other end of the phone. 'I've also heard,' he went on, 'that you've just set a new record for the Arctic Ocean front, twelve victories in one day!'

'That's not strictly accurate, Herr General,' I explained, 'but the twelve victories were achieved within the space of twenty-four hours.'

'Well, in my book every day has got twenty-four hours, and at this time of the year the sun shines day and night anyway. The bubbly is already on its way,' he added.

Two days later a case of champagne arrived.

As far as I can recall, 17 June 1944 was the most successful day in III./JG 5's entire history, with the pilots of 7., 8. and 9. Staffeln amassing a grand total of sixty-six enemy aircraft destroyed in a series of hard-fought battles. Among the most successful claimants were Oberleutnants Rudolf Glöckner and August Lübking, and Oberfeldwebel Heinz Arnold, each of whom scored nine, with Oberfähnrich Helmut Naumann and my fatherly friend and mentor, the now Oberleutnant Franz Dörr, being credited with eight apiece.

Station commander van Aaken (right), Döbrich (centre) and Ehrler

An

III./Jagdgeschwader 5 , P e t s a m o
-.-.-.-.-.-.-.-.-.-.-.-.-.-.-.-.-.-

        Zu den ausgezeichneten Erfolgen des 17.6.1944

Glückwunsch und Anerkennung. Fj.-Oberfeldwebel Walter

S c h u c k meine besondere Anerkennung für den Abschuss

der Spitfire am 18.6.1944.

                K a m m h u b e r
              General der Flieger u.
          Oberbefehlshaber der Luftflotte 5

F. d. R. d. A.

Kalinlek

Oberleutnant und Adjutant.

A note from General Kammhuber on the successes of 17 June 1944, in particular my bringing down the Spitfire

General der Flieger Josef Kammhuber

Returning after my 113th victory

On my way to the ops room

III./Jagdgeschwader 5
Jagdstaffel "Eismeer"   O.U., 18.6.1944
(Truppenteil)   (Ort, Datum)

Abschussmeldung, Zerstörungsmeldung

1. Zeit (Tag, Stunde, Minute) und Gegend des Absturzes: 18.6.44 um 05.10 Uhr (Quadrat 37 Ost U.E.4.1.d.) 45 km nordwestlich Murmansk
Höhe: 7500 m
2. Durch wen ist Abschuss / Zerstörung erfolgt? Fj.-Ofw. S c h u c k (113.Abschuss)
3. Flugzeugtyp des abgeschossenen Flugzeuges: Spitfire
4. Staatsangehörigkeit des Gegners: U.d.S.S.R.
Werknummern bzw. Kennzeichen: Britische Kokarde
5. Art der Vernichtung:
   a) Flammen mit dunkler Fahne, Flammen mit heller Fahne;
   b) Einzelteil weggeflogen, abmontiert (Art der Teile erläutern), auseinandergeplatzt;
   c) zur Landung gezwungen (diesseits oder jenseits der Front, glatt bzw. mit Bruch);
   d) jenseits der Front am Boden in Brand geschossen.
6. Art des Aufschlages (nur wenn dieser beobachtet werden konnte):
   a) diesseits oder jenseits der Front;
   b) senkrecht, flachem Winkel, Aufschlagbrand, Staubwolke;
   c) nicht beobachtet, warum nicht?
7. Schicksal der Insassen (tot, mit Fallschirm abgesprungen, nicht beobachtet).
8. Gefechtsbericht des Schützen ist in der Anlage beigefügt.
9. Zeugen:
   a) Luft: Lt. Werner G a y k o
   b) Erde:
10. Anzahl der Angriffe, die auf das feindliche Flugzeug gemacht wurden: 1
11. Richtung, aus der die einzelnen Angriffe erfolgten: hinten unten
12. Entfernung, aus der der Abschuss erfolgte: 30 m
13. Takt. Position, aus der der Abschuss angesetzt wurde: hinten
14. Ist einer der feindlichen Bordschützen kampfunfähig gemacht worden?
15. Verwandte Munitionsart: Pz.Spr.Gr.Patr., Br.Spr.Gr.Patr., Pz.Br.Gr.Patr.
16. Munitionsverbrauch: 5 Schuss MG 151/20, 30 Schuss MG 131
17. Art der Anzahl der Waffen, die bei dem Abschuss gebraucht wurden: 1 MG 151/20, 2MG 131
18. Typ der eigenen Maschine (z.)B. Me 109 E mit 2 Kanonen und 2 MG.): Bf 109 G-6
19. Weiteres taktisch oder technisch Bemerkenswertes:
20. Treffer in der eigenen Maschine: keine
21. Beteiligung weiterer Einheiten (auch Flak):

Gayko
(Unterschrift)

Leutnant u. Staffelführer

Zu Ziffer 5—7 ist Zutreffendes zu unterstreichen.

An aerial witness report and a combat witness report signed by Staffelführer Gayko regarding my 113th victory – the Russian reconnaissance Spitfire on 18 June 1944

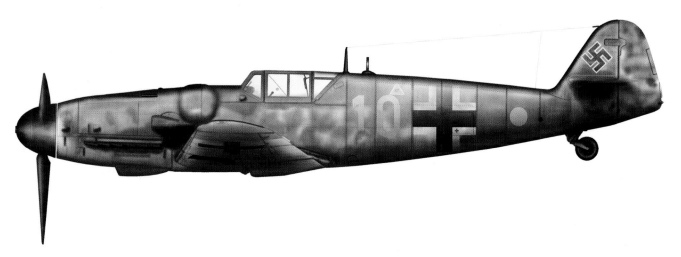

Messerschmitt Bf 109 G-6 'Yellow 10', my aircraft during the summer of 1944 at Petsamo. It was with this 109 that I achieved my twelve victories.
Kjetil Akra, 2008

„Mein 113. Abschuss..." / Wie Ritterkreuzträger Oberfeldwebel Schuck die Aufklärung fliegende Spitfire jagte

Als sie kurz nach Mitternacht bei strahlendem Sonnenschein starteten, zog der Sowjetaufklärer in 8000 Meter Höhe Kondens über dem deutschen Absprunghafen in der Tundra. Hauchdünn zeichneten sich die weissen Linien in das fahle Blau des wolkenlosen Himmels. Auf dem Liegeplatz standen die Männer des Bodenpersonals an den leeren Boxen und sahen den Staubfahnen nach, die hinter den alarmgestarteten Me 109 langsam verwehten. An einen Abschuss dieses Sowjetaufklärers glaubte niemand. Sein Vorsprung war zu gross. Zudem wusste jeder, dass es die Bild-Spitfire war, die sich hier so mutig in die Höhle des Löwen wagte.

»Der drückt kurz an, wenn er dies sieht und dann ist er über Murmansk«, sagte einer.

Ein anderer dachte sich etwas — und das war Ritterkreuzträger Oberfeldwebel Schuck. Als die Sirene heulte, war er augenblicklich von seinem Bett aufgesprungen, auf das er sich vor kaum einer Stunde todmüde hingelegt hatte. Elf Abschüsse hatte er in den letzten fünfzehn Stunden auf sein Konto gebracht und damit einen neuen Tages- und Abschusserfolg an der Eismeerfront aufgestellt. In diesen Augenblicken aber, da er die Spitfire Kondens ziehen sah, war alle Müdigkeit von ihm gewichen. Was geschehen war, gehörte der Vergangenheit an. Hier lag ein neuer Fall an. Diese Feindmaschinen, die auf »Nummer Sicher« gehen und in astronomischen Höhen den Platz anfliegen um seine Belegung bildmässig festzuhalten, hatten es ihm seit langem angetan.

So startete er aus einer Position, die nur herzlich wenig Aussicht auf Erfolg versprach...

Neben ihm flog sein Rottenflieger Lt. G. Beide hatten den Steuerknüppel an den Leib gezogen und stiegen der Spitfire nach. Von der Erde aus konnte man beobachten, wie sie langsam Höhe gewannen, wie sie schliesslich selbst Kondens zogen und die weissen hauchdünnen Streifen spiralenförmig im Blau der Himmelswiese verteilten, wie sie fächerartig auseinanderstrebten und wieder aufeinander zuliefen.

Die Waffenwarte, die Techniker, der Schreiber aus dem Gefechtsstand klopften sich auf die Schultern, lachten und deuteten immer wieder aufgeregt auf die beiden winzigen haardünnen

Streifen, die sich immer näher an die Sowjetmaschine heranschoben. In diesem Augenblick hatte jeder gemerkt, was sich nun ereignen würde. Nur der Sowjetpilot als einziger merkte nichts. Er zeigte sich als die verkörperte Ahnungslosigkeit.

Ofw. Schuck vor dem Start.
PK.-Aufn.: Kriegsberichter Kühne

Währenddessen, als die beiden Messerschmidt-Flugzeuge die letzten zwei Kilometer stiegen, entspann sich folgendes Gespräch zwischen Ritterkreuzträger Walter Schuck und seinem Rottenflieger:

»Herr Leutnant, das ist doch die Spitfire« (während des Startes waren ihm Zweifel gekommen. Es konnte auch eine Jak 9 sein), gleich sind wir dran«.

»Der Iwan merkt immer noch nichts.«
»Mensch, muss der'ne lange Leitung haben.«
»Wenn der seine Birne dreht, ist der Braten futsch«.
»Tut der nicht.«

Inzwischen waren die beiden Me 109 auf gleiche Höhe gekommen und langsam bis auf fünfzig Meter an die Spitfire herangeflogen.

»Sie ist es, sie ist es«, kam es ein wenig aufgeregt aus dem Mund des Ritterkreuzträgers. An den abgerundeten Flächenspitzen und dem Profil war klar die Spitfire zu erkennen. Oberfeldwebel Schuck sass in Schussposition.

»Wenn der wüsste, dass er gleich ins Himmelreich fährt.«
»Schiessen Sie doch endlich«...
»Eine kleine Weile noch, der Anblick ist zu schön, meine erste Spitfire, die ich vor den Rohren habe...«

Das letzte Wort war kaum ausgesprochen, als Oberfeldwebel Schuck auf die Knöpfe drückte. Glühende Fäden sprangen aus den Rohren seiner Maschinenwaffen und frassen sich in den Rumpf und die Flächen der Spitfire. Die Feindmaschine kam in eine trudelnde Bewegung, fing sich in etwa 6000 Meter Höhe wieder, trudelte weiter... zweitausend Meter tiefer löste sich ein weisser Punkt aus der abstürzenden Maschine. Der Sowjetpilot war mit dem Fallschirm ausgestiegen, während die Spitfire nun steil nach unten sauste und brennend in der Tundra aufschlug.

Als der Oberfeldwebel gelandet und ausgerollt war und wieder in seiner Boxe stand, sprang er freudestrahlend aus dem Führersitz seiner Me 109. Lächelnd lief er von einem Gratulanten zum anderen, rannte nochmals um die Maschine, klopfte seinen braven »Gaul« anerkennend auf den Rumpf und rief einem anderen Flugzeugführer entgegen, der auf ihn zukam: »Endlich mal eine Spitfire.«

So freudig erregt hatt noch keiner von uns Walter gesehen. Sämtliche sowjetischen Jagd- und Kampfmaschinen sind in seiner Abschussliste vertreten. Auch die amerikanischen Baumuster, die den Sowjets geliefert werden; nur eine Spitfire fehlte bisher. Der technische Schreiber aber rief den Gruppengefechtsstand an und meldete den 113. Luftsieg des Ritterkreuzträgers Oberfeldwebel Schuck und seinen 12. Abschuss innerhalb von 24 Stunden.

Kriegsberichter Dietrich

190

A newspaper account of my 113th victory

The next ten days were somewhat quieter, at least for us at Petsamo. On 24 June, while en route for Murmansk, I managed to bring down a Yak-9 north-west of Ura Guba, but it was not until 27 June that we again encountered a large number of Russian aircraft over Kirkenes. That afternoon III./JG 5 clashed with a formation of Boston torpedo-bombers strongly escorted by Yak-9s, Kittyhawks and Airacobras. A fierce scrap took place at altitudes ranging from 2,000 to 6,000 metres. Jockel Norz shot down five of the enemy and I returned home with four victories.

But it wasn't all one-sided. Our Geschwader was having to mourn its fallen comrades with increasing frequency. And when it was one of the 'old hares' who went missing, it was simply no longer possible to replace him. The days when a pilot would not be sent to the front

before first being given a solid foundation in flying training were long gone. The replacements we were now getting from the schools in the Reich were totally unprepared for combat. During fighter pilot training they may have practised their take-offs and landings, but they often had fewer than ten flying hours in their logbooks. These young pilots were full of fighting spirit, no question about that, but most of them lacked even the most rudimentary knowledge of flying and combat discipline, of navigation, of aerial tactics, evasive manoeuvres when under attack, and so on. The result was that we no longer had just the enemy to concentrate on, we also had to watch over the tyros entrusted to our care.

When they arrived it was relatively easy to tell from their behaviour how long each was likely to survive. This was especially so after

The cover of the 1 July 1944 issue of 'Luftflotte Nord', the air fleet's own magazine – the caption reads '12 victories in one day'

the glass or two most of them accepted to celebrate their joining our unit. Those who immediately began boasting about how they were going to show the enemy a thing or two, we practically wrote off right from the start. You could be fairly certain they wouldn't be coming back from their first mission. As we were now having to fly more and more often in the company of these youngsters instead of with the experienced wingmen of old, I tried to hammer home to each new firebrand the cast-iron rule of always sticking close together. But, unfortunately, all too many of them failed to heed my words of wisdom. Thirsting for action, fired up with ambition and full of mindless heroism, off they would go on their own, only to be promptly shot down.

After losing a number of these daredevil types in this way, and no longer being willing to watch, often without being able to intervene, as they so recklessly threw their young lives away, I sought the advice of my friend Franz Reichenbach. He was an Oberfeldwebel and chief clerk of the ops room, and thus the first to get to see the documents of all new arrivals fresh from the flying schools. As we went through the files together I spotted the name of a flying instructor that was familiar to me: Oberleutnant Heinz de Vries. We had got to know each other at Bergen during 7./JG 5's original transfer flight northwards along the Norwegian coast back in January 1942. Although he was by then already wearing the Combat Flight Clasp in Gold for his service with JG 54 on the Channel front, he confided to me that he would dearly like to be posted to a flying school as an instructor. He was not at ease with all the 'killing' and would much prefer to teach youngsters the finer points of flying and, at the same time, show them how to be able to avoid acts of senseless self-sacrifice. I arranged with Franz Reichenbach that in future he would send me only those pilots who had been trained by this one instructor – and from then on I had no further problems.

During the night of 28 June the Russians again launched a major raid on Kirkenes. Between 00.02 and 00.09 hours I shot down three Airacobras and a Boston. Three hours later, having in the meantime refuelled and re-armed, I claimed a pair of Yak-9s and another Airacobra in the Murmansk area. Jockel Norz was credited with three kills, which took him to 100 victories. Overall, in terms of enemy aircraft destroyed, June 1944 was to prove the most successful month of my entire operational career – in those thirty days I achieved more than thirty kills. One reason for this was that the Russian Air Force was now coming over into our airspace in ever larger formations and we ourselves were no longer being called upon quite so often to overfly the front lines into enemy territory. This had always been a risky business, but now the chances of our being shot down and ending up in Russian captivity were greatly reduced. Furthermore, during the period of the summer's midnight sun we were flying practically around the clock, and I had gained so much combat experience by this stage that my actions had become almost automatic. Another factor was the continued shortcomings of our opponents. They seemed incapable of coordinating the fighter escorts for their bomber, ground-attack or torpedo aircraft so that the whole formation arrived over the target at the same time. It was often the case that we were able to hack away at the bombers completely unhindered for considerable lengths of time simply because their escorting fighters turned up too late.

Fighter instructor
Heinz de Vries

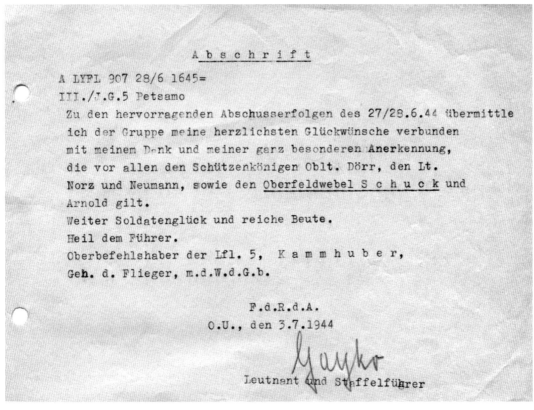

A message of congratulation and appreciation from General Kammhuber to the pilots of III./JG 5 for their successes of 27/28 June 1944

Today's aviation historians cast doubts time and time again on the high scores claimed by the Luftwaffe's fighter pilots and call into question the fact that we on the eastern front could apparently claim so many victories, one after the other, within the space of just a few minutes. But the explanation for such 'serial' kills, at least as far as the Arctic theatre was concerned, is relatively straightforward: our opponents not only appeared in such vast numbers, they also continued to stick rigidly to the same outdated combat formations that had long been proven expensive and unworkable. Instead of learning from our practice of almost invariably keeping at least a Rotte or Schwarm at height to provide top cover, they all remained so tightly packed together that when we dived through one of their formations we could bring down several machines in one pass. Even when we had

From the left, myself, Franz Dörr, Heinrich Ehrler and Jockel Norz

151

taken out two or three of their number in this way, the remainder would inexplicably immediately close up to fill the gaps torn in their ranks. And as every attack produced results, I could sometimes shoot down three or four of the enemy in very quick succession.

On the evening of 4 July over Kirkenes harbour, for example, I brought down two Bostons and an Airacobra and the whole thing took just three minutes. On 17 July I needed all of fifteen minutes to despatch seven opponents: three Bostons and four Airacobras. Although this may sound like potting at ducks in a shooting gallery, it's not to imply that the Russians didn't fight bravely and stubbornly, and their new Yak fighters were every bit the equal of our Messerschmitts. Numerically they were always superior to us. But the fighters produced by Yakovlev had one major drawback – their limited range. This was only about 1,000 kilometres, which greatly reduced their value as escort fighters on long-range bombing raids. When it came to attacking our convoys rounding the North Cape and sailing along the northern coast of Norway, the Russians were forced to employ their totally obsolete Airacobras and Kittyhawks as fighter cover simply because they possessed the necessary range of well over 1,000 kilometres.

At around 11.30 hours on 22 July we were ordered to scramble and make for Varanger Fjord, where fighter control had reported another of our Kirkenes-bound convoys coming under fighter-bomber attack. Headed by the Stabsstaffel we set course for the vessels' position. Ensuring as always that we had the advantage of height, we bounced the enemy machines. Leading us down, Leutnant Jockel Norz claimed three Curtiss P-40s. In the twenty minutes between 12.16 and 12.36 hours I managed to add another seven victories to my overall score – five Airacobras and two Kittyhawks.

However, our successes on the Arctic Ocean front, the majority admittedly gained by just a handful of the more experienced pilots, had absolutely no effect whatsoever on the overall course of the war. We had learned from the radio that the Allies had landed in Normandy on 6 June. Shortly after that the Russians had launched a major offensive in southern Finland, where they broke through the fortified 'Mannerheim Line' and captured the town of Viipuri, or Vyborg. This heralded the final dissolution of the military alliance between Finland and Germany. On top of this came the death of the legendary 'Hero of Narvik', Generaloberst Dietl, who was worshipped by the troops of his 20th Mountain Army in Finland. On 22 June Hitler had summoned Dietl to his Berghof Alpine retreat at Berchtesgaden for an urgent meeting to discuss ways of keeping Finland in the war on Germany's side. Tragedy struck shortly after Dietl had taken off for the flight back to Helsinki the following day; his machine smashed into a mountain in the Hochwechsel range in Styria, and his death was kept secret at first.

Petsamo was far removed from the events taking place in the homeland and all the other theatres of war. Perhaps it was a kind of self-protection that made us close our eyes to the bad news elsewhere. If we discussed the general situation at all, we stuck only to the basics, and if some were beginning to have misgivings, wondering what would happen to them and to Germany once the war was lost, they were careful to keep such thoughts to themselves. Nobody wanted to depress his comrades and have them brooding over such melancholy matters; after all, we had to be able to rely on each other and it was vital for everyone's chances of survival that morale be maintained.

Generaloberst
Eduard Dietl

14 Staffelkapitän of 10./JG5

At the end of July 1944 there were a number of changes of command within JG 5. Geschwaderkommodore Scholz, promoted in the meantime to the rank of Oberstleutnant, was appointed to the office of Jagdfliegerführer Norwegen, or Fighter-leader Norway. His place at the head of the Geschwader was taken by Major Ehrler, who in turn named Oberleutnant Franz Dörr as the new Gruppenkommandeur of III./JG 5. At the same time I was made Kapitän of the newly activated 10./JG 5, which was created out of 7. Staffel. I was the last remaining member of the old 7./JG 5; the original Staffelkapitän, Hauptmann von Sponeck, had been transferred to France long ago, while Bodo Helms, Kurt Philipp and Werner Schumacher were in Russian captivity, and Franz Strasser was dead. August Braun and Hans Link were officially posted missing, and my faithful wingman of earlier days, Kurt Scharmacher, was still undergoing treatment for his acute rheumatism in Germany and France.

On 31 July 1944 I was promoted to Leutnant effective as of 1 July. This wartime commission 'for bravery in the face of the enemy' was, to my mind, something rather special. A lad from the Saarland, of humble origins and with only an elementary school education, it was an achievement to be proud of; the result entirely of my own efforts. Those who had enjoyed a more privileged upbringing, or had benefited from a higher education, might not have understood my sense of personal accomplishment. For although such types did not automatically find a set of officer's insignia waiting for them in their cot at birth – and although they too had first to develop and demonstrate their qualities of leadership – it is an undoubted fact that most gained their commissions far more quickly than those who came up through the ranks. At first I found it terribly difficult suddenly being the superior officer to all my NCO comrades. I was having to walk a very fine line between exercising the kind of authority that I had never before displayed, but which was now expected of me, while at the same time being careful not to damage friendships of many years' standing. As Staffelkapitän I had been entrusted with disciplinary power over 120 men. I now had to get used to giving orders, not just receiving them.

My Luftwaffe officer's dagger, a gift from Reichsmarschall Göring engraved 'For special bravery in air combat: Hermann Göring'

153

Promotion to Leutnant

General der Flieger Willi Harmjanz, until September 1944 GOC Luftwaffe in Finland

A congratulatory teletype from General Harmjanz regarding my promotion

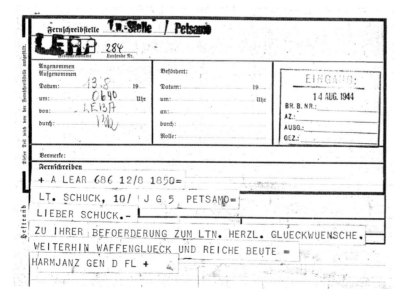

At the beginning of August the weather deteriorated again and brought all flying activity to a standstill. I was lying on my bed getting a little rest one day when Jockel Norz ambled into my room accompanied by Oberleutnant Rudi Glöckner. Jockel was the sort who got on well with everybody, fellow officers and NCOs alike. Oberleutnant Glöckner had originally flown as a member of the Gruppenstab before first transferring to 6./JG 5, the Expertenstaffel, then taking over 8./JG 5 when the Kapitän of that Staffel was killed in a crash in May 1944. Norz and Glöckner told me they had been chatting to the crew of a Ju 88 that had just landed after a weather recce flight. Apparently a huge area of low pressure was coming in from the east.

'No flying weather for the next two weeks,' Jockel said, 'so we can relax.' After a short pause he added: 'Well, come on then, Walter. Get the schnapps out!'

A congratulatory teletype from General Harmjanz regarding my promotion

I stared first at Jockel, then at Rudi Glöckner. But their expressions told me that the pair weren't joking. I had actually intended to get some sleep and didn't feel in the least like a drinking session. But Jockel hadn't waited for my reply. He'd made straight for my locker, opened it and spotted a large number of brandy bottles on the bottom shelf.

'Rudi,' he announced delightedly, 'the evening's saved!'

If we'd had a particularly successful day in combat, we would often be 'rewarded' with a bottle of spirits or the like. Because of my recent string of victories, and as I didn't drink much alcohol anyway, I must have amassed the largest collection of such bottles in the entire Staffel.

'I'd much rather get some shut-eye,' I said with a yawn, thinking to myself that the situation seemed somehow familiar.

'Now don't be a wet blanket,' Norz replied with a broad grin as he filled three glasses and handed one to me.

'Prost, comrades!' cried Oberleutnant Glöckner, emptying his glass.

The night that followed was short and horrendous. I was rudely awakened next morning by a loud voice yelling through the barracks hut: 'Immediate emergency scramble!' With aching joints, a rebellious stomach and bloodshot eyes I stumbled outside. When I put my lightweight flying helmet on it felt as if someone was jamming a pin-cushion over my throbbing head. From my cockpit I saw Rudi Glöckner climbing onto the wing of his Me 109 still clad in his pyjamas.

Next I'll be seeing pink elephants, I thought – I'm still in bed and this must all be a dream. But it wasn't. Immediately after take-off the state of my insides convinced me that I should turn straight round again. How I managed to get back down on the ground, I'll never know. But I do know that I spent the rest of the day in bed. There's a photo still in existence showing Rudi Glöckner dressed only in his pyjamas and flying jacket, which bears witness to this extraordinary and unforgettable morning.

Rudi Glöckner (left) and Werner Gayko

Oberleutnant Rudi Glöckner

155

The pilots of 10. Staffel seemed rather pleased that, after my appointment to Staffelkapitän, I still kept up a relaxed relationship with them. Instead of the more formal and correct 'Sie' form of address, they continued to use the familiar 'Du' and still called me Walter. They went along with my preference for jazz and we listened to this kind of music on various foreign radio stations. The German forces' programme from Vadsø also broadcast light entertainment music, but my comrades and I found their selection of tunes absolutely appalling. One day the female head of the Vadsø station paid us a visit in Petsamo, no doubt hoping to bask in the approval of her presumably 'delighted' listeners. Our reaction must have come as quite a shock to the poor woman. We told her exactly what we thought of her and the rubbish she was broadcasting – stuff like that was better suited to a ladies' sewing circle than a bunch of hardened front-line flyers.

The high spirits being displayed by the members of my Staffel were perhaps becoming a bit too rowdy. It wasn't long before I was hauled up in front of Major Ehrler.

'Leutnant Schuck, I am disappointed in you,' Ehrler declared. 'Perhaps it was a mistake to appoint you Staffelkapitän. Under your leadership the Staffel has become an undisciplined rabble. I'd like you to tell me what you think you're playing at.'

I wasn't at all surprised to be getting a rocket, for I knew that Ehrler was right.

'Herr Major, because of all the hard work that everybody puts in here, I wanted to allow my people a little more leeway in their spare time in the hope that it would motivate them,' I replied. 'But I have to admit that I was wrong and can assure you that I'll soon make my Staffel toe the line again.'

Ehrler then wanted to know what measures I intended to take to restore discipline.

'I'll drill them for as long as it takes to knock all this stupid nonsense out of their heads. And could you please place two other officers temporarily at my disposal so that I can put the NCOs and senior NCOs through their paces as well?'

Major Ehrler seemed to like the idea and agreed to my proposed course of action.

The next morning the personnel of 10. Staffel were more than a little bewildered when they were ordered after breakfast to fall in outside in full uniform and equipment, including steel helmet and rifle. I gave my instructions: 'Thirty minutes parade drill, then thirty minutes field exercises – after that the other ranks will dismiss to clean barracks and carry out make and mend!'

A Hauptmann took charge of the senior NCOs, a Leutnant the NCOs, and Hauptfeldwebel Böring-Schulte the other ranks.

There then began the most rigorous period of drill the men had ever undergone in their lives. When they lined up in front of me again an hour later, breathing hard and filthy dirty, I ordered: 'Other ranks, dismiss to your barracks! Herr Hauptmann, Herr Leutnant, please continue drilling your groups!'

The two officers put the shocked NCOs through another session until they were on the point of collapse. Then I had the whole Staffel back on parade.

'You miserable hounds have really put me out on limb, the lot of you,' I said in a menacing tone. 'I gave you every imaginable freedom, and what do you do – you shamelessly abuse my proffered friendship and leniency and get me in deep trouble with the Kommodore. Well, now it's going to stop. With immediate effect this is a military unit run on military lines. I no longer wish to hear the words "Du" or "Walter". From now on you will address me in the correct manner: "Herr Leutnant".'

With that I turned my back on them and marched off to the station HQ.

It obviously worked, for the Staffel soon began to operate properly and efficiently again. Even so, there was still the occasional irregularity or misdemeanour that required attention. Somebody was stealing alcohol and cigarettes from the men's barracks. I got a few trusted comrades to set a trap. A bottle of schnapps was tucked beneath a pillow with only its neck showing. A piece of string was tied around the bottle itself and attached to the pillow of the man whose bed was next to the light switch. He had been briefed what to do, and when, in the middle of the night, he felt a tug at his pillow, he immediately switched on the light. The thieves – there were two of them – were caught red-handed and brought to me the following morning. Instead of recommending them for a court-martial charged with the serious offence of stealing from their comrades, I placed them under arrest for a week.

This may not seem much of a punishment for the crime committed, but there was a sting in the tail: every morning, before they had eaten, head cook Jupp Heinrichs would turn up outside their cell with bottles of the cheapest rum, brandy or other spirits he could lay his hands on. They then had to hold their mess-tins through the bars of the cell and Jupp Heinrichs would fill each to the brim. He wasn't very careful about it either. In fact, he deliberately waved the bottles about so much that a large part of their contents ended up all over the prisoners' uniforms or sloshing onto the floor of the cell. In the evening,

before lights out, the process would be repeated. At first the pair enjoyed this treatment hugely, toasting each other and trying to work out ways of getting their sentence lengthened. But after just two days they stank so foully of cheap alcohol that they couldn't stand their own smell. It goes without saying that, while locked up, they weren't allowed to change their underwear or take a shower. The only facilities in their cell were a hand basin for washing and a bucket as a toilet. By day three Jupp Heinrichs only had to approach their cell for them to start retching. The amount of alcohol they were consuming affected not only their stomachs, but their bowels too. After a while they were finding it difficult to reach the bucket in the corner in time. The horrendous stench can be imagined, and it's no wonder that long before the week was up they had sworn off alcohol for life and were begging for mercy. After completing their sentence they were transferred as labourers to one of the heavy work gangs out on the airfield. As far as I'm aware, they didn't transgress again.

On another occasion it was brought to my attention that everybody was getting slightly less than their normal ration of 40 grammes of butter daily. Upon investigation it was discovered that two of the orderlies responsible for handing out the rations were skimming 2 grammes off each portion. This they kept for themselves, storing the accumulated butter in empty sausage tins carefully boiled clean for the purpose. Once each tin was full, the lid would be securely soldered in place and the butter taken home when they next went on leave. This pair didn't appear before a court-martial either, but were sent to join the others labouring out on the field. In both instances I had asked the men beforehand whether they would accept my judgement, or whether they would prefer to be posted to a Luftwaffe assault battalion. All had chosen to be sentenced on the spot, and with good reason. The much-feared Luftwaffe assault battalions had been set up during the winter of 1941/42, and were composed of men charged with cowardice, or other serious disciplinary crimes, who were being given the chance to 'redeem' themselves at the front with a rifle in their hands.

Then there was the Stabsfeldwebel whom I hadn't seen at roll-call for weeks. I asked around, enquiring whether anyone knew where he had gone. Somebody mentioned that he often saw him making his way down to Petsamo Joki, a river that teemed with salmon.

'The Herr Stabsfeldwebel isn't a very friendly type – he never shares his catch with us,' my informant went on to say. 'Instead he cures them in salt and preserves them in sausage tins.' Those sausage tins again! 'Then he gives the tins to people going home on leave who deliver them to his wife. She swaps them on the black market in Berlin for other items. He told me that people are so hungry they're prepared to offer a fur coat in exchange for six tins of his salmon, and that his wife's already got several of the things hanging in her wardrobe. It's been going on for quite a while now, and he never gives his comrades any salmon.'

I decided to wait at a spot that the Stabsfeldwebel would have to pass on his way back from the river. After a time the happy angler appeared bearing two buckets full of salmon. When he first saw me, he seemed a little unsure of himself. But I hailed him with an air of false bonhomie.

'Wow, now that's what I call fisherman's luck!' I exclaimed.

'Petri Dank, Herr Leutnant,' he muttered, and made to go on his way.

'Not so fast, my friend. I hope there's enough there for all the pilots of my Staffel?'

'Sorry, Herr Leutnant, but I've caught these fish for another purpose,' he stammered.

I dropped all pretence. 'If that's the case, my good fellow,' I snapped curtly, 'I know a place where you can make much better use of all your free time. How would a little fishing trip with an assault battalion on the eastern front suit you?'

Needless to say, the Staffel dined that evening on fresh salmon sprinkled with juice from mother's lemons.

When the skies over Petsamo finally cleared on 17 August a large formation of enemy aircraft was reported approaching our base. Every pilot of III./JG 5 was ordered to scramble immediately and at about 09.30 hours Russian fighter-bombers hove into view. In the ensuing attempt to prevent them from attacking the field, one of the pilots of my Staffel, Leutnant Karl-Heinz Schneider, was shot down. Then control informed us that the fighter-bomber raid was probably a feint by the Russians, intended to keep us busy and out of the way while they attacked their true objective, for in the meantime a force of Boston torpedo-bombers was heading for Kirkenes. Major Ehrler promptly ordered Unteroffizier Josef Suske and several other pilots to remain over Petsamo and keep the fighter-bombers occupied, while the rest of us split into three groups and hared off to Kirkenes, climbing to 3,500 metres on the way. A convoy had just docked there and it was vital that its cargo be protected.

While Jockel Norz and his group flew on a more north-westerly heading towards Kirkenes, Ehrler and I led the two other groups straight for the harbour. Nearing the target area we bumped into the Bostons' escorting fighters. Ehrler and I each claimed a Yak. By now we could hear Norz's voice in our headphones. He was obviously over the harbour already: 'Bostons 3,000 metres above the ships. Am attacking!' Five times we heard him yell 'Abschuß!' and every time he identified his victim as a torpedo-bomber. But he also reported that several of the Bostons had scored hits on our ships. Ehrler's group immediately disengaged from the fighter escort to go down after the bombers. East of Kirkenes I caught an Airacobra, and shortly afterwards a Boston, both of which I shot down. By this time the enemy bombers were fleeing in all directions. In hot pursuit, Ehrler managed to bring down four of the Bostons and Franz Dörr two. I claimed one last Airacobra that was attempting to attack Ehrler from below. The hard-fought battle had lasted more than an hour, and when we finally landed back at base we were so exhausted we could hardly speak.

Having no doubt judged the feint tactics of

Edition No 87 of the *Berliner Morgenpost*, August 1944, containing a report on the thirty-nine Soviet aircraft shot down during the air battle of 17 August 1944

39 Sowjetflugzeuge am Eismeer abgeschossen

Wirkungsloser Bombenangriff auf den Hafen von Kirkenes

Am 17. August vormittags zwischen 10 und 11 Uhr wurde von einem bolschewistischen Kampfverband ein Bombenangriff auf das Hafengebiet der Stadt Kirkenes durchgeführt. Zahlreiche Jagdflugzeuge begleiteten den über 100 Kampfflugzeuge zählenden bolschewistischen Verband, dessen Angriff in erster Linie den im Hafen liegenden Schiffen eines deutschen Geleits galt. Der Abwurf zahlreicher Bomben richtete keinen militärischen Schaden an. Eismeerjägern gelang es, aus dem in verschiedenen Richtungen angreifenden Kampfverband 35 Flugzeuge herauszuschiessen, während die Flakabwehr weitere vier Sowjetflugzeuge vernichtete. Dieser Verlust bedeutet den Ausfall von mehr als einem Drittel des sowjetischen Kampfverbandes. Zwei eigene Jagdflugzeuge gingen verloren.

17 June a success, the Russians tried the same thing again on 23 August. Shortly before midday their Jabos, or fighter-bombers, were again reported heading towards our base. In the meantime a force of Bostons was flying along the northern coast intent on attacking the small harbour town of Vadsø, north-west of Kirkenes. This time we were better prepared. Franz Dörr and the Messerschmitts of the Gruppenstab looked after the fighter-bombers attacking Petsamo. Dörr had been awarded the Knight's Cross just four days earlier and when, at 11.45 hours, he sent down one of the Kittyhawks from a height of 1,000 metres, he also joined the ranks of the Eismeerjäger who had scored 100 victories. But he didn't stop there. During the course of the next hour he went on to add kills 101 to 106.

Meanwhile the rest of III. Gruppe were heading for the main attacking force, which had entered the mouth of Varanger Fjord and was rapidly approaching Vadsø. We raced low above the rocky terrain of the tundra, crossed out over the coast and stumbled straight into a formation of Russian escort fighters south-west of the Rybachi Peninsula. Desperate to keep us away from the bombers, the enemy fighters got us embroiled in a stubborn, tenacious fight. After managing to bring down a Yak-9, my 150th kill, I had to return to Petsamo with my wingman David Wollmann, as we were running low on fuel.

By this time Dörr and his men had driven the fighter-bombers off and, after we had refuelled, they accompanied us back in the direction of Vadsø. Our comrades informed us over the R/T of the enemy's exact locations. Dörr and I waded straight into a gaggle of low-flying Airacobras and emerged from a lengthy battle close to sea level with three victories apiece. After landing I congratulated my wingman, David 'Fritz' Wollmann, on his splendid performance. He had stuck to me like a leech throughout and had kept my tail clear at all times, completely ignoring everything else that was going on around us.

Late in the afternoon the Russians repeated their simultaneous attack tactics yet again. Our base at Petsamo came under renewed assault while enemy bombers were sent for a second time into Varanger Fjord. Unteroffizier Josef Suske, Rudi Glöckner, Jockel Norz and I each brought down an Airacobra. But the Russians had already bombed the harbour of Vadsø, and among the buildings destroyed was our local radio station.

Shot down on 17 August 1944: Leutnant K. H. Schneider

Knight's Cross on 18 August 1944: Hauptmann Franz Dörr

Oberleutnant Kurt
Schulze joins us ...

... and later
becomes
Staffelkapitän of
16./JG 5

14 Dusk over Petsamo

At the end of August 1944 the Finnish Ambassador in Berlin informed the German Government that Finland had entered into peace negotiations with the Soviet Union, and when the Finns issued an official statement demanding that all German troops leave Finnish soil by mid-September, German-Finnish relations had reached rock bottom.

That year autumn came early to the Far North. Thick fog rolled in from the Arctic Ocean and blanketed the Petsamo region. A low-pressure area brought persistent rain showers, and low-lying cloud kept us on the ground for most of the time. The result was that there was quite a long period during which we were unable to report any victories to HQ. It was in this charged atmosphere that somebody or other decided that we needed motivating politically and sent us a national-socialist leadership officer, or NSFO.

The members of all three Staffeln, together with the ground staff – several hundred men in all – were gathered in the cinema block to await his arrival. The NSFO climbed the short flight of steps at the side of the stage. In its centre a music stand had been set up, upon which he placed the notes for his speech. We eyed the man suspiciously, noting that his uniform jacket was bare of decorations except for a plain War Service Cross. We regarded this award, the Second Class one without the crossed swords, as nothing more than a piece of tin that was doled out to just about anyone who sat behind a desk long enough. Then he began to speak, and his words hit us like a cold shower.

'You Eismeerjäger,' he declared, using the unofficial title of which we Arctic Ocean pilots of JG 5 were so proud, 'are all a bunch of cowardly swine, otherwise you would have shot down a lot more of the enemy.'

He couldn't continue, for there was an immediate angry uproar in the hall. The men started hurling insults at him, using the filthiest language imaginable, which perhaps I'd better not repeat here. Suffice to say that the whole place was seething and boiling with rage and resentment.

Alongside me were sitting Franz Dörr, Jockel Norz and several other officers, and behind us was Geschwaderkommodore Ehrler with the members of his Stab. In front of us were five groundcrew of my Staffel. Among them was the rather left-wing Stabsgefreiter Nebeling, who was one of the best aircraft mechanics we had and was greatly respected by all. Clearly worked up, he turned round to me and asked, 'Are you lot going to stand for that?'

'I mustn't take any action myself,' I replied, 'but feel free – I can and will defend you.'

My Staffel mechanics had a brief discussion, then rose to their feet as one and leaped onto the stage. This was the signal for a general uprising.

The NCOs and men of the other Staffeln had also jumped up, calling the NSFO every name under the sun and threatening him with their fists. The visiting politician was almost to be pitied. He had realised too late that he had gone too far. Panic-stricken with fear, he was running round the stage in circles like some trapped animal. But he was caught by three burly groundcrew, two grabbing his arms and the third taking hold of his wildly flailing legs. He yelled loudly to the officers for help, but no one lifted a finger. Then with one mighty swing, and to a roar of approval, the three mechanics hurled the terrified politico through the closed window at the back of the stage. Someone peered out and reported him hobbling away as fast as his feet could carry him. I never did find out whether the rough treatment handed out to the party bigwig landed our Kommodore in any kind of trouble, but another NFSO turned up in Petsamo a few days later.

He was a completely different type altogether. He had fought in the First World War, losing an arm in an action that had won him the Iron Cross. He was also wearing an Iron Cross gained in the present conflict. He seemed eminently more sensible than his predecessor and requested that only the pilots be assembled. In the course of the discussion that followed he asked Jockel Norz: 'Herr Leutnant, what do you intend to do after the war?'

'Well,' Norz replied, betraying nothing by his expression, 'after the war I'll go home and help look after my father's farm.'

'But you don't have to do that,' countered the NSFO. 'A highly successful fighter pilot like yourself will be kept more than busy travelling around the Reich giving talks and lectures.'

Jockel Norz's expression didn't change, but he looked the other straight in the eye and said very slowly in his broad Bavarian dialect, 'You know what, you can lick my arse.'

The shocked NSFO stared at Norz in utter amazement, then stalked out of the room. Jockel turned to me: 'Christ, everything's going to hell in a handcart, and then this halfwit comes along and starts spouting rubbish like that!'

On 15 September the skies over Petsamo cleared again. On this date I led seven aircraft of my Staffel against the Kittyhawk fighter-bombers that for the past few days had been keeping up a constant series of attacks on Vadsø and Kirkenes. But we were unable to get through to the Jabos, becoming caught up instead in a ferocious battle with their escorting fighters. By the time it was all over I had managed to claim a pair of Airacobras, but two of our own pilots had also gone down. Unteroffizier Heinz Lork had destroyed an Airacobra when he was himself caught by another of the Russian fighters. Despite being wounded, he was able to bale out of his burning Messerschmitt, but Leutnant Günther Fuhrmann was posted missing. It was not until later that we found out that these attacks were also part of a decoy manoeuvre by the Russians, this time to keep our attention firmly away from a force of four-engined Lancaster bombers of the Royal Air Force that were attacking the battleship *Tirpitz* berthed in Alta Fjord. Most of the bombers, which included machines from 617 Squadron that enjoyed a certain notoriety as the 'Dam Busters', were loaded with the 12,000lb 'Tallboy' bomb. The English had developed a new high-altitude precision aiming technique for this raid

and the 'Tallboys' possessed such enormous power of penetration that they could split open the battleship's heavily armoured decks. While the Russians were successfully keeping us otherwise engaged, the RAF bombers inflicted such serious damage on the *Tirpitz* that she was rendered no longer fully seaworthy.

At midday on 16 September eight of us – Major Ehrler, Jockel Norz, Oberleutnant Rudi Glöckner, Feldwebel Arnold, my wingman Wollmann and I, and two others – took off to intercept a force of Il-2s and Bostons that was reported to be heading for the harbour at Kirkenes. This time the escort consisted of Airacobras and the much more dangerous Yaks. From a distance we could already see a huge column of smoke climbing into the sky above the harbour basin. Just as I was sliding into position behind an Il-2 that was attempting to make off at an altitude of 400 metres, the rear gunner hosed a hail of bullets back towards me. To escape his fire, I dived away to the left, completed a wide circle and returned to renew my attack on him from below.

Pointing my nose up at him, I put a burst of cannon fire into his belly radiator, which burst open like a ripe tomato. For a few moments the Il-2 continued in straight and level flight, trailing a long banner of escaping coolant. Then it tipped forward and plunged head-first into the sea. I was just about to latch onto another Ilyushin when I heard Wollmann's warning yell: 'Achtung, Walter – Indians from above!' I looked up and saw three enemy fighters swooping down on us head-on. The condensation streamers at their wingtips and the dark puffs of smoke from their exhausts, clearly visible against the pale blue of the sky, told me they were bearing down on us at full throttle. In the next few minutes Wollmann and I each claimed an Airacobra.

Then suddenly we heard the voice of Jockel Norz in our headphones: 'Yellow 8 here – have shot down a Boston but he's hit my engine. Cockpit's full of smoke!'

I searched the sky until I spotted a Messerschmitt pouring black smoke. The situation didn't look at all good, so I broke into the R/T chatter with an urgent call to my friend: 'Bale out, Jockel! Get out of there immediately!'

'Nothing doing – I'm going to try and make it back to base,' Norz gasped.

At that we all broke off from the fight and prepared to cover Jockel and his shot-up Me as we led him back to Petsamo. We were only a few minutes' flying time away from the field and hopefully Jockel would be able to hold out.

I informed base, asking them to get everything ready for an imminent emergency landing.

When 20 kilometres south-east of Kirkenes we heard his hoarse voice say, 'Damned smoke … the elevators are jammed.'

'Jockel, for God's sake, what's wrong?' I demanded, filled with foreboding. By this time his Me 109 was much too low for him to bale out safely.

'Elevators, nothing's working any more!'

As I watched the Messerschmitt sinking at a shallow angle closer and closer to the rock-strewn ground below, a sense of fear and foreboding gripped me. 'Jockel, you've got to trim her!'

Back came the despairing reply, 'Trim's as far as it'll go already!'

Everyone fell silent. Helplessly we had to watch the machine's inexorable descent as it sank ever lower. 'I'm going to try a belly-landing!' Jockel cried. I held my breath. There wasn't a single patch of clear ground below us. The surface of the trackless tundra was a solid jumble of high, jutting rocks and boulders. Now, just a few seconds before impact, we all knew there was no longer any hope. Although I realised the inevitability of what was about to happen, a sense of deep shock ran through me as the Messerschmitt flew straight into a large rock and was smashed to pieces. Leutnant Jockel Norz, the victor of 117 aerial battles, was killed instantly.

When we were scrambled again that afternoon I could hardly concentrate on what I was doing. My head was filled with thoughts of Jockel and his terrible end. After shooting down an Airacobra, I called it a day and headed back to base, not bothering to indicate my latest victory to the assembled groundcrew. In the evening a recovery team returned from the crash site with the remains of the comrade who had been so popular and well-liked by us all. Such was the force of the impact against the rock that there had been little of him to find. His burial, I felt, was an undignified sham of an affair, stones being placed in his coffin to make up for the weight of the missing body parts, and the funeral oration upset me immensely. Although everyone knew that Norz had been a devout Catholic all his life, this aspect was not accorded the respect it deserved when he was laid to rest in the cemetery at Parkkina. The main theme of the oration was the usual claptrap about heroism and suchlike pathos.

The burial of Jakob Norz. Kurt Schulze is in the front row left and I am in the middle, holding Jockel's medals

Not forgotten: Jockel Norz

The death of Jockel Norz represented an enormous personal loss. Self-assured, possessed of a great inner strength, Jockel had always been a very good friend to me. When he was no longer there it was as if the sparkle had gone out of the unit. In the weeks that followed nobody felt like celebrating anything any more. The mess was deserted, the record player remained silent, and there was none of the usual chat and banter between missions.

The day after Jockel's death six pilots of my Staffel – Oberfeldwebels Heinz Arnold and Martin 'Martl' Villing, Unteroffiziere Josef Suske and Heinrich Dreisbach, my wingman Wollmann and myself – tangled with a sizeable formation of Sturmoviks escorted by Yaks and Kittyhawks. It was already late in the afternoon and the Russians had once again been attacking the harbour of Kirkenes. By the close of this 17 September we had brought down thirteen enemy aircraft; four of the Yaks falling to my guns. Three days later, in the same area and at around roughly the same time, we clashed with another enemy group and I was able to add an Il-2 and an Airacobra to my score.

It was on 25 September that the Russians launched their next twin-pronged attack. While a force of Sturmoviks, with an escort of Yaks, was heading at low-level for Kirkenes, Airacobras were approaching our field at Petsamo. We scrambled just as they were beginning their attack. While still climbing I managed to get behind an Airacobra and bring it down. I caught another, slightly higher at 800 metres, and despatched that too before we tore off after the Sturmoviks raiding Kirkenes. By the time we arrived over the harbour only some fifteen minutes later, however, most of the attackers were already making off. We pursued them north-eastwards towards the coast and in the course of the brief chase I claimed both a third Airacobra and an Il-2. In the early afternoon of 26 September the Russians targeted the ports of Vardø and Vadsø on the Varanger Peninsula. The fighters of the Stab, 10. 11. and 13. Staffeln destroyed twelve of the attacking force, but we lost four of our own pilots reported missing. One turned up again later after having spent two days at sea bobbing about in his dinghy.

Next day the Russians repeated their attack on Vadsø, this time with twenty Bostons escorted by more than thirty Airacobras. The raiders came in from the north-east shortly before noon, flying at an altitude of 3,000 metres. They were after the barges lying in the harbour as well as the artillery emplacements ringing the town. While three Schwärme of Me 109s launched an attack on the bombers below, I led my six Messerschmitts down on them from above. Suddenly I spotted a solitary Boston flying on its own some 2,500 metres higher

than the rest of the formation. Suspecting that this could be the bomber leader, I ordered four of my pilots to continue their dive on the main force while Wollmann and I went after the singleton. Planning to take him by surprise we made our approach though a bank of clouds. Experience told me how long we would have to remain hidden in order to get close enough to him. When I emerged from the cloud I saw the Boston off to the right immediately ahead of me. I sent several short bursts into his engine and into the fuselage close to the cockpit. He immediately started to emit smoke and tumbled earthwards. This Boston was my 170th victory.

But even before it had slammed into the ground near Vadsø, Wollmann and I were already on our way down to join the main action. We were aiming for a bunch of Airacobras that were harrying a Messerschmitt flying below them. I picked out the two leading enemy fighters, but they quickly climbed away, seeking refuge in some thin cloud. But it didn't do them any good. When the Airacobras reappeared we were waiting for them. Wollmann immediately sent one of them down. When the other saw that his wingman had gone, he skidded into a tight turn and dived back into the cover of the cloud. I decided to let him go, turning my attention instead to the remaining Bostons. Shortly afterwards I added number 171 to my scoreboard.

Our military situation in northern Finland was deteriorating rapidly. The Finns had already ceased fire on all fronts on 4 September 1944, and at the end of the month open hostilities broke out between our two countries. Not long after that the bombers of our erstwhile allies began attacking our positions. The worst of it was that the Finns, our recent brothers-in-arms, naturally knew all there was to know about us. They not only knew where our rear-area depots were situated, the routes followed by our lines of supply and the strengths of our units, they also knew our weaknesses. And there was every danger that they would pass this knowledge on to the Russians. While we were hastening to complete the withdrawal of our troops from Finland, the Soviets were preparing to stage a massive advance into northern Norway.

At least I was spared the ordeal of witnessing the tragic end at Petsamo. We had again been given the order to scramble, and again the Russians were employing their tactics of sending over two raids simultaneously. But this time it was us the Sturmoviks were after. They came roaring in low across our field with their heavy machine-guns hammering. I was just on the point of lifting off when a bullet came through my cockpit roof and smashed into the instrument panel. With blood streaming down my face I managed to bring my machine to a stop. I jumped out and dived for cover. Splinters of flying glass had ripped open my cheek and buried themselves in my nose. Later, at station sick quarters, the MO was able to remove all the glass splinters except for one which had embedded itself in the root of one of my teeth. The doctor told me I was not allowed to fly any more ops as this could possibly cause my upper jaw to suppurate. So two or three days later I received instructions to fly to Bardufoss, where I would be seen by a qualified dental surgeon. I packed a few things together and set off in a Fieseler Storch, the long trip to western Norway requiring several refuelling stops along the way. At Bardufoss the splinter of glass still in the root of my tooth was successfully removed by a professor who had travelled up from Oslo especially for the purpose.

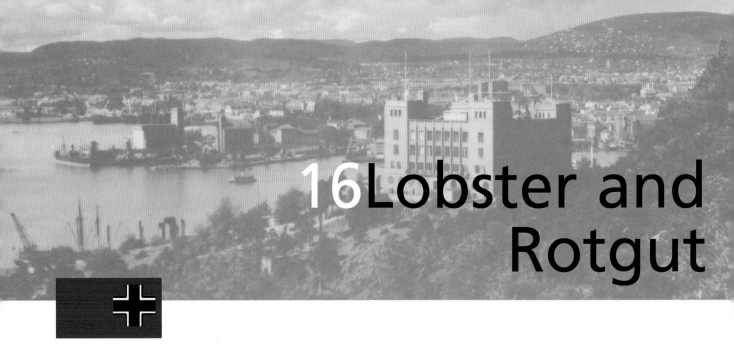

16 Lobster and Rotgut

While I was at Bardufoss recovering from the operation on my tooth, I learned that on 30 September 1944 I had been awarded the Oak Leaves to the Knight's Cross of the Iron Cross. The doctors at the clinic were so pleased on my behalf that they promptly fashioned a set of Oak Leaves for me out of dental silver, which they attached to my Knight's Cross as an interim measure. After my convalescence I was to go to Berlin for the award ceremony proper. Since the attempt on Hitler's life on 20 July 1944, the Führer was now represented on such occasions by Reichsmarschall Göring.

General Josef Kammhuber had only recently relinquished his post as GOC Luftwaffe Forces in Norway and Northern Finland. He had begun his operational career as a bomber pilot, serving as Kommodore of KG 51 'Edelweiß' during the French campaign, although today he is best known as the founding father of Germany's night-fighter arm, which he commanded from 1940 to 1943. The chain of radar defences protecting the Reich even bore his name: the 'Kammhuber Line'. He also championed the Heinkel He 219 'Uhu' night-fighter, although this may have been his undoing, for it brought him into conflict with Generalfeldmarschall Milch, who wanted the He 219 programme scrapped. This was probably the reason why he was shunted off to the Far North late in 1943, initially as GOC Luftflotte 5. But now the dire situation in the Reich had demanded his return. By the war's end he was discharging two offices, employing his expertise as both 'Plenipotentiary for Jet and Rocket Aircraft' and 'Special Plenipotentiary for the Defence against Four-engined Bomber Formations'.

In October, after I had fully recovered, I flew to the Norwegian capital Oslo, where I was to report to Kammhuber's successor, the new GOC Luftwaffe Forces in Norway, Generalmajor Eduard Ritter von Schleich, at his official residence on the Holmenkollen heights on the outskirts of the city. Also known as the 'Black Knight', General von Schleich had been one of the leading aces of the First World War, winning the Pour le Mérite for his thirty-five victories in that conflict. As it was nearing midday, Ritter von Schleich invited me to lunch, and some twelve members of the General's staff joined us at table. I wasn't allowed to leave afterwards, as Ritter von Schleich wanted to ask me about my time on the Arctic Ocean. During the course of the afternoon he suggested I should stay and join him and his guests for dinner as well. Around 6 o'clock Reichskommissar Josef Terboven, Hitler's highest appointed representative in Norway, arrived on the Holmenkollen with his staff. Just to show who was really in charge in Norway, Terboven had set up his HQ in the building of the

A teletype from Führer HQ announcing the award of the Oak Leaves

Norwegian Government, or Storting, and had moved into Skaugum, the seat of the Norwegian Crown Prince, which he had appropriated as his own private quarters.

At dinner we were served lobster. For me, this immediately brought back memories of those quiet days in France with Ergänzungsjagdgeschwader 3 and the delight Oberleutnant Freiherr von Metzingen had taken in showing us how to deal with these awkward crustaceans. I dismembered the lobster placed in front of me with such casual aplomb that you would have thought this delicacy had formed part of our daily diet up on the Arctic Ocean. It was amusing to note how taken aback the staff officers were as they watched my expertise with the lobster fork. After the meal Ritter von Schleich led us downstairs to a well-stocked cellar bar, which his predecessor Kammhuber had had decorated as a Bavarian beer-garden. We were served by three charming ladies, who offered us beer, wine, whisky, cognac and champagne. Two of the ladies were Terboven's secretaries, the third was one of Generalmajor Ritter von Schleich's receptionists. Then Terboven suddenly suggested that each of us should tell a story, the youngest first. And at just twenty-four years of age I was, of course, the youngest among this august gathering. Under normal circumstances I would have found the prospect hugely embarrassing, but having drunk more than a few glasses of champagne during the course of the day, I found that my normal bashfulness had been transformed into rashness. It would perhaps have been better had I been able to hold on to my natural reserve.

Without regard to the exalted company, I allowed my words free rein. 'I'd like to tell you something about the Eismeerjäger,' I began, as my listeners settled back comfortably. But as I went on, their expressions changed rather rapidly. I told them of the harsh conditions under which we fought in the Far North, that we fighter pilots were always greatly outnumbered by the enemy, that we were inadequately or badly supplied, and that we had recently suffered heavy losses at the hands of the Russians. After a while Terboven seemed to have heard enough.

'You Eismeerjäger,' he interrupted me, 'are an ungrateful bunch. I've always sent you the very best of everything – cigarettes, Italian red wine, French cognac and I don't know what else. And I don't get a word of thanks from you in return.'

I had definitely drunk one glass too many, for I heard myself daring to contradict him.

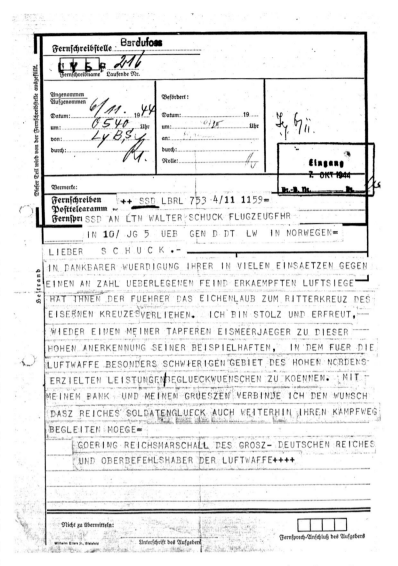

A teletype from Reichsmarschall Göring congratulating me on my award

Reichskommissar Josef Terboven

View of Oslo. The Holmenkollen is visible in the background.

The 'Black Knight', General von Schleich

'Herr Reichskommissar, I've no doubt that's what you despatched from Oslo, but what reached us up there? Mouldy Salem cigarettes, sour red wine, and the so-called cognac was the most evil rotgut imaginable!'

Terboven jumped up out of his chair and turned to a middle-aged man in a brown uniform: 'Ministerialdirigent Müller! I want to see a report on the supplies sent to the Arctic Ocean front on my desk at 9 o'clock tomorrow morning!'

Georg Müller, who was head of the Department for Propaganda and International Understanding in Norway, turned pale and nodded. That should really have settled things for the time being, but I thought the Reichskommissar still required convincing and that I needed to make one final point.

'Please calm yourselves, meine Herren. The war will soon be over. If we win it, we won't need to concern ourselves over the matter any more. But if we should by any chance lose it, I'll be without a profession. All well and good – in that case I've at least been taught how to drive a car and fly a plane. But I've no other skills to my name. Perhaps I can become a taxi-driver.'

A deathly hush descended on the room. Everyone had stopped drinking and put down their glasses. Even the secretaries seemed to have been turned to stone. Everybody except me was expecting Terboven to explode at any moment. Instead, an anonymous-looking character in a blue-green uniform spoke up. He had been sitting next to Terboven the whole evening and had scarcely uttered a word. Now, with Terboven's permission to take the floor, he rose to his feet, looked me in the eyes and said in a condescending tone of voice: 'From the Leutnant's words it is clear that the Eismeerjäger have become a bunch of defeatists. It's shocking to discover that we've got people like that at the front!'

I now noticed that this previously silent individual was wearing no decorations. I waited until he had finished speaking before requesting the Reichskommissar for permission to say something more. Without even waiting for Terboven's response, I too stood up and replied in the same dismissive tone, mimicking the unknown man's voice: 'Herr Reichskommissar, unfortunately I wasn't quite able to understand what the gentleman sitting next to you was implying, as he used a word that was entirely foreign to me, one that isn't in my vocabulary. Nor am I aware of the gentleman's position. I have only seen him sitting here, with no medals, decorations, collar patches or epaulettes to give us any indication of his military rank. From this I can only assume that he is one of those types who keep themselves busy flying a desk safe and sound in the rear areas. You have my sympathy, Herr Reichskommissar, at being surrounded by people such as this who have never heard a shot fired in anger. If this man wishes to refute my remarks again, I would ask that he show us his papers so that we can arrange his immediate transfer to the front. He's obviously just the kind, Herr Reichskommissar, that we need up there!'

I noted with satisfaction that the unknown man had turned a bright shade of red. I looked at Terboven and was surprised at what I saw behind his round-framed glasses. I got the distinct impression that there was a glint of amusement in his eyes. He rescued the situation by bringing the proceedings to a close with the words: 'Meine Herren, it's already getting late and we all have a lot to do. Leutnant Schuck is one of our most successful pilots in the Far North and he is, besides, an honoured guest of Herr Generalmajor Ritter von Schleich.'

Everybody rose from their chairs and I was driven back into Oslo. Terboven had placed a Buick and a Norwegian driver at my disposal, and had reserved me a room in the Grand Hotel. I greatly enjoyed the comfort of my overnight stay there. But breakfast next morning was continually interrupted by my having to get to my feet to salute the steady stream of senior officers passing by. After a while, tired of standing to attention so often, I solved the problem by changing to the other side of the table and sitting with my face to the wall.

At about 8 o'clock Ministerialdirigent Müller appeared. He urged me to finish up and drive out with him to the supply depot where all the documentation relating to deliveries to JG 5 were kept. However, as I explained to him, 'Herr Müller, where I come from it's said that breakfast is the best season of the year. I'd like to stick to that rule, otherwise I won't be fit for anything for the rest of the day.'

Müller resignedly lowered himself into a chair. Time passed, the clock on the wall was showing 8.20 and Müller was becoming visibly more and more restless. At last he burst out, 'Man, I've got to report to my superior!'

So we drove out by car to a large stores depot where the office staff had already dug out all the necessary paperwork for our inspection. Then I asked for a telephone in order to contact my Geschwaderkommodore, Major Ehrler. 'Put me through to Holmenkollen please, the office of General Ritter von Schleich!'

After a brief wait I had von Schleich's secretary on the line. 'Leutnant Schuck speaking. I expect you will remember me from yesterday evening. Would you please be so kind as to put me through to the Geschwaderkommodore of JG 5, Major Ehrler.'

'One moment please, Herr Schuck!' I was in luck. In only a matter of seconds I heard the familiar voice of Major Ehrler.

'Herr Major, Leutnant Schuck. I am speaking to you from Oslo. Yesterday evening we had a discussion with Herr Reichskommissar Terboven and Ministerialdirigent Müller. These gentlemen maintain that in the past our Geschwader has been supplied with only the best cigarettes, choice red wine, French cognac and other such luxury items. I took the liberty of explaining to the gentlemen what actually turned up at our end. Furthermore, I have told them that we are forever fighting against superior numbers and that we have suffered severe losses.'

With that I passed the receiver over to Müller. This time I had every reason to be confident of my actions. Since the autumn of 1944 the catastrophic supply situation had been the cause of deep dissatisfaction among us up on the Arctic Ocean, and with very good reason. Ehrler therefore didn't just allow us to voice open criticism, he actually encouraged us to do so in outside circles. Also, I knew that Ehrler always supported his people, especially when one of them got into difficulties.

I pricked up my ears and was able to overhear what Ehrler was saying in a loud voice at the other end of the line.

'Herr Müller, I'm glad you've listened to what Leutnant Schuck has had to say. I regard him as one of my most reliable men. Have you any idea what things are like up here? I can assure you that it's been a very long time since we've received anything really useful. When the Herr Reichskommissar came up to visit us in the north once before, we provided his aircraft with a fighter escort. We got on very well with each other then. But, as I say, that was a long time ago. Please tell Herr Reichskommissar Terboven that he should come up and pay us a second visit. We'll gladly escort him in again. But we won't need to bother with fighter cover for his return flight, because there won't be a return flight...'

Müller's eyes grew wide and his face turned chalk-white. What Ehrler was saying to him he found absolutely unbelievable and disgraceful. That this Major was actually daring to express himself about the Herr Reichskommissar in such a manner. His superior was supposed to fly to the front just so that he could be shot down by the enemy!

Müller and I drove back to Oslo without exchanging a word. The journey took us straight to Terboven's HQ, where Müller ran up the stairs and went into the anteroom. When the two secretaries who had been serving drinks the evening before recognised me, they looked at me sympathetically, their eyes full of concern. Then Müller was summoned into the inner sanctum. Through the open door I caught a brief glimpse of Terboven seated behind a large desk.

As soon as the door closed behind Müller the two secretaries introduced themselves. One was a Fräulein Graf from Berlin, the other a Fräulein Hettich from Wiesbaden. They produced a pot of coffee and poured three cups. They addressed me with the familiar 'Du'.

'Ach, you young pilots,' they said. 'Let's just hope that things turn out well in the end!'

'Why?' I was completely mystified. 'What is it you're trying to say?'

And then they explained to me. 'The man without any badges of rank who was sitting next to the Reichskommissar yesterday, the one you gave a good ticking-off to, is the personal representative of Reichsführer Himmler, the head of the SS!'

Now it finally sank in – I really was in deep trouble. The two ladies went on.

'We've seen lots of people come here who have expressed criticism of the leadership. Highly decorated naval officers, Knight's Cross wearers and the like. After they left we never heard anything of them again.'

I was by now feeling pretty miserable, but said, 'Oh well, it doesn't really matter a lot where you get shot down – whether here and now or later at the front!'

After about twenty minutes the door to Terboven's room opened again. Müller appeared in the doorway and said, 'Herr Schuck, please!' I entered the room, heard the two huge doors closing behind me and prepared myself for the worst. But Terboven came out from behind the desk, shook me by the hand, apologised for keeping me waiting and thanked me for the important information I had given him regarding the supply situation and the Eismeerjäger. Now I was thoroughly confused. Terboven then said to me, 'Herr Schuck, would you be my guest this evening?'

'Delighted, Herr Reichskommissar,' I replied, still somewhat bewildered.

That evening the Norwegian chauffeur drove me out to Skaugum in the Buick. It was about a 25km trip from Oslo and the road ran through a thick forest. I had already heard stories about the Norwegian resistance and their habit of ambushing single vehicles, so I was prepared for just such an attack. Suddenly there was a loud report. The driver slammed on the brakes and the car skidded off the road into a ditch, coming to rest against a tree. Because the trunk of the tree was blocking my door, I thought I had been somehow led into a trap, so pulled out my pistol and levelled it at the driver. He seemed absolutely terrified and shouted something at me in Norwegian: 'Punktering!'

As I obviously didn't understand, he tried again in French and English: 'Pneu, tyre!' I heaved a sigh of relief. Just a puncture.

After the driver had changed the wheel we continued our journey, arriving at Terboven's residence rather late. After dinner Terboven asked me if I fancied a game of table-tennis. Certainly – this was something I prided myself on being good at. I quickly won the first set 21:9 and could see from my opponent's expression that he wasn't a good loser. I therefore let him take the next two sets. Terboven threw his bat on the table, complaining, 'I can see right through you – you're only allowing me to win out of politeness!'

While Terboven went off to freshen up, I thought I heard a noise behind a door leading out into the hallway. I threw it open, sending one of Terboven's orderlies crashing to the floor. He had clearly been eavesdropping and was now holding one hand to his eye where the door handle must have caught him. Terboven's secretary put a finger to her lips, indicating that I should ask no questions and not mention the incident. Next day she told me a really outlandish story. Apparently this orderly had been recruited as a spy by the British before the war and was informing them of everything that went on at Skaugum. Not a picture could be re-hung on the walls without his being sure to report it. And as the people here wanted to keep feeding him false information for as long as possible, knowing it would all be dutifully passed on to the English, he was being left strictly alone for the time being.

17 Oak Leaves, Ehrler and the *Tirpitz* tragedy

Before I went to Berlin to be presented with the Oak Leaves, I was scheduled to give an interview to members of the Norwegian and German press in Oslo. There I was asked how it was possible to hold out for so long on the Arctic Ocean front, one of the most desolate and inhospitable places on earth. I didn't need long to consider my answer. It came from the heart and was based upon the unshakeable bond of trust between us Eismeerjäger.

'It's all down to a strong sense of comradeship,' I replied. 'Comradeship comes before all else.'

The next day I flew to Berlin in a Junkers Ju 52 transport. We landed at Tempelhof at around midday, having been exceptionally lucky to have escaped the attentions of the many hundreds of American fighters that were escorting more than a thousand heavy bombers to targets in the Reich on this 2 November 1944. It was only after our arrival that we learned of the devastating American attacks on our synthetic oil refineries, which had apparently cost the defending Luftwaffe fighters more than a hundred casualties. Up on the Arctic Ocean front we had known next to

nothing about the true situation within the Reich. It wasn't until I saw the ruins of Berlin for myself that I suddenly realised that our once so proud Luftwaffe had practically ceased to exist. Over the past five years of war many of our best fighter pilots had been killed and now, with the widespread shortages of fuel and equipment, we no longer had anything left with which to combat the non-stop streams of Allied bombers invading our airspace.

On 6 November I reported to Göring's IA, Oberst von Brauchitsch, at the Reichsluftfahrtministerium. He ran me through the details of the awards ceremony, which was scheduled to take place the following day. The next morning at 8 o'clock I was back at the RLM, where I met twelve other Oak Leaves winners. Most of them, the likes of Generalmajor Heinz Trettner, Oberst Karl-Lothar Schulz and Major Friedrich von der Heydte, were from the paratroops. Four were ground-attack or bomber pilots; these including Hauptmann Franz Kieslich, the Kommandeur of III./SG 77, and Hauptmann Dieter Lukesch from KG 76. I was the only fighter pilot present and also the only Leutnant among the high-ranking gathering. The whole ceremony was very nearly scuppered by the paratroopers, who at first refused to surrender their service pistols before entering the presentation hall. Since the attempt on Hitler's life everyone, irrespective of rank, had been forbidden to carry arms during discussions or official meetings with those holding high office within the Reich's leadership. It was only after

Göring's adjutant warned them that they would be excluded from the ceremony altogether if they did not submit to the regulations, that the paratroop officers gave in and handed over their sidearms.

A teletype ordering me to report to the RLM in Berlin at 09.00 hours on 6 November 1944 in preparation for the Oak Leaves award ceremony

Hauptmann Franz Kieslich, Kommandeur of III./StG 77. His Ju 87 wears the family coat of arms of Kommodore Major Graf von Schönborn

The Oak Leaves to the Knights Cross being awarded by Reichsmarschall Hermann Göring to Lieutenant Walter Schuck, in the Reichsluftfahrtministerium Berlin, November 7 1944. *Barry Smith*

A newspaper cutting regarding the Oak Leaves award ceremony. From the hands of the Reichsmarschall and not yet turned to ice

„Und noch nicht vereist . . .?"

Das Eichenlaub für den Eismeerjäger Walter Schuck

PK. Wer lange Zeit unter den Fliegern im hohen Norden gelebt hat, dem ist die Einsamkeit dieser Breiten, dem ist das spöttelnde Wort von Polarkoller und Tundrafieber, von dem sie sich manchmal befallen glauben, dem ist aber auch das „kriminelle" Fliegen, der unsichtbare Kampf gegen die Naturgewalten der polaren Bezirke, geläufig. Hier über dem nördlichen Polarkreis haben deutsche Jagdfliegerstaffeln mehrere Jahre, von der Offentlichkeit weniger beachtet, weil man immer von einer stillen Eismeerfront hörte, einen zähen und verbissenen Kampf gegen zahlenmäßig immer überlegene Sowjetgeschwader geführt.

Man müßte beschämt bekennen, daß man vielleicht die Namen der Eichenlaubträger Major Ehrler oder des Hauptmanns Weißenberger (beide haben inzwischen je 200 und mehr Luftsiege errungen) gehört hat, aber von den übrigen Männern, die jahrelang auf scheinbar verlorenem Posten standen, vernahm man doch nur sehr selten. Von dem inzwischen im Zuge unserer Absetzbewegungen geräumten Petsamo und Kirkenes starteten diese Handvoll Männer tausende Male gegen den Feind, der von Murmansk herüberkam und die deutschen Geleite an der Eismeerküste angriff. Hier, über Kola und Fischerhals, über der Varanger-Halbinsel, der menschenfeindlichen Tundra und über dem offenen Meer haben sich, besonders in den beiden letzten Jahren, Luftkämpfe und -gefechte, ja, wie der Wehrmachtbericht mehrfach melden konnte, Luftschlachten klassischen Ausmaßes abgespielt, die ein einmaliges Ruhmesblatt der deutschen Luftwaffe sind.

Walter Schuck, 1920 in Frankenholz an der Saar als Sohn eines Bergmanns geboren, ist einer dieser Eismeerjäger. 1942 kam er als unbekannter Unteroffizier ans Eismeer. Keiner ahnte den fast kometenhaften Aufstieg dieses damals Zweiundzwanzigjährigen. Von schmächtiger, fast zierlicher und kleiner Gestalt, mit schwarzem Haar und beinahe verträumten Augen ist er doch von einem sprühenden, überschäumenden Temperament. Die Vorzüge seines persönlichen Wesens, die seltene Bescheidenheit und doch diese Zähigkeit und Härte sich selbst gegenüber, der Schwung seiner Jugend und das rücksichtslose Draufgängertum, das ließ den geborenen Jagdflieger bald erkennen. Im Sommer 1943 schoß er nahezu 70, in der vergangenen „Sommersaison", wie sie nennen (denn der Polarwinter mit der ewigen Nacht bringt den Eismeerjägern ungewollte Ruhe), mehr als 100 Sowjetmaschinen ab. 1 Luftsiege hat er insgesamt errungen.

Wir trafen ihn nach langer Zeit als frischgebackenen Leutnant beim Reichsmarschall wieder, der ihm am 7. November das Eichenlaub zum Ritterkreuz persönlich überreicht. „Zwei Jahre am Eismeer und noch nicht vereist?" fragte ihn der Reichsmarschall scherzend. Das könne er nicht sagen, entgegnete Schuck in seiner liebenswerten Art lächelnd. Wegen seines unerschrockenen Mutes, seines vorbildlichen Angriffsgeistes und seiner überragenden Erfolge beförderte ihn der Reichsmarschall auf der Stelle zum Oberleutnant.

Oberleutnant Schuck, der Bergmannssohn, ist einer der Männer, die aus dem Unbekannten kommen, mit sich tragen das Echt eines starken, männlichen Herzens, die begeisterungsfähig sind und die immer wieder hinaufsteigen in die Lüfte und den Gott des Zweikampfes herausfordern. Und auch immer wieder, bei jedem Einsatz, wie der Reiter sein Herz als erstes über Graben und Hürde werfen.

Kriegsberichter Walter Henkels

Obviously in a good mood, Göring chatted to each of the recipients as he presented them with their awards. When he got to me he said: 'So, you're Schuck then. I've already sent you my congratulations by teletype to the Far North. How long have you been up there on the Arctic Ocean?'

'For two and a half years now, Herr Reichsmarschall,' I replied.

Göring let out a peal of laughter, exclaiming loudly to the assembly: 'Two years on the Arctic Ocean front and not yet turned to ice?'

I assumed that the Herr Reichsmarschall simply wanted to make a witticism and wouldn't be all that interested in my actual answer, so I merely replied: 'Turned to ice? No, I can't say that I have.'

As nobody was sure how long Göring's good humour would last, all those standing around joined in the laughter, some more self-consciously than others.

After the presentation ceremony an excellent meal was served. Still in a jovial mood, Göring must have decided that a little surprise was called for. 'Schuck, put up a star on each shoulder – as of now you are the youngest Oberleutnant in the Luftwaffe.' By the word 'youngest', I'm sure he meant 'most recent' and was not referring to my actual age, for although I still looked like the 'Sohndel' of 1941, I was by now 24 years old. Hauptmann Kieslich promptly asked one of the group to help him remove a star from each of his own epaulettes and attach them to mine. I was deeply touched by this spontaneous and comradely gesture.

Göring's assistant aide, Major Müller, had paid no apparent heed to his chief's last remarks, so Walter Henkels, a war correspondent who was covering the event, turned and whispered to him, 'Didn't you hear that the Herr Reichsmarschall has just made Herr Leutnant Schuck up to Oberleutnant? You've got to get that down on record!'

The adjutant hastened to rectify the omission, adding almost apologetically in an aside to Göring, 'Herr Reichsmarschall, there is also the matter of Herr Oberleutnant Schuck's additional victories to be discussed, the ones since reported to us by the Navy.'

I was aware that I had downed some thirty or forty aircraft more than the 171 I had been credited with to date. But I had never regarded it as important to chase up subsequent confirmation of my successes. After a period of time the clocking up of victories had even acquired a certain air of routine about it and, besides, in the interim other things had become of much more concern than mere numbers on a scoreboard. Nonetheless, Göring made a point of going through the lists of enemy aircraft shot down as witnessed and recorded by the naval personnel on board their ships. In order to prevent false or duplicate claims being submitted, the Navy often made a note of the markings of the German machine that had scored the kill. After Göring had checked the Navy's lists against the relevant combat reports submitted by JG 5, and found irrefutable evidence of my hitherto unconfirmed successes, victories 172 to 196, most of them Bostons, were subsequently credited to me by the RLM.

After the meal Göring asked if I would care to accompany him to Karinhall, his country estate on Schorfheide Heath, 65km north-east of Berlin. Because of my success in air combat he wanted to take me on a stag hunt. This invitation was a special privilege, but I declined it politely, explaining that I had to get back to my unit as quickly as possible. In fact, I wanted first to go home and visit my family. But the excuse allowed me to escape any further friendly overtures on the part of the Reichsmarschall and also rescued me from the dubious pleasure of having to take part in his stag hunt. Later, however, I did come to regret my decision somewhat when I discovered that everyone who was invited to join one of Göring's hunting parties was presented with a souvenir of the occasion: a hand-crafted shotgun inlaid with chased silver worth several thousand Reichsmarks.

From Berlin I caught the train for Paris, which ran via Frankfurt and Saarbrücken. As it also stopped at Homburg, I would be able to change there on to a local line that would get me to Oberbexbach where my parents lived. When I boarded the train in Berlin and took my reserved seat in a heated sleeping compartment, I found myself opposite a Feldwebel whose face I had never forgotten: it was the erstwhile Obergefreiter Dürr, who had treated us so sadistically during basic training in Quakenbrück and had made us climb those imaginary trees. He didn't recognise me; presumably too many other unfortunate recruits had passed through, and suffered at, his hands in the intervening years. He must have spotted my Oak Leaves, however, for he immediately jumped up, saluted me punctiliously and remained standing until I had taken my seat. I asked him in a friendly manner where he was from, where he was travelling to, what job he did and what his daily duties were. With great eagerness he immediately launched into all the details: he was a platoon leader serving with a training company stationed near Berlin and had been given a few days leave after all his recent hard work.

'Herr Oberleutnant, you simply can't imagine how pampered today's recruits are. But the young gentlemen have me to reckon with first,

The official Oak Leaves award certificate

175

The only known Oak Leaves photo with the original wartime signature

The Oak Leaves to the Knight's Cross of the Iron Cross (the full and official title of the decoration)

and I soon knock the stuffing out of all the mummy's little darlings,' he prattled on gleefully.

When I could stand his boasting no longer, I let the mask drop. Contorting my face into the most intimidating scowl I could muster, I yelled, 'You loathsome slave-driver, leave this compartment at once. You can freeze your arse off outside as far as I'm concerned, but don't let me set eyes on you in here again!'

He stared at me in complete amazement. 'But Herr Oberleutnant, we've just been having such a pleas–,' he stuttered.

'Get yourself out of here, you foul swine!' I raged at him.

He quickly grabbed his things and stumbled hurriedly out of the compartment. I leaned back with a contented smile. It had done me a power of good to be able to give the bully a taste of his own medicine at last. He would have plenty of time during his leave to think over what had just happened to him.

At home I became aware of just how worried my friends and neighbours were about what would become of them if we lost the war. What they feared above all else was a renewed occupation of the Saarland by the French. There was also some bad news on the radio about events in the Far North: on 12 November bombers of the Royal Air Force had sunk the *Tirpitz* in Norwegian waters. Despite all the grim tidings, however, the civil population still clung to the hope of a change in fortune and were awaiting the new wonder weapons that, the propaganda of Dr Goebbels was assuring them, would bring final victory. In fact, the weekly newsreels were showing impressive film reports of the daily firing of V1 flying bombs against London and also footage of the even bigger A 4 rockets, better known as V2s. Typically, the leadership had taken the letter V, which indicated Versuchsreihe – or prototype series – and neatly turned it into V for 'Vergeltungswaffe' – reprisal weapon. And when I heard that the Luftwaffe was now being equipped with a revolutionary new jet-powered aircraft, I wanted to join one of these new units immediately. Despite being most secret, breathtaking stories were already circulating about the miracle jet and I had to fly one at all costs!

On New Year's Day 1945 I was invited to the wedding of my old Arctic Ocean comrade-in-arms Theo Weißenberger. He was getting married at Langenselbold, not far from Frankfurt, to his childhood sweetheart Cilly, née Vogel, and I had the honour of being a witness.

The solemnity of the ceremony was interrupted by the pitiful wailing of a child. It later turned out that Cilly's little brother Dieter had eaten a lot of fruit and then drunk milk on top of it. The results could be clearly heard and smelled throughout the church. The last time I had seen Theo Weißenberger had been after he had risen from the ranks to become Kapitän of 6./JG 5, the Expertenstaffel. Since then his career had taken off like a comet. After first being appointed Kommandeur of II./JG 5, he had then taken over I./JG 5, which he led during the fighting over the Normandy invasion front. There he had scored twenty-five victories in just twenty-six missions, raising his overall total to 200. Promoted to Major, he was now commanding I./JG 7, a Gruppe equipped with the brand-new Me 262 jet fighter. Weißenberger let drop that he had already requested my transfer to the unit.

'Bit by bit I want to get all the old successful Eismeerjäger flying with me. It's proving quite expensive, though,' he said with a wink. 'To get you I'm going to have to give up three of my officers to other units.'

After we had said our farewells, I took the train back to Berlin early in January, then caught a flight from Tempelhof to Oslo. On arriving in the Norwegian capital I reported to Reichskommissar Terboven. I was hoping I could persuade him to help Heinrich Ehrler, who had been held responsible for the sinking of the *Tirpitz* and who, after an unfair trial, had been sentenced to three years and two months imprisonment. In times like these it was perhaps not particularly surprising that the BBC in London had already broadcast details of the sentence the evening before judgement was announced. This led to the court's reducing the term of imprisonment – perhaps not least to prove to the English that they had been wrongly informed – to two years and two months. In addition, Major Ehrler was to be reduced to the ranks and stripped of all awards and decorations. Because rumours persist to this day that Ehrler was to blame for the loss of the *Tirpitz*, and because there are many false reports still in circulation that cast a dark shadow on Jagdgeschwader 5, I would like to take this opportunity to go a little more thoroughly into the actual events leading up to the events of 12 November 1944.

Terboven greeted me with the words, 'Well, we've got your Geschwaderkommodore to thank for the sinking of the *Tirpitz*. The military court established that he completely failed in his duty on 12 November 1944. All he was concerned about was getting his 200th victory, rather than remaining at his operational HQ to coordinate fighter protection for the *Tirpitz*. That's why he's now locked up here in Akershus prison.'

Although I was inwardly seething, I kept control of myself. 'Herr Reichskommissar, I find that very hard to believe. Herr Major Ehrler would already have far more than 200 victories by now had he not gone out of his way in the past to help his younger pilots gain confidence by holding back himself and allowing them to achieve their first kills. Might I request that you please have a visitor's pass made out for me so that I may speak to him in person.'

That afternoon I drove to Oslo's Akershus Fortress accompanied by Fräulein Anneliese Sprenger, who was a member of the Kommissar's press office and the daughter of Jakob Sprenger, the Gauleiter of the Frankfurt-on-Main region. At Akershus I found my Geschwaderkommodore a broken man. I asked him to tell me the whole story, while Fräulein Sprenger took down every word.

He first explained to me that no naval department had informed either Luftflotte Nord or JG 5, let alone him personally, to which anchorage the *Tirpitz* had been moved. Up until 15 September 1944 she had been lying in the long and narrow Alta Fjord in northern Norway, whose steep rocky sides gave such good protection that it was almost impossible to sink her there. But after the Lancaster attack of 15 September the *Tirpitz* had left Alta and been transferred further south to a location 5km off Tromsø between the islands of Haakøy and Grindøy. Because of the severe damage she had suffered, she was no longer fully seaworthy, and was now to be employed more in the deterrent role as a floating coastal artillery battery. But here in her new berth, where the water was far too shallow and lacked the natural cover the Alta Fjord had provided, she was, in effect, a sitting duck, almost inviting further attack. Her position was now some 300km closer to the British Isles, which would greatly facilitate operations by RAF bombers despatched against the vessel from their home bases.

Ehrler, however, knew nothing of any of this. On 9 November 1944 he was ordered by the Fliegerführer Nord to fly from his operational HQ at Banak the several hundred kilometres south-west to Bardufoss, where he was to organise the transition of the Staffel stationed there from Me 109s on to the Fw 190. The Fliegerführer had given him just one

Major Heinrich Ehrler, who was unfairly held responsible for the sinking of the *Tirpitz*

Oslo's Akershus Fortress, where Ehrler was imprisoned

day (!) to do this job, and he was to return to his operational HQ at Alta/Banak on 11 November. Hauptmann Franz Dörr was to accompany Ehrler to Bardufoss, where he would remain to oversee the change-over after the latter's departure. Then Ehrler showed me a copy of the sentence that had been passed on him by the court at the end of the trial, which had lasted from 17 to 20 December 1944. This document clearly contains all the proof necessary to exonerate Ehrler but, because a scapegoat was needed for the sinking of the *Tirpitz*, the court simply ignored these facts in arriving at its verdict.

The following extracts are taken from the judgement of the Reich's court-martial proceedings and are reproduced here verbatim:

'On 9.11 the accused Ehrler, the Kommodore of the Geschwader, arrived at Bardufoss from his operational HQ at Banak on the orders of his Fliegerführer. His duties were: the reorganisation and re-equipment of 9. Staffel and IV. Gruppe. This entailed handing over aircraft of the Fw 190 type to 9. Staffel. In addition, a number of the younger and not yet combat-experienced pilots of IV. Gruppe were to be retained to serve as replacements to make good any operational losses suffered by 9. Staffel and the rest of III. Gruppe. On 10.11.1944 the accused Hauptmann

Dörr, together with his adjutant and an advance party of his III. Gruppe, likewise arrived at Bardufoss. The accused Ehrler had been ordered by his Fliegerführer to return to his operational HQ at Alta on 11.11.1944 immediately upon completion of the handover. During handover of the new Focke-Wulf aircraft to 9. Staffel, Ehrler became aware that almost all members of the Staffel were unfamiliar with the type. In particular, the Staffelführer and Schwarmführer had never flown it. He was furthermore made aware that the young pilots intended as replacements possessed no front-line experience and did not yet know the area, the prevailing weather conditions and other such operational prerequisites; nor had they yet flown together as a unit. He therefore ordered that 9. Staffel were to familiarise themselves with the [new] aircraft, and that the young pilots, whom he had organised into a "Kommandostaffel", should fly circuits and practice formation flights. In order to supervise these activities he extended his stay at Bardufoss and postponed his return flight until the morning of 12. 11.1944.'

There now occurred the gravest and most far-reaching mistakes in the entire *Tirpitz* tragedy:

'Shortly before 08.00 hrs on 12.11.1944 the Divisional Communications Centre at Bardufoss received a report that 3 Lancasters had been sighted in the Mosjøen area at 07.39 hrs heading eastward at medium altitude. Immediately thereafter came a report of another Lancaster somewhat more to the north and on a north-easterly heading. The reason for the delay in these two reports reaching the Div. Comms. Centre was the fact that the Mosjøen sightings had first to be routed via Bodø and Fauske to the Main Observer Post at Narvik, which only then could report them to the Div. Comms. Centre. The accused Beniers [Leutnant Beniers, officer on duty at Bardufoss Communications Centre] thereupon immediately passed on both messages at 08.00 hrs to the Main Observer Post at Tromsø for onward transmission to the *Tirpitz*. He neglected, however, also immediately to inform fighter operational HQ. It was not until 08.18 hrs that the

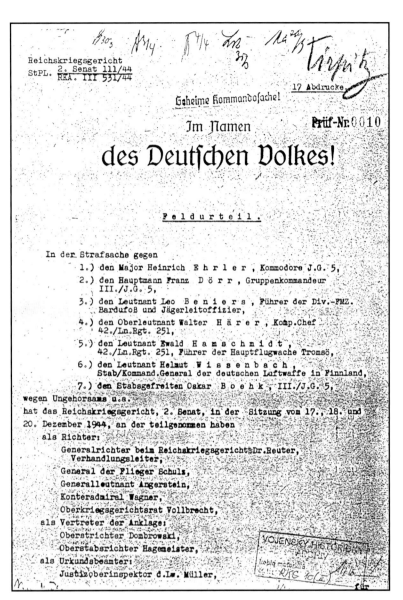

accused Beniers put out the two reports over the general net, which resulted in their receipt by both the Corps Communications Centre and Operational HQ "Meise". There then followed the "Air warning for Bodø" and "Termination of air warning for Bodø", the latter being given at 08.58 hrs. At 08.34 hrs had come a report of 4 further Lancasters flying at medium altitude on course OI/MK 4/LL2 between 07.54 and 08.26 hrs.

Out of all these reports of incursions in the southern area, Div. Comms. Centre only appended the area designation Large Grid Quadrilateral 16 N to the first one, ie. to the report of 3 Lancasters at 07.39 hrs. At this time the accused Boehk [Stabsgefreiter on duty at Fighter Operational HQ in Bardufoss] was on duty; he was responsible for plotting the

'In the name of the German People!' The first page of the court-martial judgement against Major Heinrich Ehrler et al, stamped 'Secret!'

incoming reports on the situation map at Operational HQ. But this map did not cover Large Grid Quadrilateral 16 N – in other words, the area around Mosjøen and Bodø. This large Grid Quadrilateral only appeared on a smaller-scale general overview map of the entire region that hung next to the main situation map, but which was not used for plotting purposes. Boehk erroneously entered the report received as being in Large Grid Quadrilateral 27 S. This gave the impression that the 3 Lancasters were in the area to the north-west of Hammerfest and were retiring northwards. Unteroffizier Ulrich, the clerk at Operational HQ, assumed from the position plotted that the aircraft were in fact retiring eastwards out of the Hammerfest area. And as he knew that the airfields of Alta and Banak, both of which housed fighters, were located there [roughly 300km north-east of Ehrler's actual position on 12 November!], he presumed that the report would be of no interest to the fighters stationed on the airfield down at Bardufoss. He therefore informed neither his Kommodore Major Ehrler, nor any other fighter officer, of this report. As Div. Comms. Centre did not repeat [the reference to] Large Grid Quadrilateral 16 N in any of its following reports, the accused Boehk remained ignorant of his mistake. Rather, he continued to plot these new reports in Large Grid Quadrilateral 27 S too, showing them in the Hammerfest area and retiring eastwards. The accused Boehk and the witness Ullrich therefore placed no importance on these reports. This meant that neither Major Ehrler nor Hauptmann Dörr, nor any other fighter officer, was informed about the incursions in the south and thus knew nothing of the English bomber formation flying [across Norway] towards Swedish territory.'

At Bodø, where the Lancasters actually crossed the coast, Norway is only some 70km in width. They could therefore disappear into Swedish airspace within a matter of minutes without being tracked by our radar. When they then reappeared over Norway, flying up from the south, they were thus already nearing Tromsø and only a few minutes' flying time away from both Bardufoss and the anchorage of the

Tirpitz. At this time Ehrler, misled by the false plots on the map in fighter control HQ, must have been under the impression that the bombers were several hundred kilometres to the north and heading away north-east towards the Alta area. The judgement continues:

'Of those fighters based at Bardufoss on 12.11.1944, the accused Major Ehrler had ordered 9.Staffel to 3-minute readiness to protect the field and the aircraft carrying out practice flights from surprise attack. The Kommandostaffel was at 15-minute readiness, as it was still under training and could not be scrambled so quickly. Major Ehrler had issued these orders earlier without either knowledge of, or regard to, the situation on 12.11.1944. As he himself – as already stated – wanted to fly back to Alta, he went to Operational HQ [at Bardufoss] at about 08.50 hrs to prepare for his departure. When he got there he still had no knowledge of the incursions in the Mosjøen area. As he had forgotten something, he returned to Operational HQ a second time prior to his departure. Just as he was about to leave HQ, a message from Div. Comms. Centre was received, relaying a report from the *Tirpitz* about the enemy bomber formation. According to the testimony of the accused, however, this did not read "Enemy bomber formation approaching from south" but "Aircraft noise. Location and height unknown". At this the accused immediately – 09.18 hrs – ordered 9.Staffel to cockpit readiness and the Kommandostaffel to 3-minute readiness. Ehrler instructed Unteroffizier Schoppe to contact Div. Comms. Centre for further details, but Schoppe was unable to obtain any clear information. Between 09.21 hrs and 09.23 hrs another message was received from Div. Comms. Centre, and again this was a report of aircraft noise, giving the position as 16 N B S 8. Upon receipt of this second report of aircraft noise Ehrler ordered 9. Staffel to scramble at 09.23 hrs.

Meanwhile, in his quarters, the accused Hauptmann Dörr had also received the reports of aircraft noise from Operational HQ. He immediately drove to Operational HQ, and arrived there just as Ehrler was taking off at 09.25 hrs. Dörr himself now took over the Kommandostaffel, while 9. Staffel, initially under the command of its Staffelkapitän, Leutnant Gayko, prepared to take off after Major Ehrler. 9. Staffel's take-off was held up, however, because, immediately after Ehrler had become airborne, a Ju landed and obstructed the runway for about five minutes. This delayed 9. Staffel's take-off by about five minutes. When Ehrler had reached an altitude of about 2,000 metres, he saw all the aircraft still on the ground below him with their engines running. At the same time he discovered that his R/T was not functioning and that he had no contact with either fighter control or the aircraft of the Gruppe. He therefore decided to set off on his own immediately in the hope of finding the enemy formation and thereby being able to claim his 200th victory. He first flew to Bals Fjord, which he reached in the area between Storesteinnes and Vollan, on the assumption that the [enemy] attack was aimed at the *Tirpitz*. He knew that the vessel was anchored somewhere in the Tromsø area, but was ignorant of its exact location. From Bals Fjord he flew at a height of 6,000 metres due north to the islands north-east of Tromsø, and from there westwards along the outer chain of islands before turning south-east, increasing speed and flying at between 5,000 and 6,000 metres, returning via Malangen to Bals Fjord. During this flight he observed no signs of the enemy, but neither could he see the *Tirpitz*'s anchorage. He flew at this high altitude on the assumption that the English would be flying high in such good weather conditions.

As he had noticed no enemy aircraft throughout the whole flight, he decided to fly on to Alta. While turning to the north-east over Storesteinnes he saw in the distance off to the left a column of white smoke some 100 metres high and above it, at a height of some 4,000 metres, bursts of Flak. Having flown up towards the *Tirpitz* from the south-east and south behind the accused Ehrler, it was at this precise moment [09.42 hrs] that the English were releasing their bombs on the *Tirpitz*. The accused flew towards the Flak bursts, but could see no enemy aircraft there either, nor anything of the *Tirpitz*. He then flew to

the left, past the bursts, and gradually descended to low level in order to cut off the enemy's escape route, his assumption being that they would have to retire westwards at low level. He searched the coast to north-east and south-west and then flew via Malsnes to the area of Heia, without making contact with the enemy. Finally he continued his flight to Alta.

9. Staffel took off five minutes after the accused Ehrler. The Staffelkapitän, Leutnant Gayko, had to take off last, as the engine of his aircraft did not start immediately. The Staffel was therefore led first by the witness Oberfeldwebel Bössenecker and later, when he was forced to turn back with engine trouble, by Oberfähnrich Höhn, while Leutnant Gayko flew independently. They too observed the Flak fire in the Tromsø area, but saw no enemy, with the exception of Leutnant Gayko, the latter encountering a Liberator south of Tromsø, which he attacked several times without success.

Before taking off with the Kommandostaffel, the accused Hauptmann Dörr received a report from Div. Comms. Centre: "16 N P T – 20 Lancasters direction Bardufoss 09.25 hrs." Thereupon he decided not to take off straight away, as this report could mean that the airfield itself might be the target and he felt that he should not leave it entirely defenceless. He therefore delayed take-off until receipt of the next, unequivocal report: "17 S enemy formation U.U. 4/T. U 4 course Tromsø." Now realising that the attack was aimed at the *Tirpitz*, he ordered his Kommandostaffel to scramble immediately; he himself was the first to take off at 09.36 hrs. He led his Staffel towards Tromsø and on approaching the area observed Flak bursts at a height of 4,000 metres. He saw nothing of the *Tirpitz*, but did spot a twin-engined enemy aircraft retiring north-westwards, which he was, however, unable to pursue. Shortly before reaching base on the return flight, ground control directed him towards an enemy machine, which he shot down approximately 20km north-east of Bardufoss. During the flight he had been receiving position reports from the fighter control officer, the accused Beniers, from which he assumed that he would arrive over the *Tirpitz* before the enemy formation.'

Now Ehrler provided me with further details:

'Although by 09.23 hours at Bardufoss Operational HQ I still hadn't been given any clear information by the Divisional Communications Centre – their reports containing mention only of "aircraft noises" – I gave the order to scramble. After taking off at 09.25 hours, radio malfunction prevented me from contacting 9. Staffel, whose machines I could see on the ground with their engines running. As they still hadn't taken off after five minutes, in other words at 09.30 hours, I had to assume that they had encountered a major problem and so set off on my own. All I knew was that an enemy bomber formation was approaching and I could only surmise that its target was the *Tirpitz*. But not one of us knew exactly where she was. Even if we had known, and the scramble had gone without a hitch, the time from the report being received at 09.23 hours would never have allowed us to take off, get into formation, gain altitude and arrive over the *Tirpitz* in time to stop the bombing from taking place at 09.42 hours.

After the whole affair was over the search began for someone to pin the blame on. Accusations were levelled at me and Gruppenkommandeur Hauptmann Franz Dörr in particular. But I swear that neither the GOC of the Luftwaffe in Norway, nor we had the slightest inkling that the *Tirpitz* was located practically on our doorstep, so secretive had the Navy been about her

position. Then we started hearing ominous phrases such as "cowardice in the face of the enemy" and "refusal to obey orders". Hitler himself ordered an enquiry into the matter.

Dörr and I were at first quite calm and collected about the whole episode. We had done no wrong and had nothing to reproach ourselves about. Franz Dörr was exonerated, but I was made the scapegoat. It was held that I had gone against Göring's express order to control the operation from the ground, and that I had taken off solely in order to get my 200th kill, instead of remaining on the ground to coordinate the air defence of the *Tirpitz* from our fighter control room. I was so shocked by the court's refusal to hear any evidence in my favour, in fact by the whole proceedings, with my continually being interrupted in mid-sentence or having my words twisted, that I couldn't defend myself properly.'

As later became known, a force of thirty Lancasters of Nos 9 and 617 Squadrons RAF had taken off from Lossiemouth in Scotland on that 12 November 1944. The English bombers were again carrying the 5.4-ton 'Tallboy' bombs that they had used in the 15 September attack on the *Tirpitz*. When the battleship capsized 1,204 crewmen, twenty-eight officers and commanding officer Kapitän zur See Robert Weber perished. It was scant consolation that 880 sailors were able to be saved.

I took my leave of Ehrler, promising him that I would do everything I could to have the sentence overturned.

I drove back to Terboven fuming with rage. 'This is monstrous, Herr Reichskommissar,' I said, not bothering to weigh my words this

The capsized *Tirpitz* after the RAF attack of 12 November 1944

time. 'It was wholly and solely the fault of the stuck-up Navy, who are so obsessed with secrecy that they don't even trust themselves any more. The *Tirpitz* had previously been anchored under excellent cover at Alta Fjord. Then the Navy moves her to Tromsø, but doesn't think it necessary to inform the Luftwaffe of her new location where, incidentally, she's laid out on a plate just asking to be attacked. And the whole sorry mess – the incomplete reports from the Divisional Communications Centre, the catastrophic situation in the fighter control room, where inadequate maps result in the wrong coordinates being plotted, the inexperienced pilots in the middle of converting from the Me 109 on to the Focke-Wulf Fw 190, the lack of R/T communication between the two types because the sets haven't been tuned properly – is then judged to be the fault of just one man, Herr Major Ehrler, so they simply lock him up!'

My words had obviously made an impression on Terboven. He told me that he was flying to Berlin that night as he had been invited to attend the celebrations on 12 January 1945 marking Göring's fifty-second birthday. I should prepare a full report, which he would need to have by 3 o'clock in the morning at the latest, the time of his departure, if he was to achieve anything with Göring on Ehrler's behalf. This written statement would be going to the highest quarters, but as I had no idea of proper legal terminology, I found myself faced with an insoluble problem. While I was still racking my brains over it, one of Terboven's secretaries, Fräulein Hettich, had a brainwave: she knew a Protestant minister who had studied law and who, she was sure, would be willing to help us. We met him that evening and explained the events surrounding Major Ehrler.

The minister explained: 'We've got to take the facts exactly as described by Ehrler and formulate them in such a manner that they cannot be contested. We will need six originals, plus several copies of each of the six. Because of all the petty jealousies and jostling for authority that goes on at leadership level, there is no point in directing just the one document to Hitler and appending the names of the other "important high-ups" at the bottom for distribution only. There's much too great a risk that the other gentlemen, the likes of Göring, Himmler, Speer, etc, and their adjutants or private secretaries will feel slighted and not give the matter any, or at best only half-hearted, attention.'

We worked away for hours on the report, trying to get it just right, and poor Fräulein Hettich almost typed her fingers to the bone. Shortly before three in the morning we delivered the documents to Terboven. I am still proud to this day of our night's work. Whether our efforts were alone responsible for securing Ehrler's release, or whether they were but part of a larger picture, who can tell? Either way, the following announcement, reproduced here word for word, was issued shortly afterwards by Führer HQ:

'I declare the sentence against Major Ehrler commuted insofar as the term of imprisonment be replaced by 3 months confinement. The loss of rank is rescinded. I suspend the period of confinement in order to give the convicted party the opportunity to rehabilitate himself in front-line service, sgd. Adolf Hitler.'

When I left Oslo to travel on to my unit, I knew that I would no longer find them at Petsamo. Shortly after I had left there back at the beginning of October 1944 the Russians had launched a major offensive and had taken the narrow Finnish corridor. Stab/JG 5 had then been transferred to Trondheim, and 9. and 12. Staffeln to Herdla. 11 Staffel, led by Oberleutnant Rudi Glöckner, and my 10. Staffel were now based at Gossen, which lay on the Norwegian coast some 1,200km to the south-west of Petsamo. The transfer of JG 5 from the Arctic front to the west coast meant that the aircraft we were fighting carried a different set of national markings. Previously our enemies had worn the Soviet red star; now we were facing Spitfires, Mustangs, Mosquitos, Beaufighters and Lancasters bearing the roundels of the Royal Air Force. The RAF, which had been operating against our ground installations along the coast of Norway more or less undisturbed since 1940, now faced tougher resistance with our presence in the area. After a raid by 'Tallboy'-laden Lancasters on the fortified U-boat pens in Bergen on 12 January 1945, for example, our III./JG 5 and the Flak defences between them claimed twelve British aircraft destroyed.

When forty-four aircraft of the RAF's Dallachy Strike Wing took off on 9 February 1945 to attack a group of vessels, including the destroyer Z 33, in Förde Fjord north of Bergen, twelve Fw 190 Jabos of 9. and 12./JG 5 were scrambled from Herdla to intercept them. Ten English machines were brought

down on this occasion, but the success carried too high a price: north of Herdla 9. Staffel lost Feldwebel Otto Leibfried, who crashed and was killed, together with Unteroffizier Heinz Orlowski, wounded in Fw 190F-8 'White 1'. Two pilots of 12. Staffel were shot down: Leutnant Karl-Heinz Koch in his 'Blue 9' and Unteroffizier Herbert Schäfer. And in Leutnant Rudi Linz, who failed to return after claiming his 70th victory, we lost one of our best aces. Flying his Fw 190A-8 'Blue 4', he had already destroyed a Beaufighter and a P-51 near Meistadt before fate overtook him. He was awarded a posthumous Knight's Cross.

Unteroffizier Heinz Orlowski

Leutnant Karl-Heinz 'Charly' Koch of 12. Staffel has a lady visitor in the cockpit of his 'Blue 9'

This unit badge only came to light when Fw 190A-2 'Yellow 16' of 12./JG 5 was recovered in Norway in November 2006

Leutnant Rudi Linz, Staffelkapitän of 12./JG 5, in his Fw 190A-8 'Blue 4', a machine handed down from JG 54 'Grünherz'

On the afternoon of 16 February an incoming enemy formation was reported out to sea heading towards Ålesund, and my 10. Staffel was ordered to take off from nearby Gossen. We found the English force flying at an altitude of 4,000 metres between Orsta and Hjorund Fjord. It consisted of about ten to twelve twin-engined Beaufighter strike aircraft protected by several elements of Mustangs, and they were approaching us very rapidly. I was flying my usual Me 109G-6 and led our attack formation past the screen of escorting Mustangs straight at the Beaufighters. After our first pass I saw four of the Beaufighters go down into the water. Thoroughly alarmed, the remaining machines jettisoned their bombs and went into a circle. Manoeuvring sharply, I managed to insert myself into the circle and get on the tail of one of the Beaufighters. When it was almost completely filling my windscreen, I opened fire. The English machine shuddered under the heavy impact of my shells, then the fuselage broke in two behind the wings.

As the two halves of the Beaufighter went tumbling down, I started searching for my next target. Suddenly I heard the voice of my wingman yelling in my headphones: 'Walter, look out, Mustangs behind you!' At the same moment something exploded close to my cockpit. Instinctively, I hurled my Messerschmitt around and saw two Mustangs coming at me. My abrupt evasive move had thrown them off their aim and I was able to escape into the clouds. While still hidden I climbed several hundred metres higher, and when I re-emerged into clear sky I spotted the two Mustangs below me. I tipped over onto one wing, firing as I swooped down on the left-hand Mustang of the pair. Flames and clouds of black smoke belched from its engine, then the machine went spinning earthwards in ever-quickening spirals. These victories of 16 February 1945 were to be the last two I would score in the trusty Me 109, an aircraft that over the years had grown dear to my heart.

The pilots of 10. Staffel, Gossen, 1945

The last days of JG 5 at Gossen. From the left, Lübking, unknown, Lobald Andresen, myself, Amend and Wiegand

187

9. Staffel in front of the Fw 190F-8 'White 1' that Heinz Orlowski had to bale out of on 9 February 1944. The machine was recovered in Norway in 1983 and restored in the USA, where it is now on display in a museum

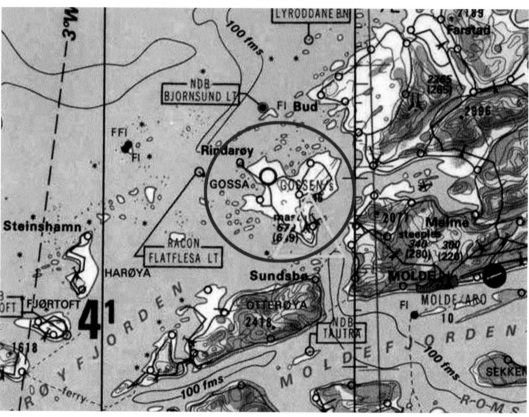

The island airfield of Gossen near Molde in Norway

On 19 February the order for my transfer to I. Gruppe of Jagdgeschwader 7 arrived at Gossen. I said my farewells to my comrades of JG 5 and packed my things into a Ford that Terboven had given me; he obviously hadn't forgotten that evening on the Holmenkollen when I'd said that I would have to become a taxi driver after we lost the war. My driver and my orderly were to put the vehicle on board a train and bring it to Oslo for me. I myself took a flight from Trondheim-Vaernes to Oslo as I wanted to say goodbye to Luftflotte chief Ritter von Schleich and to Terboven. When the vehicle still hadn't arrived after three days of waiting, I telephoned Trondheim only to discover that the freight train had been requisitioned by the Army for the transport of war material, and the car had therefore not been loaded. I later heard that the driver and orderly had driven the vehicle to Oslo, and had arrived on the third night, but didn't want to disturb me as it was so late. What they didn't know was that I had already boarded a Lufthansa machine that night and had departed for Berlin, where I was to report for duty with Jagdgeschwader 7 at Brandenburg-Briest. Having been left in the meantime with Herr Brinkmann, the head of the Reichskommissariat for Shipping, the vehicle was subsequently taken by ferry to Denmark, where it was stored in a large Wehrmacht car park. From later enquiries it transpired that while there the car had been completely ransacked and all the personal possessions I had packed into it were gone.

18 From the Me109 to the Me262

Within the upper hierarchy of the Luftwaffe there had been arguments for more than a year as to whether the Me 262 should be employed as a pure interceptor fighter or as a fighter-bomber. Hitler's brilliant idea, that here at last was the Blitzbomber of his dreams, quickly proved to be pure folly. Suspending two 250kg bombs beneath it robbed the machine of its advantage of speed and brought it back down into the speed range of Allied fighters. Initially, however, the experimental Erprobungskommando Schenk achieved considerable successes with its Me 262 Jabos, whereas the fighter operations flown by the Kommando Nowotny failed to produce the quick victories hoped for. It was clear that a new set of combat tactics would have to be developed. The fighter pilots were on their knees begging Göring not to relegate this advanced machine to the bombing role; it was only with a fighter of such superior speed that there was any hope of combating the Allied bomber streams and their escorting fighters. But Hitler regarded the early successes of the Kommando Schenk as confirmation of his policy and by the war's end more Me 262s had been delivered to the KG(J) fighter-bomber units than to the Jagdgeschwader. On the other hand, because he had fallen into disfavour with Hitler, Göring desperately needed to come up with some successes. Reversing his earlier stance that the jet fighters were best employed as fast bombers, he now supported their use in purely fighter operations. If heavy losses could be inflicted on the Allied aircraft now flying into German airspace in their thousands, he would be able to regain Hitler's respect and demonstrate to him the power and might of his fighter arm.

Göring decided to set up a new jet Jagdgeschwader under the designation JG 7.

Formed from the original Kommando Nowotny, III./JG 7 was now commanded by Major Erich Hohagen, and Göring appointed Oberst Johannes Steinhoff as Geschwaderkommodore. But success continued to elude the unit, not least because III./JG 7 was seriously under strength. Göring laid the blame for this on Steinhoff and Hohagen, accusing them of dereliction of duty, and alleging that they had paid scant attention to the matter of aircraft deliveries. Weißenberger was then ordered to activate the brand new I./JG 7 from scratch. No longer trusting the rather prickly Steinhoff and Hohagen, this was probably Göring's way of temporarily sidelining them. In addition, he instructed Weißenberger to work out new and effective tactics for the Me 262 as quickly as possible so that the results expected from this machine could finally be achieved.

Göring then went one step further. Having incurred his displeasure yet again, Oberst Steinhoff and Major Hohagen were now summarily dismissed, and Göring named Theo Weißenberger as the new Geschwaderkommodore of JG 7 in January 1945. Hohagen's successor at the head of III./JG 7 was my erstwhile CO during my time with Erg./JG 3, the now Major Rudolf Sinner.

On 5 March 1945 I reported for duty with the Gruppenstab I./JG 7. After passing the sentry outside the guardhouse at the entry to Brandenburg-Briest airfield, I noticed an airman walking a greyhound on a lead. On the way to the Staffel ops room I saw that the machines parked alongside the runway

Introduced by Theo Weißenberger: the badge of JG 7

189

carried a badge on their forward fuselages also depicting a leaping greyhound. When I reported to Major Theo Weißenberger, I was again struck by the painted shield with the greyhound motif hanging on the ops room wall. When I asked Weißenberger what the connection was, he told me the following story:

'Close to the airfield there's a large estate belonging to a countess, who owned two greyhounds that used to sneak on to the airfield every day to be made a fuss of by the men or to beg for food. Each evening the two dogs would be returned to the countess, only to turn up back here again the moment they could get away. Realising that they preferred our company to hers, the countess presented me with the two animals. That's when I got the idea of calling our unit the "Greyhound Geschwader", and since then we've included a greyhound in our badge.'

Major Theo Weißenberger, Geschwaderkommodore of JG 7

A day or two later General Kammhuber paid a visit to the ops room and was clearly pleased to see me again. When I heard that Heinrich Ehrler, who had arrived at Brandenburg-Briest on 27 February 1945, was to be made Geschwaderkommodore of JG 51 'Mölders' at Danzig-Neufahrwasser, I said to General Kammhuber, 'Herr General, you know what Herr Major Ehrler has been through lately. Herr Major Weißenberger and he are good friends, and I believe that Herr Major Ehrler would be best served if he were to stay with us. Could you not arrange for another Kommodore to take over Jagdgeschwader 51 and allow Major Ehrler to remain here as acting Kommodore?'

This manner of obtaining postings by pulling strings and personal intervention could hardly be described as going through the proper channels, but it was one that was sometimes resorted to within the Luftwaffe, especially towards the end of the war. Kammhuber called somebody in Berlin, then informed me that Major Heinz Lange would be taking command of JG 51 and that Major Ehrler could stay here.

When I am asked today how we transitioned from the Me 109 on to the Me 262, people either find my reply unbelievable or regard all those of us who went through the process as completely crazy. But it was exactly as I describe here. JG 7 didn't have a single Me 262 two-seat trainer on establishment, and every pilot who was to fly the jet on operations began his training by being a spectator!

I must have looked pretty dumb when I asked Weißenberger how the Me 262 conversion training programme was organised and he replied: 'Go and stand outside next to the runway and watch how the others do it!' So I spent the best part of my first week at Brandenburg-Briest watching the take-offs and landings of those who could already fly the jet fighter. I made a careful mental note of the spot where they lifted off, the angle of approach and the point of touchdown on landing, and estimated their speed as they came in. No doubt everyone can appreciate that there is a huge difference between being pulled along by a propeller and pushed along by a jet-turbine. Quite apart from the sluggish reactions of the Me 262 during take-off, when power had to be applied to the two engines carefully and evenly to avoid overheating the turbine blades, a totally different angle and method of approach had to be employed when coming in to land. In the air, too, a whole new book of aerodynamic rules came into play. In

'Dawn Intrusion', a painting by Robert Bailey showing me being attacked by Mustangs when coming in to land at Brandenburg-Briest

the Me 109 you could turn quickly and steeply, and if you suddenly needed to slow down at high speed you merely had to pull back on the throttle to produce the desired braking effect in an instant, whereas the jet engines would still continue to produce thrust for a considerable time after the throttles had gently been eased off. Moreover, when flying the Me 262 at low speeds you had to be devilish careful not to stall, or to make any jerky throttle movements that would cause the power plants simply to flame out altogether.

One day during the course of my initial training, which was spent standing at the end of the runway, a very smart car, its long bonnet secured by stylish leather straps, pulled up not far away from me. A driver in a fur jacket was behind the wheel with an Oberstleutnant sitting in the passenger seat next to him. The driver called something across to me, but as a jet was just coming in to land I couldn't make out what he was saying. Visibly annoyed, the Oberstleutnant promptly climbed from the vehicle, demanding to know why I didn't answer when I was asked a question.

'I am very sorry, Herr Oberstleutnant, but I could not hear what your driver wanted of me because of the noise,' I apologised.

The Oberstleutnant turned on his heel without a word, climbed back into the car and the pair sped off with a squeal of tyres. I noticed that it then pulled up next to a group of pilots gathered around General Galland, who also happened to be present on that day.

Shortly afterwards Galland drove across to ask me what I had said to annoy the two gentlemen so much. I explained to him about the driver and my not being able to answer his question because of the amount of noise. Galland roared with laughter.

'What – you didn't recognise Generalmajor Peltz?'

I had to admit that I hadn't, excusing myself by pointing out that the 'driver' had no insignia of rank on his fur jacket. I had come from the Arctic Ocean front, where we all of course knew who General Galland was, but had otherwise been privy to next to no information on high-ranking officers of the bomber arm. It was only after the war that Galland told me about his strained relationship with Peltz and why he had laughed so heartily at the thought of an Oak Leaves-wearer having the temerity not to recognise Herr Generalmajor Peltz. He disliked Peltz, who to his mind was insufferably conceited, and had withheld the jet fighters so desperately needed by the fighter arm, allocating them instead to the KG (J) fighter-bomber units. As a result of Galland's open criticism of the Luftwaffe leadership, Göring had removed him from his post as Inspector of Fighters, but, realising that he couldn't let such a famous fighter pilot just sink into obscurity, he had given him the job of setting up a new jet fighter unit, which received the designation JV 44. Galland had, in fact, taken the opportunity while speaking to me to ask if I wouldn't like to transfer to this new unit of his. I thanked him, but said

191

Heinz Arnold ...

... and August
Lübking (right),
who introduced me
to the Me 262

that Herr Major Weißenberger had specifically requested that I be sent here, and I didn't want to let him down now. Also, several of my old friends from the days of the Eismeerjäger were at Brandenburg-Briest; as well as Ehrler and myself, Weißenberger had previously gathered August Lübking and Heinz Arnold into the fold. The two Oberfeldwebel already had several hours' flight time on the Me 262 and thus belonged to the ranks of the 'old hares'.

When, after many boring days watching others, I finally lowered myself into the cockpit of an Me 262 for the first time, I was immediately struck by the roominess it offered in contrast to the cramped cabin of the Me 109. My initial nervousness was quickly dispelled when I saw Lübking and Arnold approaching the machine. While Arnold remained on the ground to carry out final checks, Lübking swung himself up onto the left wing and calmly began explaining the functions of all the various individual instruments. Compared to the jet's profusion of switches, levers and push-buttons, the Me 109's instrument panel had all the complexity of a training glider. Lübking now began to tell me what I had to watch out for:

'You've got to have a little patience at take-off – the turbines need quite a while to wind up to the necessary revs. While they are doing so, keep an eye on the engine temperature gauges, and don't let the turbine blades overheat. Treat the throttle levers like raw eggs. Always move the two together, and never abruptly. When you're on final approach, make absolutely sure that the turbines have sufficient thrust. If you find they're sinking down towards idle and you want to increase power again, there's every chance that they'll choke, or flame out, and stop altogether. So now start engines, but keep the machine's brakes on until you get clearance to take off.'

With these words Lübking jumped down from the wing and pulled the chocks away from the wheels.

I closed the cockpit canopy and was amazed at how smoothly it slid shut. What an improvement on the 109's frequently tricky hinged hood! When I put my earphones on I heard the reassuring voice of Arnold, who by now had gone back to the ops room. He was watching everything through binoculars and proceeded to run through all the points with me one last time.

'You're cleared for take-off. But keep those brakes firmly on. Flaps to take-off setting of 20 degrees, put your oxygen mask on. Push the throttle levers slowly forward and bring the engines up to 3,000 revs. Now release brakes, continue to accelerate steadily and "Hals and Beinbruch" ["Break a leg"] Walter!'

When I released the brakes the Me 262 took a leap forward, then began screaming down the runway. It gathered speed effortlessly and when the nosewheel lifted off I applied gentle pressure to the elevators. It was 20 March 1945, and I was fulfilling a dream that had occupied my mind for months past: I was making my first flight in a jet fighter! After retracting the undercarriage, I checked instruments while still

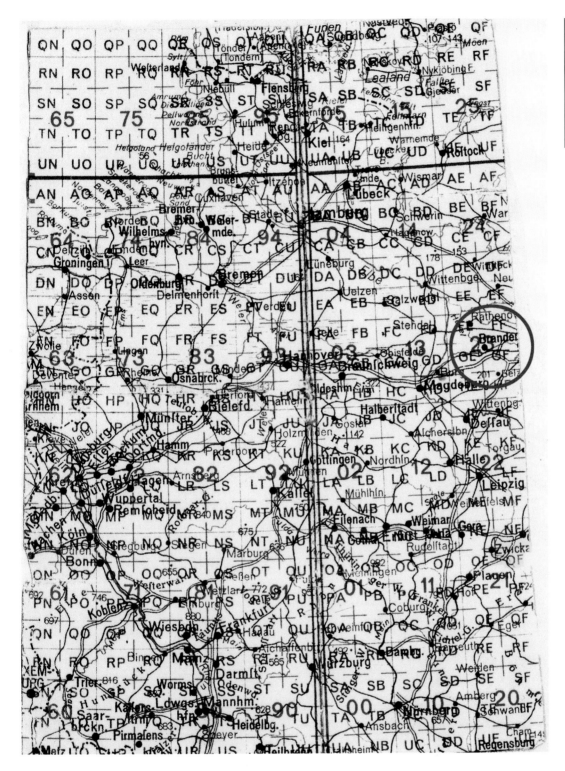

An original Me 262 flight map, covering the area from the Danish border in the north down to Regensburg (bottom right) in Bavaria

climbing. I was already at a height of 3,500 metres. That couldn't be right! I had never imagined such a rate of climb possible and was completely unprepared for it. What a bundle of power! A moment ago I was filled with nothing but exaltation, but now the first twinges of apprehension were beginning to creep in. I had been flying in a straight line for only a very short while, and already I'd lost sight of the field. A glance at the instruments told me that I was on a south-westerly heading and doing 700kmph. I pulled into a 180-degree turn and registered how wide a radius the jet required in comparison to the Me 109. Then the Hannover-Berlin Autobahn, a narrow white band snaking through the countryside, appeared below me. I followed it eastwards and soon, much to my relief, spotted the Brandenburg-Briest runway.

With Lübking's words of warning in my mind, and not wanting to risk a flame-out, I

throttled back the power to 50%. Because I was still too high and much too fast, I must have flown at least half a dozen nerve-wracking circuits. But I had to get this bird down somehow or other. At about 300kmph and with the angle of approach looking good, I reduced power to 25%, pressed the undercarriage switches on the side console to my left, and at 250kmph gradually lowered the flaps. Now at the correct height, I swept in over the treetops and set the machine down on the landing cross at 190kmph. After taxiing in, I retracted the flaps again and switched off the engines. As I was climbing out of the cockpit, Lübking and Arnold came running up to congratulate me on my first jet-powered flight. Only then did I realise how badly my knees were shaking and that my overalls were soaked in sweat.

In the three days that followed I made a number of practice flights, all of which proved trouble-free. On 24 March, four days after my maiden flight, I wanted to carry out a high-altitude test to see how the machine would behave at 10,000 metres. As it was forbidden for safety reasons to undertake such flights alone, Major Weißenberger assigned an Oberleutnant to accompany me as my wingman. The two of us took off and first climbed to a height of 9,000 metres. Once again I was struck by the sheer power of the jet fighter; without apparent effort it stormed upwards with no loss of performance and

Me262 A-1a as flown by Walter Schuck in defence of Germany

proved to be perfectly at ease at this high altitude. Stormed – that's the only word to describe its unprecedented rate of climb. No more of the wretched, seemingly endless scrabbling for height as in the Me 109, no more propeller labouring in the rarefied air, no more spongy controls – ach, if only we'd had these jets up on the Arctic Ocean front!

'Enemy reconnaissance aircraft in the Berlin area, height 6,000 metres, retiring south-west,' the voice of the controller suddenly sounded in my headphones. As we just happened to be to the south of Berlin, I signalled to my wingman that I'd like to take a closer look. We turned on to the given heading, diving down to an altitude of 7,000 metres. In the area of Leipzig, approximately 120km south-west of Berlin, I spotted three black dots some 3-4km ahead of us. As we closed in on them at top speed I recognised them as two American P-51 Mustangs and a P-38 Lightning. In a fluid diving curve I positioned myself behind the trailing Mustang of the trio and opened fire. The shells from the four 30mm cannon grouped in the nose of the Me 262 smashed with tremendous impact into the enemy machine, which was literally torn apart; the pilot of the Mustang was just able to bale out before it exploded in mid-air. I immediately manoeuvred on to the tail of the second Mustang, which was continuing on its way, seemingly quite oblivious. Either the pilot had noticed nothing of his comrade's fate, or the suddenness of the attack had taken him so much by surprise that he was still sitting in his cockpit paralysed with shock. The explosive rounds from my MK 108 cannon chewed

through the right wing of the Mustang. I must have hit its engine too, because it suddenly reared skywards, flipped onto its back and went down trailing a long plume of smoke. In the meantime the Lightning had made good its escape by diving away at full throttle. Now I wasn't just enthusiastic about the Me 262's clean lines and amazing performance, I was also hugely impressed by its devastating firepower.

After we landed, my wingman submitted his aerial witness report to Weißenberger. 'Herr Major!' he exclaimed. 'I've been flying in defence of the Reich for more than two years now, but never have I experienced anything quite like it. Just four days' training on the jet and he promptly goes and shoots down two Mustangs!'

Weißenberger replied laughingly, 'You shouldn't be that surprised. This man comes from the Arctic Ocean front and it's the sort of thing they do up there.'

But then he grew serious, informing me that the Staffelkapitän of 3./JG 7, the Knight's Cross-wearer Oberleutnant Hans 'Waldi' Waldmann, had been killed in a crash shortly after take-off from Kaltenkirchen airfield. The incident had occurred on 18 March when his Me 262 'Yellow 3' had been rammed by the machine of his wingman, Leutnant Hans-Dieter Weihs, while both were climbing away through low-lying cloud. And while 'Hadi' Weihs was able to land his crippled jet, Waldmann's body was found, parachute unopened, close to the scene of the accident near Schwarzenbek.

19 Staffelkapitän of the Greyhounds

On 26 March 1945 Weißenberger appointed me as Waldmann's successor and instructed me to take over 3. Staffel at Kaltenkirchen near Hamburg at once. I climbed into a twin-engined Siebel Si 204 courier machine and arrived at Kaltenkirchen at about 10 o'clock that evening. My first impression of my new base was not particularly good. I made my way to the Staffel's barracks and asked the duty NCO where I might find my quarters. He led me to a room containing a bed that showed clear signs of recent occupation by somebody else. By the time I had unpacked and finally been provided with fresh bed linen it was well past midnight. I had hardly dropped off to sleep when the light was switched on again and an obviously drunken Leutnant was standing by my bed.

'Get out of my bed at once – this is my room!' he yelled at me.

I was absolutely speechless; where on earth had I landed up? Before the situation got completely out of hand, the duty NCO came running into the room. He explained to the Leutnant that the man lying in his bed was the new Staffelkapitän. The night was short and cold.

As I was getting dressed the next morning I heard a soft female voice coming from the adjoining room. It was asking whether anything new had been happening. Another female voice, presumably a room mate replied, 'Yes, the new Old Man has arrived.'

'What's he look like?' enquired the first gentle voice.

'No idea, I haven't set eyes on him yet,' came the response.

'Never mind. I'll get to work on him and make sure he doesn't cause us any bother,' said the first speaker.

I could well imagine what the woman meant by 'getting to work on'. I marched angrily out of my room and went looking for the Staffel's senior NCO. When I asked him who the two women in the room next to mine were, the Chiefy, a Hauptfeldwebel, explained that they were female auxiliaries provided by Berlin to work here as clerks.

'That's of no interest to me – have travel orders made out and send the two ladies back where they came from,' I said.

The Hauptfeldwebel looked at me dumbfounded. 'I can't carry out such order, Herr Oberleutnant. According to regulations laid down by the Herr Reichsmarschall, as we are based within the Reich our Staffel establishment officially includes two female secretarial clerks,' he replied in an insolent, almost arrogant tone of voice.

This can't be true, I thought to myself – an NCO dressing down a superior officer! Abandoning all further discussion, I asked him where I could find the Gruppenkommandeur, Major Rudorffer.

After he had given me directions, I grabbed a motorcycle parked outside the quarters and set off across the field. Major Erich Rudorffer had set up his HQ in an old omnibus standing close to the runway. He acknowledged my reporting for duty by saying sarcastically, 'Ach, not another one from the Eismeerjäger.' He indicated a group of people in flying gear leaning lazily against the bus. 'That motley crew over there, that's your new Staffel!'

I looked more closely, and could hardly believe my eyes: a bunch of unshaven, long-haired pilots lounging around in their flying overalls. A thought went through my mind: what a cheerful prospect – I've just been made Staffelkapitän of the most degenerate bunch of men I've ever seen in my life. I couldn't understand Rudorffer's indifference to the state that 3. Staffel was in; after all, as Gruppenkommandeur he was ultimately responsible for the unit. I introduced myself to the pilots, at the same time asking whether there was a barber on the base. When assured that there was, I sent one of them to fetch him and to be sure that he brought all the tools of his trade with him. Then I asked one of the pilots, who clearly hadn't shaved for weeks, 'Tell me, does your oxygen mask still fit properly over your beard?'

'Certainly, Herr Oberleutnant,' he retorted with a grin.

I turned to the next, whose hair was nearly down to his shoulders. 'And what about you? Mask still fit?'

'Mine's fine too,' came the cheeky reply.

By now I'd had enough. 'Just how dumb do you think I am?' I retorted angrily. 'You're seriously trying to tell me that with your beards and long hair you have no problems putting your oxygen masks on? What altitude do you fly at then – only ground level? Let me tell you, you're not going to sit in an Me 262 ever again looking like you do now. I take it you have no objection to the barber smartening you up a little bit? Because if you do, you'll soon find yourselves parading your fancy hairstyles in an assault battalion.'

The grins and all the previous arrogance were wiped away at a stroke. At that moment the barber arrived and I ordered him to shave every man and cut his hair to regulation length. As he set about his task, I got back on the motorcycle and rode across to the orderly room, where I wanted to take up the matter of the two female auxiliaries with the Gruppenadjutant, a Hauptmann Trübsbach. In his office he explained to me that a transfer of the women was out of the question. I leaned towards him and said, 'Herr Hauptmann, please listen to me most carefully. I know someone who will sort this whole tiresome business out for me very quickly. What you cannot be expected to know is that I am on extremely good terms with Herr General Kammhuber. I would therefore recommend that you accede to my request and have the two ladies sent back to Berlin immediately.'

My words must have made quite an impression on Trübsbach, for all at once he became very amenable. 'If that's the case, I will get on to it straight away,' he replied in a tone that was almost friendly. After this showdown with Trübsbach and the measures taken against the scruffy state of the pilots, I had no further problems with the Staffel.

On 30 March 1945, which happened to be Good Friday, fighter control reported that more than a thousand American bombers, escorted by many hundreds of Mustang and Thunderbolt fighters, were approaching over the North Sea heading towards Hamburg. Around midday I./JG 7 received the order to scramble and we lifted off from Kaltenkirchen. I was one of a group of twelve Me 262s that was then sent off in the wrong direction by ground control.

Hauptmann
Trübsbach (right)

197

Consequently only about twenty of our number made contact with the enemy and the successes achieved were correspondingly few. Having been given the wrong coordinates, I was searching for the bombers much too far to the south. It was only after control had corrected their mistake that we abandoned our fruitless criss-crossing high above Lüneburg Heath and immediately altered course for Hamburg. By the time we arrived over the Hanseatic city, the enemy aircraft had all disappeared. But what I saw below me almost froze the blood in my veins. The once thriving Hamburg, home to more than a million people, was nothing but a vast expanse of smoking ruins. During my time on the Arctic Ocean I had, of course, heard news over the radio about the aerial bombardment of our towns and cities, but never in my worst nightmares had I imagined devastation on such a massive scale. Here and there individual walls still stood, each one seeming to be crying to the heavens in pain and grief at the death and destruction all around them. It was such a horrific sight that tears welled in my eyes and I howled like a little child. A feeling such as I had never experienced before rose within me: an indescribable anger at all those who had ordered these criminal attacks against defenceless civilians and strategically unimportant towns simply in order to spread terror, death and endless suffering.

Arriving back at Kaltenkirchen I lowered my undercarriage and prepared to land. However, of the three indicators only the two outer ones, those for the mainwheels, were showing green – the middle one had not lit up. This meant either that the nosewheel had failed to lower, or that it wasn't locked properly. I repeated the undercarriage retraction and lowering procedure several more times, but always with the same result. A glance at the fuel contents gauge then warned me that there was no time for any further attempts and that I had to land at once. After touchdown I held the Me 262 on just its two mainwheels for as long as possible, with the consequence that the nose of the machine was pointing to the sky, while the undersides of the engine nacelles were scraping along the concrete surface of the runway. For a moment the long fiery tail of sparks I was dragging in my wake, and the very real danger of an explosion, almost persuaded me to lower the aircraft down onto its nosewheel after all. But I was still going too fast and decided that the risk of the machine digging its nose in and somersaulting was greater than letting it simply carry on spraying

showers of sparks behind it. As it finally lost speed, however, the nose inevitably sank down towards the ground almost as if in slow motion. To my amazement the nosewheel leg didn't collapse. I jumped from the cockpit, saw the smoking engine nacelles, and ran for my life. At that instant somebody yelled, 'Achtung, ground strafers!' Out of the corner of my eye I saw a bunch of enemy fighters swooping in at low level and threw myself into the nearest slit trench. The Flak guns ringing the airfield were hammering away for all they were worth and soon forced the attackers to break off. But an earlier group of American Mustangs had already strafed the field shortly before my return; several men had been killed and a number of jets had gone up in flames.

On 31 March air reconnaissance reported another large force of enemy bombers coming in across the North Sea. Shortly after 8 o'clock in the morning about a dozen Me 262s of I./JG 7 were scrambled and vectored towards a formation of RAF bombers between the Bremen and Stade areas. The Staffelkapitän of 2. Staffel, Oberleutnant Stehle, succeeded in bringing down two Lancasters. As more and more groups of Lancaster and Halifax bombers began appearing on the scene, the original dozen or so Me 262s were joined by another fifteen from III./JG 7, which had taken off from Parchim and Oranienburg. By mission's end we had shot down at least eight Lancasters and three Halifaxes from the various attacking groups. Other sources even give the total of enemy bombers destroyed as thirteen, to which must be added a further six victories claimed during another operation later that same afternoon. Oberleutnant Fritz Stehle, one of the Me 262 aces, was again among the claimants and would amass eleven kills on the jet before the war's end. This was one of the most successful days in the history of Jagdgeschwader 7: even more welcome that the almost twenty victories was the fact that they had not cost us a single casualty.

When, early on the morning of 1 April, a military station broadcast a warning that Kaltenkirchen airfield was shortly to be the target of a major bombing raid, the order to evacuate all units stationed there was given immediately. Without waiting for further details as to the time, manner and scale of the attack, the jets were got into the air in great haste and dispersed to other fields. I landed with my 3. Staffel at Brandenburg-Briest, where Theo Weißenberger greeted me with some sad news. Our mutual friend, Oberfeldwebel August Lübking, the victor in thirty-eight air combats and one of the pilots who had helped to familiarise me on the Me 262 only days before, had been killed. On 22 March, near Neustadt in Saxony, he had attacked a Boeing B-17, but its bomb load exploded just as he was pulling away immediately above it.

The state of depression that Heinrich Ehrler was in was also giving cause for great concern. The once so strong and rock-steady Ehrler was becoming increasingly dejected and seemed no longer to enjoy any peace of mind. When talking to him it emerged time and time again that he was finding it impossible to get over the disgrace of the humiliating treatment to which he had been subjected: that he was only here with us now simply because every man was needed, not because people were convinced of his integrity and complete innocence in the loss of the *Tirpitz*.

Oberleutnant Fritz Stehle of 2./JG 7

An Me 262 of 3. Staffel at Kaltenkirchen

At Brandenburg-Briest 3. Staffel was quartered in a remote corner of the field. Close by was a brickworks that was no longer in operation, but the entrances to which were still under close guard. This aroused the men's curiosity and they decided to find out what there could be of such importance inside the abandoned works. When the sentries were withdrawn on one occasion they managed to get into the building, where they discovered huge quantities of cigarettes and cigars stored inside one of the ring kilns. Needless to say, the delighted finders of this treasure stuffed their pockets full of the products of the giant Reemtsma tobacco company, which they 'confiscated' for their own use.

One of the main responsibilities of JG 7 was now to protect the airspace above Berlin. While Weißenberger's Stabsstaffel remained at Brandenburg-Briest together with Oberleutnant Hans Grünberg's 1. Staffel, Oberleutnant Fritz Stehle was ordered to take his 2. Staffel to Burg bei Magdeburg, some 100km south-west of the capital, and I was instructed to deploy with my 3. Staffel to Oranienburg, which lay to the north of Berlin.

From the gun camera of an American fighter ...

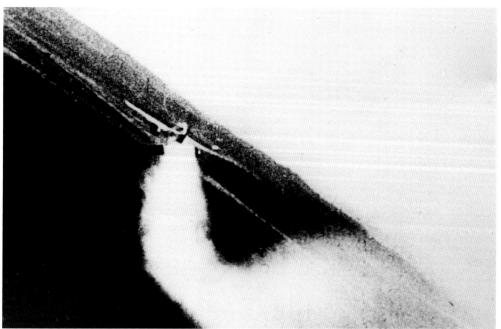

... the downing of Leutnant Schulte

20 Auf Wiedersehen, see you in Valhalla

When fighter control reported a large formation of four-engined bombers in the Stendal area on 4 April, Major Weißenberger scrambled from Brandenburg-Briest with the Geschwaderstab to intercept them. At the time I was with a number of other pilots in the ops room and we followed the R/T exchanges over the loudspeaker. Weißenberger had just reported the destruction of a B-17 when we recognised Ehrler's voice on air: 'Theo, Heinrich here. Have just shot down two bombers. No more ammunition. I'm going to ram. Auf Wiedersehen, see you in Valhalla!'

As Weißenberger told us after landing, he had immediately looked in the direction where he imagined Ehrler to be, but apart from an Me 262 going down pouring smoke, he saw no signs of any explosion or of a bomber displaying the kind of damage that would be inflicted by a mid-air collision. Whether Ehrler actually did ram, or whether his machine was shot down before he could do so by the tail gunner of the B-17 he was aiming at, will remain just one of the many unexplained mysteries of the war. But his reputation as an officer and consummate fighter pilot cannot be tarnished, and the drama of his last words will never be forgotten. Heinrich Ehrler was not the first, nor would he be the last, to bring down – or attempt to bring down – an enemy bomber by ramming.

On 7 April almost 200 fighters of the Luftwaffe's recently activated ramming unit, the Sonderkommando Elbe, took off to intercept a huge force of American aircraft. The specially lightened Me 109s hurled themselves against a superior enemy who were more than ten times their number – more than 1,200 bombers and 800 fighters. But sacrificial missions of this nature were worse than useless. Although seventeen American bombers were apparently claimed by ramming, the bloody operation had cost the lives of more than seventy of our own pilots. With just a handful of Me 262s we were supposed to keep the escorting Mustangs and Thunderbolts off their necks, but against such a weight of enemy fighters we were simply unable to break through to them. My bringing down of a Mustang on this date was thus nothing more than the proverbial drop in the ocean.

It was at Oranienburg that I first set eyes on the unusual combination of two aircraft, one sitting on top of the other. A kind of trestle framework had been mounted on the fuselage of an unmanned Ju 88, upon which was perched an Fw 190. This combination was known as the Huckepack – or 'piggyback' – system, but was more commonly referred to as the Mistel device. It was the fighter's job to get the bomber, which was packed with a ton of high explosive, up to a certain height, then release it. Because of the scatter effect of the weapon's warload, it was expected to prove effective in destroying bridges and breaking up concentrations of Soviet troops and armour. On the evening of the costly ramming operation several of these 'piggybacks' trundled out from their dispersal areas at Oranienburg, but after the first had difficulty in taking off and effectively blocked the runway, the mission was scrubbed.

In these final weeks of the war our supply system had, to all intents and purposes, collapsed. As we were receiving hardly any replacement parts for our jet fighters, the mechanics cannibalised damaged machines for usable spare parts in order to keep the others flying. Due to engine damage to his Me 262, one of my pilots had been sitting on the ground for three days. Although there was a perfectly good engine in stores, the chief engineer in charge of the workshops still hadn't had it made serviceable. Repair work in the shops was already being carried out with no great sense of urgency, and I could only assume that he wanted to slow things down even more. Nonetheless, I asked him why the engine hadn't been changed yet. All I got in response was an unfriendly, 'These things take time, you know.'

We usually spent the periods between ops in the mess, still wearing our flying overalls. But this didn't go down at all well with the station commander, an Oberstleutnant, who ordered that, even when we were at readiness, correct uniform was to be worn in the officers' mess. When I saw the station liaison officer, a Major, who was responsible for the interests of the pilots, sitting in the mess with the chief engineering officer, I had a word with him about the current state of affairs regarding servicing and repair work, and went on to ask him if he could intervene on our behalf in the matter of uniform in the mess – could we not be spared the time-consuming change out of flying gear, then back into it again, at least during our two-hour periods of readiness?

He replied with some asperity, 'The people in the workshop are already overstretched these days. And the station commander's orders are not a subject for discussion – they are to be obeyed without question.'

That did it for me. I reached for a telephone and demanded to be put through to General Kammhuber. At a neighbouring table the 'piggyback' pilots, who had been listening to what had been going on, started whispering to each other.

'Who does the little Oberleutnant think he is? How can he just call General Kammhuber like that?'

After being connected I made my report: 'Herr General, Oberleutnant Schuck here. I am at present based with 3./JG 7 at Oranienburg, and we have a slight problem here.' By the time I had finished outlining the difficulties we were encountering, the 'piggyback' pilots, unable to curb their curiosity, had almost climbed into the receiver. After no more than two hours a Hauptmann arrived, announced himself as the new liaison officer, and handed orders from Kammhuber to the station commander. I was absolutely astounded at the results produced by my telephone call: the previous liaison officer had to pack his bags immediately and was transferred to another unit. Furthermore, Kammhuber had decreed that pilots awaiting the order to scramble could enter the mess in their flying gear.

The new liaison officer asked the chief engineer, 'How long do you require to change an engine?'

'No more than six hours, Herr Hauptmann,' he replied in an almost servile manner.

The Hauptmann made a point of checking his watch. 'Well, see that you stick to that. And while you're doing so, think over why it has taken three days in the past.'

That did the trick. Well before the six-hour deadline the jet was already up carrying out an air test.

While 10 April 1945 dawned as a sunny spring morning, the sky a radiant blue, it was to end as the blackest of black days for JG 7. On airfields in eastern England the crews of 1,315 B-17 Flying Fortresses and B-24 Liberators were preparing for another major assault on the Reich. The heavies would be escorted by 801 P-51 Mustangs and sixty-two P-47 Thunderbolts. Their main targets were our Me 262 bases at Rechlin-Lärz, Parchim, Brandenburg-Briest, Burg bei Magdeburg, Zerbst and Oranienburg. Against this overwhelming display of aerial might, more than two thousand enemy aircraft in all, JG 7 and KG(J) 54 could between them put up a total of just sixty-three jet fighters. The preparations for such a massive operation did not escape our wireless intercept services and radar stations. Around midday, when the bomber stream began crossing the English coast at a height of some 3,000 metres, we were brought to cockpit readiness – my 3. Staffel had all of seven jets serviceable!

Because of the good weather, I expected Berlin to be the target of such a major effort. At around 13.40 hours fighter control reported that the enemy formations were approaching Osnabrück. As British and Canadian forces had taken the Lüneburg Heath area some days earlier, the bombers no longer had to fear any Flak in that region. In any case, the Allies had long enjoyed air superiority in the skies of Germany and were flying their bomber and fighter-bomber raids around the clock.

Leaving Osnabrück, the bomber stream began to split up and climb to 8,000 metres. The B-17s of the 1st Air Division headed for Oranienburg, while those of the 3rd divided into two, with one group making for Neuruppin and the larger force aiming for Zerbst, Brandenburg-Briest and Burg bei Magdeburg. The targets for the B-24s of the 2nd Air Division were Rechlin, Rechlin-Lärz and Parchim. At 14.15 hours, as the Burg force neared its objective at a height of 7,000 metres, the jets of Oberleutnant Fritz Stehle's 2.

Staffel and KG(J) 54 were scrambled. Although they succeeded in bringing down several of the attacking B-17s, the remainder were able to unload more than 400 tons of high-explosive and incendiary bombs almost undisturbed, putting every runway out of action. Meanwhile, the air-raid sirens began to wail at Rechlin-Lärz, Parchim, Brandenburg-Briest and Oranienburg. As the Me 262s of 9. and 10./JG 7 were taking off from Parchim they were set upon by American fighters and two jets were shot down. Shortly afterwards a group of Liberators marched overhead, leaving Parchim's main runway pocked with bomb craters to mark their passing. When Oberleutnant Franz Schall, the Kapitän of 10. Staffel, attempted an emergency landing, his Me 262 ran into one of the craters, was hurled onto its back, and exploded. Schall, a Knight's Cross winner with 133 victories to his credit, was killed instantly.

Some 60km further to the south-east the main force of Liberators, together with an errant squadron of Flying Fortresses, ploughed up the runways at Rechlin and Rechlin-Lärz. Twenty-nine aircraft were destroyed on the ground and a further twenty-one severely damaged. III./JG 7 hardly had a chance to get at the bombers, being harried and involved in a succession of violent clashes with the screen of escorting fighters. They claimed just four of the enemy: a B-17, two Mustangs and a Thunderbolt. Oberleutnant Walter Wever of the Gruppenstab was brought down in his Me 262 after combat over Dierberg near Neuruppin.

Now the condensation trails of the B-17s were pointing menacingly towards Brandenburg-Briest. Down below, the teardrop canopies of the Messerschmitts were slid shut, and the engines coughed and whined into life, pouring out clouds of smoke that quickly dissipated in the clear spring air. The runway trembled under the thunder of the jets as the machines of the Stabsstaffel and 1./JG 7 took off in rapid succession. Oberleutnant Hans Grünberg, an ace who had gained most of his victories while serving with Jagdgeschwader 3, shot down two B-17s. As bombs rained down on Brandenburg-Briest, the field's Flak defences continued to pump fire up at the attackers.

Meanwhile I was in my 'Yellow 1' climbing hard into the skies above Oranienburg at the head of 3. Staffel. Fighter control had reported enemy bombers coming in from the north-west at an altitude of 8,000 metres. I kept my pilots in tight formation, knowing from past experience that enemy fighters would be patrolling above the bomber force like a swarm of hornets. To avoid becoming entangled with the Mustangs, I zigzagged the Staffel up to a height of 10,000 metres and led it in a wide curve behind the bomber stream. Once in position, and with the advantage of height, we launched our attack on the Flying Fortresses. The difference in speed between our jet fighters and the lumbering heavies was so enormous that I had come up with a special tactic for dealing with them.

A stream of several hundred bombers, even when flying in close formation, stretched quite a few kilometres from nose to tail. In order to reduce the risk of massed defensive fire from the bombers' gunners on the one hand, and to use as little fuel as possible on the other, it made no sense to carry out a series of separate, lengthy, curving passes each time you made an attack. As there were more than enough targets to hand, I decided that I would 'surf-ride' along the length of the bomber stream: dive on the enemy from a height of 1,000 metres above, select a bomber flying out on one of the flanks, put a short burst of fire into an inboard engine, pull up and away while still at least 200 metres above the bomber in order to ensure safe recovery, climb back to 1,000 metres and repeat the process. Even though a 'ride' of this kind above the bombers took up several kilometres, such was the length of the average stream that it was usually possible to achieve multiple successes in the course of the one roller-coaster pass.

However, the bombers had to be hit in or near the inboard engines, for it was through this area of the wing that the fuel lines ran. I simply couldn't understand why other pilots would choose to attack a bomber box from the side, from below or from the front. It was against tactics such as these that the B-17 really lived up to its name as a 'Flying Fortress'. Only if one flew with, and not against, the bomber stream, and only if one attacked from above, could one escape the worst of its concentrated firepower. Furthermore, the B-17s' gunners could open fire on us with their heavy machine-guns from an effective range of 700 metres, whereas our four Mk 108 nose cannon were calibrated for a range of only about 300 metres.

When I saw the flashes of the bombs exploding on Oranienburg far below me, the picture of the rubble and ashes of what had once been Hamburg rose again before my eyes. At this moment I didn't spare a thought for the pain and suffering that my cannon shells would soon be inflicting upon the enemy bomber crews. Vengeance, hate, retribution? No, those are the wrong words to describe the unbridled fury at the hundred-thousandfold deaths of innocent German women and children that filled my entire being as I opened fire on my chosen target. The 30mm shells gnawed greedily through the giant tail unit of the B-17. It broke away from the fuselage as if severed by a chainsaw and fell away earthwards. I pulled up the nose of my machine, gaining height before swooping back down on the bombers. I hit the next B-17 between the two starboard engines. As it tiredly lifted one wing prior to going down, I thought I caught a glimpse of a name written on the exposed nose section: 'Henn's Revenge'. With the mortally wounded bomber already practically filling my entire windscreen, I quickly had to break upwards to avoid colliding with it.

The Flying Fortresses had by this time unloaded their bombs, but the stream continued to fly stoically eastwards despite the Flak still exploding directly in its path. Then I spotted a lone B-17 that had sheered out of formation and was heading north dragging a long banner of smoke behind it. At first I intended to give it the coup de grâce, but as I drew closer I could see that a shell had ripped the starboard side of the fuselage open from the cockpit to behind the wing. As the bomber's fate was already sealed, I flew a wide circle around it, not wanting to shoot at the defenceless crew members: the co-pilot was slumped forward in his seat harness and the rest of the crew had gathered in the fuselage clearly preparing to bale out as none of the guns were manned. As I turned back towards the bomber stream I saw the crew leaving the stricken bomber – nine parachutes blossomed in the sky behind me.

The wing of my third victim seemed to attract the tracer shells from my cannon like a magnet. The 30mm incendiary and HE rounds slammed into the bomber's engines with colossal force. With an enormous hole punched in its wing, the B-17 turned onto its side and went down burning fiercely. As I selected my fourth target and dived down to position myself on its tail, I couldn't help noticing a triangle bearing the letter 'U' painted on the fin. After my shells had mangled the inboard engine of the Flying Fortresses to so much scrap, large sheets of metal began whirling back through the air, then the complete wing was torn off. I later discovered that this B-17 was named 'Moonlight Mission' and that most of the crew had been able to bale out before she exploded at a height of 5,000 metres.

The crew of 'Henn's Revenge' of the 303rd Bomb Group.
Maxine Bradshaw

Boeing B-17 'Moonlight Mission' before the raid on Oranienburg

The crew of 'Moonlight Mission', of the 457th Bomb Group

I was by now out of ammunition and searched the sky in vain for signs of my comrades. Right, let's get out of here, I thought. That ride along the bomber stream had certainly paid off, I was just thinking to myself, when suddenly a line of bullet holes stitched themselves across the surface of my port wing and into the front of the engine nacelle. As I wrenched the Me 262 to the right to get out of the line of fire, a Mustang hurtled past me, all guns still blazing. A hasty glance at the instruments told me I was at 8,200 metres, but that the left-hand engine was losing power. A thousand thoughts raced through my mind: was the prophecy made during that long-ago dalliance in Bad Schachen about to be fulfilled today. Should I start smiling now? Forget it – the most important thing at the moment was to get into the safety of some cloud. None up here, so down into one of those low-lying banks as quickly as possible. And then where? I decided to make for Jüterbog airfield, but was the runway there still intact? At 1,500 metres, just before descending into scattered cloud, I looked behind me. At least there was no sign of the Mustang, but the bad news was that smoke was pouring from my port engine. While I was still weighing up the chances of reaching Jüterbog, the panels of the engine cowling started to peel back as if somebody was opening a tin of sardines.

I flew Me 262 A-1a 'Yellow 1' during my time in the Reichsverteidigung in the spring of 1945, and was flying it when I was shot down on 10 April 1945. *Kjetil Akra, 2008*

'Escort Fury', a painting by Robert Bailey of events on 10 April 1945 between Brandenburg-Briest and Jüterbog. A P-51D Mustang escorting the 1st Air Division is attacking my Me 262, hitting the port engine

'The oil tank around the Riedel starter motor must have been hit,' I thought.

Then there was a dull bang as the 'Zwiebel' – or 'onion', as the exhaust cone was commonly called – detached itself from the port turbine. This meant that I had to get out immediately – the engine could explode at any moment and rip the wing off.

What happened next no doubt lasted just split seconds, but to me it seemed like an eternity. At an altitude of 1,200 metres I jettisoned the canopy, levered myself up on the edge of the cockpit and tried to bale out. But the jet was still going too fast and the airstream kept pushing me back down into my seat again. Then I remembered the advice of a comrade, who had once baled out of an Me 262: 'You've got to take the power right off, and the moment you've pulled yourself up on the edge of the cockpit, immediately put one foot on the stick and give a hefty push away from it. That way the crate points her nose downwards and you're thrown clear and won't hit your head or body on the tailfin.'

So I took the machine back up a little higher again, placed my right foot on the stick, trod down hard and flew unscathed out of the cockpit. After tumbling unchecked through the sky for a while, I decided it was high time to pull the ripcord of my parachute. And that's when the next problem arose. In my haste to get out of the burning machine, my posture had been anything but controlled. Now I discovered that my right arm was stretched out horizontally from my body like a policeman directing traffic. The high g forces were holding it rigid and preventing me from moving it across my body to reach the left

strap of the parachute harness where the ripcord release grip was situated. With a strength born of desperation, not to say mortal terror, I tugged desperately with my left hand at the outstretched right sleeve of the leather flying jacket until I had bent my arm sufficiently to enable me to get at the ripcord release.

Below me the countryside was a patchwork of extensive paddocks and meadows. By the time my 'chute had finally opened I was not far off the ground. But then I found myself facing yet more calamity. The paddock I was drifting towards was heavily fenced off with barbed-wire. To get over this wicked-looking barrier, I tried heaving myself up on the shroud lines, scrabbling and jigging about like a puppet on a string. Anybody watching my antics would undoubtedly have died laughing. But it wasn't funny to me. Somehow or other I just managed to clear the wire, only to then hit the ground very hard and – exactly as we had been warned not to do – heels first. Still shocked by recent events, I didn't notice right away that I had badly sprained both ankles on landing. As I had heard a number of stories of downed Luftwaffe pilots being shot at on the ground by Allied fighters, I quickly bundled the revealing white folds of my parachute together and tucked them beneath my body. I lay motionless until the droning of the departing bombers ebbed away westwards, and the hammering of guns and the shrill whistle of jet engines was stilled. As the shock began to wear off my whole body trembled and intense pains shot up through my legs.

I don't know how long I lay on the ground in this condition. At one point I heard the

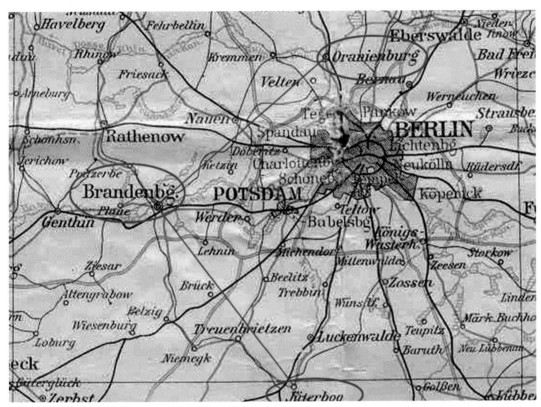

The final mission: the Oranienburg to Brandenburg-Briest and Jüterbog flight path

creaking sound of a horse-drawn cart on one of the nearby roads and called for help to the farmer driving it – but without success. As only my head was poking out of cover, perhaps he hadn't heard me, or maybe he thought I was a shot-down enemy flyer. For whatever reason, he paid me no attention whatsoever, but simply put the whip to his horse and continued on his way. Some time later a young lad wearing a baker's white cap came pedalling along a path through the fields. I struggled up on my now badly swollen legs and hobbled a few steps in his direction.

'Hey, baker's boy – please help me!' I called out to him.

He got off his bicycle and yelled back, 'I'm not a baker's boy – I'm a miller!'

Then he helped me to squirm my way under the barbed-wire entanglement. With my rolled-up parachute under my arm, I perched on the luggage rack of his bicycle and we rode to a mill not far away. While placing a cup of weak malt coffee and a few corn biscuits in front of me, the miller's wife told me that her husband had been called up into the infantry but that she hadn't heard from him for weeks. After I had forced down the worst coffee and just about the most awful biscuits I had ever tasted in my life, the miller's lad took me on his bicycle to the nearest main road. There I flagged down a truck carrying a group of soldiers into Berlin and asked the driver to give me a lift to the next suburban railway station.

How I managed to make my way through the ruins of Berlin to the house of my childhood girlfriend puzzles me to this day. But make it I did, and when her mother opened the door and stared at me in utter amazement, I was still carrying my parachute under my arm. She looked me up and down and said with tears in her eyes, 'Ach Walter, put that thing down. It's all over, the war is lost.'

Later that evening I set off for Oranienburg, reaching the bomb-damaged field at around 10 o'clock. At least my quarters were still standing, and after all the excitement of the day I was looking forward to a stiff shot of cognac. There was a bottle of Hennessy in a suitcase in my room that I kept for special occasions, but when I opened the case the carefully hoarded treasure had disappeared. Absolutely fuming, I summoned Chiefy and asked him who had rifled through my suitcase and where the cognac had gone. With his eyes firmly fixed on the ground he stammered, 'Herr Oberleutnant, I didn't think you'd be coming back. And so I allowed myself the liberty of drinking to your memory.'

'But not with my own cognac! Get out of my sight, you lousy corpse-looter!' I yelled furiously.

That day, 10 April 1945, had cost the lives of many fighter pilots and went down in JG 7's Geschwader history as 'Black Tuesday'.

21 Tomorrow you polish your own shoes

Being unable to operate the rudder pedals on account of my badly bruised and swollen ankles, I couldn't fly any missions for the time being. A few days after Black Tuesday, because of the destruction of all the jet bases in the immediate area, Jagdgeschwader 7 was transferred to the still intact airfield of Prague-Rusin. After some hair-raising take-offs from pitted and cratered runways, my comrades flew down to Bohemia, while I was faced with a long and bumpy ride by motorbike. At one of my intermediate stops I chanced to meet an old acquaintance: it was Waldemar Jung from Saarbrücken, now a Major, who had wangled the home leave for me after I had been awarded the Knight's Cross at Pontsalenjoki. Hugely delighted to have met again, we brought each other up to date on what had been happening since our last encounter.

Bad news again awaited me when I got to Prague-Rusin. My friend of many years, and second of the pair who had helped me convert to the Me 262, Oberfeldwebel Heinz Arnold, had failed to arrive in Prague from a ferry flight on 17 April. To this day I don't know what caused the crash that ended the life of my erstwhile Eismeerjäger comrade, whose score at the time of his death was standing at forty-nine. He was buried in the cemetery at Großröhrsdorf, north-east of Dresden, presumably close to the spot where he came down.

At Prague JG 7 only flew operations when fuel was available. Given the catastrophic supply situation, even the most fanatical must by now have realised that we no longer had anything left to send up against the thousands of enemy bombers and fighters that were parading through Reich airspace on a daily basis, and that the last hopes for some sort of wonder-weapon had disappeared into thin air. On 1 May 1945

the Gauleiter of Bohemia and Moravia came to the field to announce in a voice choked with emotion, 'The Führer is dead!' Most of the men of JG 7 were able to contain their grief at Hitler's passing – they were far more worried about what the future might bring.

Our situation at Prague-Rusin was becoming more and more precarious. Open uprisings and attacks on our soldiers by the Czech population were a daily occurrence and growing increasingly serious. The Czechs were supported in their actions by the troops of the former Soviet General Vlasov who, after being captured on the eastern front, had sided with the Wehrmacht. He had gathered enough ex-Russian prisoners of war to his cause to form two divisions, his eventual aim being to defeat the Red Army and topple the Stalin regime. But now that the end was approaching fast, Vlasov's men had decided that their only hope was to turn on their erstwhile German masters and this they proceeded to do, often in the most bestial fashion.

One day a Hauptmann turned up in a very agitated state. He reported that a column of Vlasov troops, equipped with some antiquated tanks and tracked vehicles, had taken up position in a narrow valley, or ravine, close to the airfield. They were demanding that we vacate the area within four hours. If not, they would move in and slaughter the lot of us. At this an Oberstleutnant Kern declared that he personally knew General Vlasov very well and that he would go down and parley with him. What he couldn't know as he set off with the Hauptmann was that Vlasov wasn't with this particular bunch of renegade Russians. After about two hours the Hauptmann returned alone with the Oberstleutnant's bloody genitals in his hand. In a deep state of shock at what he had just witnessed, he described how the Vlasov soldiers had hung the Oberstleutnant from a tree by his feet and then cut off his sexual organs. He had been instructed to tell us that we could expect the same treatment if we hadn't disappeared within three hours. We weren't going to stand for this, and in retribution for the atrocity it was agreed there and then that four Me 262s would be scrambled to ground-strafe the troops in the ravine. The jets split into pairs and it was quickly over. After two firing passes each, one from the left, one from the right, blazing armoured vehicles blocked the floor of the valley and the bodies of dead Vlasov troops lined the walls of the ravine.

wide red stripes from his uniform trousers. So, I thought to myself, it's not just the lower ranks that are getting nervous about the coming collapse, the fine gentlemen up top are taking precautions too. But I doubted that he would be able to hide evidence of his former high office simply by unstitching a pair of trouser stripes.

Before departing in the Storch the General approached me again. 'I am notifying you herewith that at midnight tonight the unconditional surrender comes into force. Make sure you get back to Germany!'

'But where in Germany, Herr General?' I enquired, given the imprecise nature of his instructions.

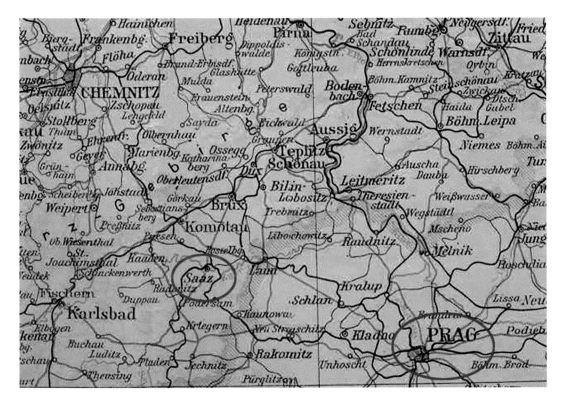

JG 7's last bases: Prague-Rusin and Saaz

When, some little while later, the first rounds of artillery fire came crashing down on Rusin airfield, destroying a good dozen of our few remaining Me 262s, our unit moved to Saaz in northern Bohemia. It was around midday on 8 May 1945 that I watched a Fieseler Storch come floating in at Saaz. From it clambered a General who asked me where he might find my superior officers. I directed him to a barracks hut where I knew several staff officers and bomber pilots were gathered. When I took a closer look at the Fieseler Storch I noticed that it contained a passenger, an Oberstleutnant of the General Staff who had already removed the tell-tale

He simply shrugged his shoulders. 'Where? Ja, that you'll have to decide for yourself.'

After the pair had taken off again at about 14.00 hours, I went into the hut where the bomber pilots were sitting waiting for their lunch. However, the mess orderlies were arguing the toss as to whether they still had to serve us, so the meal – Eintopf, or plain hotpot again as always – had not yet been brought out. I therefore went into the kitchen, ladled the hotpot into a tureen and carried it, together with some soup plates, to one of the tables where an Oberst was sitting. When I took a chair next to him and invited him to help himself first, he said with a smile, 'I'd never

209

have imagined that I'd have my soup brought to me by someone wearing Oak Leaves.'

'But tomorrow you'll have to start polishing your own shoes again, Herr Oberst,' I answered.

He looked at me with a puzzled expression on his face. It took ages before it sank in and he grasped the underlying meaning of my words. From tomorrow – no, from midnight tonight – there would be no more orderlies to light the stove for him in the mornings, to run his bath water, lay out his uniform, or polish his shoes…

22 The last flight

The whole field was a scene of near panic as troops and civilian employees, fearful of the avenging Czechs, rushed about in complete confusion throwing whatever they thought could be of use to them into a long line of waiting trucks. But when the convoy attempted to set off, it was stopped at the gates by military police backed up by heavily armed infantry. An angry confrontation broke out, with words like 'deserters' and 'traitors to the Fatherland' being hurled about. Before the situation could escalate any further, I grabbed a motor-cycle and rode to the head of the column where I showed the MPs a special pass that General Kammhuber had once issued to me and that I had since hung on to. This document stated, in the name of the Führer, that the bearer was to be allowed free passage and provided with every assistance to enable him to carry out his operational duties. Naturally, I declared the present evacuation of our people to be an operational duty.

Once the convoy had finally been allowed to pass, I went back out on to the airfield. In the meantime all eleven of our remaining serviceable jets had taken off, heading in the direction of Lüneburg Heath, to Fassberg, or some other destination in Germany. For example, Leutnant Wolfgang Müller – known to us all simply as 'Kondens-Müller' for the sharp way he flew his Me 262, which nearly always had ribbons of condensation streaming from its wingtips – put down at Munich-Riem, with Oberleutnant Hans Grünberg landing at Kaltenkirchen, and Oberleutnant Fritz Stehle, Leutnant Hans Dorn and Unteroffiziere Anton Schöppler and Günther Engler all opting for Fassberg. Apart from Leutnant Klaus Schulze and two Feldwebels, one an armourer, the other a radiolocation technician, there was nobody else about. But still standing around on the field were eighteen or so He 111s, Do 17s and Ju 88s that we didn't want to allow to fall into the hands of the Russians. The armourer dragged across a crate of stick incendiaries, which he loaded into a Kübelwagen. We then drove to each of the abandoned aircraft in turn, where we banged the fuse of one of the incendiary bombs against the machine's fuselage or wing before lobbing it up into the cockpit.

It was now high time for Leutnant Schulze and I to make for Fassberg too. We were going to fly there in an Me 108 Taifun courier aircraft that was standing fully fuelled in the maintenance hangar. The two Feldwebels had decided against coming with us, preferring instead to take the Kübelwagen and set off after the road convoy. We asked them to delay their departure for a few minutes until we were safely in the air. But just as we were about to climb into the Me 108, there was a shrill whistling noise and an Me 262 came in over the treetops to make a landing on one engine. The pilot scrambled out, rummaged around in the cockpit for all his baggage and came hurrying across to us. He introduced himself as Major Döhler from one of the disbanded KG(J) units. He had taken off for Fassberg at the same time as our JG 7 pilots, but one of his engines had packed up, so he had decided to return to Saaz. When he saw that there was no one around except us, and realising there was no chance whatsoever of an engine change or of laying his hands on a replacement machine, he demanded that we hand over the Taifun.

'I really am very sorry, Herr Major,' I replied, showing him my special pass, 'but a General was here this morning and he has ordered us to fly to Germany. If you wish to accompany us, we will have to move some of our things to make room for you. But that means you will also have to leave part of your luggage behind here.'

Knowing only too well that the disintegration of the Wehrmacht had effectively robbed him of all authority, the Major didn't bother to argue any further and readily agreed. I therefore took off on my last flight with two passengers on board. As I threaded my way north-westwards at treetop height I kept a sharp lookout for Allied fighters, but a thousand thoughts were going through my head: once you were a proud fighter pilot, flying more than 500 operational missions in the Me 109 and Me 262, and victor in 206 aerial combats. Before every mission you thought it would be your last. But time and time again you had incredible luck and you have survived the war relatively unscathed. Now you're flying back to a homeland that doesn't exist any more. There you'll be hunted down like a wild animal and at the end of the pursuit all that awaits you is captivity.

Late in the evening of 8 May 1945 we touched down at Fassberg. The field had already been occupied by the British and we were immediately surrounded by English soldiers.

My war was over.

My awards. Top row, from left: German Cross in Gold, Oak Leaves to the Knight's Cross of the Iron Cross, Combat Flight Clasp in Gold with Bar for 500 operational missions. Bottom row, from left: Wound badge in black, Pilot's Badge, Iron Cross 1st Class, Finnish Mannerheim Cross

23 The man who shot me down

I dedicate the closing lines of this book to the man who shot me down on 10 April 1945 and who, paradoxical as it may sound, probably saved my life by so doing. It is an indisputable fact that during the final weeks of the war more Me 262 pilots than ever before were shot down and killed, lost their lives while attempting to take off from, or land on, bomb-cratered runways, or died in crashes as a result of either technical or maintenance shortcomings in the chaos of the last days. I am still firmly convinced that the pilot who brought me down on that 10 April, and who was indirectly responsible for my bruised ankles, saved me from taking part in any more senseless air combats and thus from death itself.

For many years after the war I was still being bombarded with correspondence from historians, authors, aviation enthusiasts and former American fighter pilots who wanted to know, or themselves professed to know, who had shot me down. But none of their theories or suppositions matched the actual events in terms of times, locations or aircraft types involved. Some maintained that my machine crashed near Magdeburg, in other words more than 120km from Oranienburg. Others stated quite categorically that it was a P-47 Thunderbolt or a P-38 Lightning that had shot me out of the sky. My personal feelings about all this pedantic quibbling wavered between distaste and indifference. I simply couldn't understand why so much fuss was being made about the whole business.

I was therefore delighted when, in May 2005 – almost sixty years to the day since the end of the war – during a visit to my old Eismeerjäger comrade Kurt Schulze, who now lives in California, I was finally able to meet the man who had brought me down so long ago. It turned out to be the then 20-year-young 1st Lieutenant Joseph Anthony Peterburs, who was a member of the 20th Fighter Group's 55th Fighter Squadron and who, on that 10 April, was flying his P-51D Mustang as part of the fighter screen escorting more than 400 B-17 bombers of the 1st Air Division to Oranienburg. He had seen me shooting down the bombers, knew the exact location, the correct time, knew where my hits had struck home, the results they had produced, and what my subsequent evasive moves had been.

The man who shot me down: 1st Lieutenant Joseph Anthony Peterburs

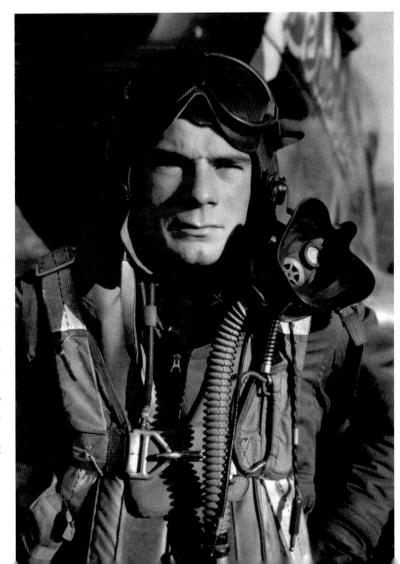

The reason why nobody had known for so long just who had shot me down is easy to explain. Joseph 'Joe' Peterburs had been unaware that I had been forced to bale out of the burning Me 262. After he had lost sight of me in cloud, he and his wingman had gone on

Joe Peterburs and his P-51D Mustang 'Josephine'

Joe Peterburs' P-51D Mustang 'Josephine'

to strafe Jüterbog airfield. Both had been brought down by the field's Flak defences and had become prisoners of war. By the time he returned to his unit stationed in England the war was long over. Nobody was particularly interested any more in his combat report, or whether the jet he had attacked had actually crashed, let alone the identity of the pilot flying it. So he didn't claim the hits he had scored on the Me 262 as a kill, nor did he mention any such possibility in his combat report, which reads as follows:

'I was in "B" group led by Capt Riemensnider. I filled the #4 position in Black Flight flying wing to Capt Dick Tracy. The bombers visually bombed the target at Oranienburg at 1438 with excellent results. Then all hell broke loose with 10-15 Me 262s barrelling through the formation. I saw one Me 262 hit at least two B-17s and I proceeded to attack it. I had about a 5,000-foot altitude advantage and with throttle wide open and .50 calibre machine-guns blazing I engaged the jet from the 6 o'clock position and was getting some hits and saw smoke. The jet headed for the deck with me in hot pursuit and Capt

Dick Tracy following close behind me. We chased the jet to an airfield. As I approached I could see the airfield was loaded with all types of German aircraft. I called Dick and said, "Do you see what I see?" He said, "Yes – let's go!" The Me 262 had entered a bank of low stratus clouds and we broke off the chase and started to strafe the airfield.'

When we met in the USA Joe Peterburs also told me a little more of what had happened to him after our brief aerial encounter:

'From above I saw this jet tearing through the formation of our B-17s shooting them down one after the other. I knew I had to stop the sonofabitch fast. I opened up the throttle of my Mustang, which was named "Josephine" after my then fiancée and future wife, and dove down on you. The rest you know. After you disappeared into the cloud there was no more point in chasing you. Then I saw an airfield jammed full of aircraft. I led Dick Tracy down for a strafing attack and opened fire on the closely packed machines. But we made the mistake of carrying out three or four low-level

passes one after the other. And as we were the only ones attacking, the Flak gunners were able to concentrate their fire on us and we were shot down. We both managed to bale out and were captured by the Germans. A few days later we were freed by the advancing Russians and I had some pretty crazy experiences with them as they pushed on through Germany. At the end of a lengthy odyssey right across Germany and France I boarded a ship for England where, after many weeks, I finally arrived back at my unit.'

The insanity of war had almost brought us to the point of killing each other. Today Joe and I, former adversaries in air combat, have become inseparable friends.

P-51D Mustang 'Josephine', flown by Joe Peterburs on 10 April 1945 when he damaged my Me 262. *John R. Doughty Jr*

Our first meeting in California after sixty years: Joe Peterburs (right), with Kurt Schulze in the background

Once opponents in the air, now firm friends: Chino, USA, 2005

'Only with the heart does man see well.
The essential things are invisible to the eye.'
Antoine de Saint-Exupéry

Appendix **1** The aircraft of our opponents

| Bell P-39 Airacobra

Airacobras of 2 GIAP at Varlamovo, Rudi Müller's opponents in the air combat of 19 April 1943. *Militaria Magazyn*

Curtiss P-40
Kittyhawk.
*E. Pilawski via
A. Brekken*

Hawker Hurricane

Supermarine
Spitfire PR IV high-
altitude
reconnaissance
aircraft

Douglas A-20
Boston. *E. Pilawski
via A. Brekken*

Douglas Boston.
P. Petrick

Ilyushin Il-2
Sturmovik.
*E. Pilawski via
A. Brekken*

Ilyushin Il-4.
*E. Pilawski via
A. Brekken*

Lavochkin LaGG-3.
(here and below)
*E. Pilawski via
A. Brekken*

Lavochkin LaGG-3.
P. Petrick

Mikoyan-Gurevich
MiG-3. *E. Pilawski
via A. Brekken*

A captured MiG-3.
P. W. Cohausz

Petlyakov Pe-2.
*E. Pilawski via
A. Brekken*

Polikarpov Po-2.
*E. Pilawski via
A. Brekken*

Polikarpov I-16
Rata. *Horst Kube*

Yakovlev Yak-7

223

Yakovlev Yak-9T.
P. Petrick

Yakovlev Yak-1.
E. Pilawski via
A. Brekken

A ski-equipped
Yak-1. *P. Petrick*

Boeing B-17G
'Flying Fortress'.
P. Petrick

A shot-down B-17.
P. Petrick

Victories scored with Jagdgeschwader 5 'Eismeer' ('Arctic Ocean')

Number	Staffel	Date	Time (hours)	Opponent	Location/area
1	7./JG 5	15.05.1942	18.18	Mikoyan-Gurevich-3	NW of Murmansk at 600m
2	7./JG 5	28.05.1942	16.36	Ilyushin DB-3 (Il-4)	Luostari/Lake Shulgul
3	7./JG 5	28.05.1942	16.40	Hawker Hurricane	Lake Shulgul area
4	7./JG 5	13.06.1942	17.02	Hawker Hurricane	Murmansk area
5	7./JG 5	22.06.1942	22.25	Polikarpov I-180	Murmansk area
6	7./JG 5	22.06.1942	22.30	Hawker Hurricane	Murmansk area
7	7./JG 5	28.06.1942	16.40	Hawker Hurricane	Rosta area
8	7./JG 5	08.07.1942	14.05	Curtiss P-40 Kittyhawk	Songui area
9	7./JG 5	20.07.1942	08.32	Petlyakov Pe-2	Litza Bay at 3,200m
10-12*	7. or 9./JG5	08-10.1942	?	?	?
13	9./JG 5	12.11.1942	12.10	Curtiss P-40 Kittyhawk	Murmansk at 4,000m
14	9./JG 5	26.12.1942	10.58	Lavochkin LaGG-3	Murmansk at 1,300m
15	9./JG 5	27.12.1942	10.45	Curtiss P-40 Kittyhawk	Murmansk at 3,500m
16	9./JG 5	31.12.1942	09.10	Petlyakov Pe-2	Litza area at 50m
17	9./JG 5	31.12.1942	09.14	Petlyakov Pe-2	Litza area at 50m
18	9./JG 5	31.12.1942	10.50	Curtiss P-40 Kittyhawk	Kola Inlet at 3,000m
19	9./JG 5	10.01.1943	11.23	Curtiss P-40 Kittyhawk	near Kirkenes at 1,500m
20	9./JG 5	10.01.1943	11.30	Ilyushin Il-2	near Kirkenes at 50m
21	9./JG 5	24.11.1943	09.12	Curtiss P-40 Kittyhawk	Rybachi Peninsula at 2,000m
22	9./JG 5	24.11.1943	09.16	Curtiss P-40 Kittyhawk	Rybachi Peninsula at 2,000m
23	9./JG 5	26.02.1943	08.42	Petlyakov Pe-2	Kola Bay at 2,000M
24	9./JG 5	28.02.1943	11.12	Curtiss P-40 Kittyhawk	near Petsamo at 600m
25	9./JG 5	02.03.1943	12.30	Douglas Boston	Afrikanda airfield at 30m
26	9./JG 5	14.03.1943	17.50	Polikarpov (Po-2) U-2	Litza front
27	9./JG 5	19.03.1943	06.03	Curtiss P-40 Kittyhawk	Rybachi Peninsula at 6,000m
28	9./JG 5	19.03.1943	06.05	Curtiss P-40 Kittyhawk	Rybachi Peninsula at 6,000m
29	9./JG 5	25.03.1943	17.40	Ilyushin Il-2	Murmansk at 30m
30	9./JG 5	25.03.1943	17.47	Curtiss P-40 Kittyhawk	Murmansk at 50m
31	9./JG 5	04.04.1943	13.25	Curtiss P-40 Kittyhawk	near Petsamo at 20m
32	9./JG 5	04.04.1943	13.27	Curtiss P-40 Kittyhawk	near Petsamo at 50m
33	9./JG 5	14.04.1943	18.25	Hawker Hurricane	near Vaenga at 5,000m
34	9./JG 5	14.04.1943	13.27	Hawker Hurricane	near Vaenga at 5,000m
35	9./JG 5	07.05.1943	04.01	Bell P-39 Airacobra	Murmansk at 1,200m
36	9./JG 5	22.05.1943	18.15	Hawker Hurricane	Motka Bay at 1,200m
37	9./JG 5	22.05.1943	18.25	Bell P-39 Airacobra	Motka Bay
38	9./JG 5	22.05.1943	19.42	Bell P-39 Airacobra	Rybachi Peninsula at 1,200m
39	9./JG 5	22.05.1943	19.50	Bell P-39 Airacobra	Rybachi Peninsula at 300m
40	9./JG 5	18.08.1943	16.16	Hawker Hurricane	Rybachi Peninsula at 300m
41	9./JG 5	18.08.1943	16.22	Bell P-39 Airacobra	Rybachi Peninsula at 600m

Number	Staffel	Date	Time (hours)	Opponent	Location/area
42	9./JG 5	03.09.1943	19.11	Hawker Hurricane	Litza at 20m
43	9./JG 5	03.09.1943	19.13	Hawker Hurricane	Litza at 50m
44	9./JG 5	12.09.1943	14.25	Curtiss P-40 Kittyhawk	Kola East at 20m
45	9./JG 5	12.09.1943	14.26	Curtiss P-40 Kittyhawk	Kola East at 20m
46	9./JG 5	12.09.1943	17.02	Curtiss P-40 Kittyhawk	Kola East at 30m
47	9./JG 5	14.09.1943	18.22	Bell P-39 Airacobra	Varanger Fjord at 1,200m
48	9./JG 5	14.09.1943	18.25	Bell P-39 Airacobra	Varanger Fjord at 1,200m
49	9./JG 5	14.09.1943	18.37	Ilyushin Il-2	Varanger Fjord at 500m
50	9./JG 5	14.09.1943	18.40	Bell P-39 Airacobra	Varanger Fjord, low
51	9./JG 5	18.09.1943	13.04	Curtiss P-40 Kittyhawk	Murmashi at 1,000m
51**	9./JG 5	20.09.1943	15.21	Douglas Boston	Kongs Fjord, low
52**	9./JG 5	20.09.1943	15.24	Douglas Boston	Kongs Fjord, low
53**	9./JG 5	20.09.1943	15.26	Bell P-39 Airacobra	Kongs Fjord, low
54	9./JG 5	23.09.1943	13.02	Curtiss P-40 Kittyhawk	SW of Murmansk at 600m
55	9./JG 5	23.09.1943	13.07	Curtiss P-40 Kittyhawk	SW of Murmansk at 200m
56	9./JG 5	23.09.1943	13.08	Bell P-39 Airacobra	SW of Murmansk at 500m
57	9./JG 5	23.09.1943	13.10	Curtiss P-40 Kittyhawk	SW of Murmansk at 600m
58	9./JG 5	24.09.1943	08.56	Curtiss P-40 Kittyhawk	Murmansk at 600m
59	9./JG 5	24.09.1943	08.58	Curtiss P-40 Kittyhawk	Murmansk at 200m
60	9./JG 5	13.10.1943	12.53	Douglas Boston	Kiberg-Vadsø, low
61	9./JG 5	13.10.1943	12.54	Curtiss P-40 Kittyhawk	Kiberg-Vadsø, low
62	9./JG 5	29.01.1944	12.08	Yakovlev Yak-7	Songui at 3,800m
63	9./JG 5	29.01.1944	12.25	Yakovlev Yak-7	Songui at 2,000m
64-65*	9./JG 5	01-02.1944		Further details unknown	
66	9./JG 5	17.03.1944	10.55	Douglas Boston	Vardø-Kiberg at 50m
67	9./JG 5	17.03.1944	11.00	Douglas Boston	Vardø-Kiberg at 100m
68	9./JG 5	17.03.1944	11.03	Yakovlev Yak-7	Vardø-Kiberg at 1,100m
69	9./JG 5	17.03.1944	11.07	Yakovlev Yak-7	Vardø-Kiberg at 1,100m
70	9./JG 5	17.03.1944	15.35	Curtiss P-40 Kittyhawk	Rybachi Peninsula at 500m
71	9./JG 5	17.03.1944	15.39	Curtiss P-40 Kittyhawk	Rybachi Peninsula at 800m
72	9./JG 5	17.03.1944	15.47	Curtiss P-40 Kittyhawk	Rybachi Peninsula at 500m
73	9./JG 5	23.03.1944	13.02	Yakovlev Yak-9	S of Litza at 500m
74	9./JG 5	01.04.1944	13.07	Curtiss P-40 Kittyhawk	Rybachi Peninsula at 5,000m
75	9./JG 5	01.04.1944	13.10	Curtiss P-40 Kittyhawk	Rybachi Peninsula at 5,000m
76	9./JG 5	02.04.1944	16.38	Yakovlev Yak-9	Rybachi Peninsula, low
77	9./JG 5	02.04.1944	16.42	Yakovlev Yak-9	Rybachi Peninsula, low
78	9./JG 5	02.04.1944	16.45	Yakovlev Yak-9	Rybachi Peninsula, low
79	9./JG 5	07.04.1944	06.07	Curtiss P-40 Kittyhawk	Varanger area at 800m
80	9./JG 5	07.04.1944	06.11	Curtiss P-40 Kittyhawk	Varanger at 300m
81	9./JG 5	07.04.1944	06.13	Curtiss P-40 Kittyhawk	Varanger, low
82	9./JG 5	07.04.1944	06.14	Ilyushin Il-2	Varanger, low
83	9./JG 5	07.04.1944	10.18	Bell P-39 Airacobra	Varanger, low
84	9./JG 5	07.04.1944	10.21	Bell P-39 Airacobra	Varanger, low
85	9./JG 5	25.05.1944	21.32	Douglas Boston	N or Varanger at 1,000m
86	9./JG 5	25.05.1944	21.35	Curtiss P-40 Kittyhawk	NE of Berlevåg at 800m
87	9./JG 5	25.05.1944	21.38	Douglas Boston	NE of Berlevåg at 800m
88	9./JG 5	25.05.1944	21.40	Curtiss P-40 Kittyhawk	NE of Berlevåg at 800m
89	9./JG 5	25.05.1944	21.43	Douglas Boston	NE of Berlevåg, low
90	9./JG 5	25.05.1944	21.45	Douglas Boston	NE of Berlevåg, low
91	9./JG 5	26.05.1944	04.56	Ilyushin Il-2	NE of Vardø, low
92	9./JG 5	26.05.1944	04.58	Curtiss P-40 Kittyhawk	NE of Vardø, low
93	9./JG 5	26.05.1944	04.59	Curtiss P-40 Kittyhawk	NE of Vardø, low
94	9./JG 5	26.05.1944	05.02	Curtiss P-40 Kittyhawk	SE of Vardø, low
95	9./JG 5	12.06.1944	15.11	Curtiss P-40 Kittyhawk	Murmansk at 200m

Number	Staffel	Date	Time (hours)	Opponent	Location/area
96	9./JG 5	15.06.1944	02.31	Curtiss P-40 Kittyhawk	Petsamo, near Liinakhamari harbour
97	9./JG 5	15.06.1944	02.33	Curtiss P-40 Kittyhawk	Petsamo, near Liinakhamari harbour
98	9./JG 5	15.06.1944	19.11	Curtiss P-40 Kittyhawk	Petsamo, near Liinakhamari harbour
99	9./JG 5	15.06.1944	19.13	Curtiss P-40 Kittyhawk	Petsamo, near Liinakhamari harbour
100	9./JG 5	15.06.1944	19.14	Curtiss P-40 Kittyhawk	Petsamo, near Liinakhamari harbour
101	9./JG 5	15.06.1944	19.15	Curtiss P-40 Kittyhawk	Petsamo, low
102	9./JG 5	17.06.1944	07.43	Curtiss P-40 Kittyhawk	SE of Vardø at 1,000m
103	9./JG 5	17.06.1944	07.44	Curtiss P-40 Kittyhawk	SE of Vardø at 800m
104	9./JG 5	17.06.1944	07.50	Ilyushin Il-2	SE of Vardø, low
105	9./JG 5	17.06.1944	07.52	Ilyushin Il-2	SE of Vardø, low
106	9./JG 5	17.06.1944	07.59	Curtiss P-40 Kittyhawk	SE of Kiberg at 800m
107	9./JG 5	17.06.1944	08.02	Douglas Boston	SE of Vardø at 1,000m
108	9./JG 5	17.06.1944	08.14	Douglas Boston	SE of Vardø at 1,500m
109	9./JG 5	17.06.1944	21.12	Bell P-39 Airacobra	W of Kirkenes at 1,300m
110	9./JG 5	17.06.1944	21.12	Ilyushin Il-2	Kong Oskar, low
111	9./JG 5	17.06.1944	21.14	Ilyushin Il-2	SE of Kirkenes at 400m
112	9./JG 5	17.06.1944	21.19	Ilyushin Il-2	SE of Kirkenes at 50m
113	9./JG 5	18.06.1944	05.10	Vickers Supermarine Spitfire PR IV	45km NW of Murmansk at 7,500m
114	9./JG 5	24.06.1944	04.05	Yakovlev Yak-9	Ura Guba at 1,200m
115	9./JG 5	27.06.1944	16.55	Curtiss P-40 Kittyhawk	Kong Oskar at 4,500m
116	9./JG 5	27.06.1944	16.58	Curtiss P-40 Kittyhawk	NW of Kirkenes at 4,000m
117	9./JG 5	27.06.1944	17.00	Bell P-39 Airacobra	Kong Oskar at 3,500m
118	9./JG 5	27.06.1944	17.03	Bell P-39 Airacobra	Kong Oskar
119	9./JG 5	28.06.1944	00.02	Bell P-39 Airacobra	NE of Kirkenes at 4,500m
120	9./JG 5	28.06.1944	00.05	Bell P-39 Airacobra	Kong Oskar at 4,000m
121	9./JG 5	28.06.1944	00.07	Douglas Boston	Kong Oskar at 5000m
122	9./JG 5	28.06.1944	00.09	Bell P-39 Airacobra	Kong Oskar at 5000m
123	9./JG 5	28.06.1944	03.50	Bell P-39 Airacobra	Murmansk area at 3,500m
124	9./JG 5	28.06.1944	04.15	Yakovlev Yak-9	Murmansk area at 800m
125	9./JG 5	28.06.1944	04.17	Yakovlev Yak-9	Murmansk area at 3,000m
126	9./JG 5	04.07.1944	19.00	Douglas Boston	Kirkenes harbour at 3,000m
127	9./JG 5	04.07.1944	19.02	Douglas Boston	Kirkenes at 3,000m
128	9./JG 5	04.07.1944	19.03	Bell P-39 Airacobra	Kirkenes at 3,000m
129	9./JG 5	17.07.1944	19.06	Douglas Boston	Kirkenes at 4,000m
130	9./JG 5	17.07.1944	19.08	Douglas Boston	Kirkenes at 4,000m
131	9./JG 5	17.07.1944	19.10	Douglas Boston	Kirkenes at 4,000m
132	9./JG 5	17.07.1944	19.12	Bell P-39 Airacobra	Petsamo at 3,500m
133	9./JG 5	17.07.1944	19.14	Bell P-39 Airacobra	Petsamo at 3,500m
134	9./JG 5	17.07.1944	19.19	Bell P-39 Airacobra	Petsamo at 2,000m
135	9./JG 5	17.07.1944	19.21	Bell P-39 Airacobra	Petsamo at 2,000m
136	9./JG 5	21.07.1944	06.04	Curtiss P-40 Kittyhawk	Varanger at 100m
137	9./JG 5	22.07.1944	12.16	Bell P-39 Airacobra	N or Kirkenes at 1,200m
138	9./JG 5	22.07.1944	12.21	Bell P-39 Airacobra	Kirkenes, Cape King Oskar
139	9./JG 5	22.07.1944	12.23	Bell P-39 Airacobra	E of Kirkenes at 600m
140	9./JG 5	22.07.1944	12.24	Bell P-39 Airacobra	E of Kirkenes at 600m
141	9./JG 5	22.07.1944	12.32	Bell P-39 Airacobra	Eina Bay, Rybachi Peninsula
142	9./JG 5	22.07.1944	12.35	Curtiss P-40 Kittyhawk	Eina Bay, Rybachi Peninsula
143	9./JG 5	22.07.1944	12.36	Curtiss P-40 Kittyhawk	SE of Rybachi Peninsula
144	9./JG 5	28.07.1944	12.50	Bell P-39 Airacobra	S of Litza Bay at 4,000m

Number	Staffel	Date	Time (hours)	Opponent	Location/area
145	9./JG 5	28.07.1944	12.52	Bell P-39 Airacobra	S of Litza Bay at 4,000m
146	10./JG 5	17.08.1944	09.38	Yakovlev Yak-1	E of Kirkenes at 2,800m
147	10./JG 5	17.08.1944	09.55	Bell P-39 Airacobra	E of Kirkenes at 2,000m
148	10./JG 5	17.08.1944	10.00	Douglas Boston	E of Kirkenes at 3,500m
149	10./JG 5	17.08.1944	10.03	Bell P-39 Airacobra	E of Kirkenes at 2,800m
150	10./JG 5	23.08.1944	12.03	Yakovlev Yak-9	E of Kirkenes, Rybachi Peninsula at 800m
151	10./JG 5	23.08.1944	12.58	Bell P-39 Airacobra	SW of Rybachi Peninsula, low
152	10./JG 5	23.08.1944	13.01	Bell P-39 Airacobra	SW of Rybachi Peninsula, low
153	10./JG 5	23.08.1944	13.03	Bell P-39 Airacobra	SW of Rybachi Peninsula, low
154	10./JG 5	23.08.1944	16.44	Bell P-39 Airacobra	N of Kirkenes at 1,500m
155	10./JG 5	15.09.1944	07.05	Bell P-39 Airacobra	NW of Petsamo at 1,500m
156	10./JG 5	15.09.1944	07.20	Bell P-39 Airacobra	NW of Petsamo, low
157	10./JG 5	16.09.1944	12.06	Ilyushin Il-2	Kirkenes at 400m
158	10./JG 5	16.09.1944	12.10	Bell P-39 Airacobra	Kirkenes at 1,300m
159	10./JG 5	16.09.1944	16.28	Bell P-39 Airacobra	Kirkenes at 3,000m
160	10./JG 5	17.09.1944	17.33	Yakovlev Yak-9	Kirkenes at 300m
161	10./JG 5	17.09.1944	17.36	Yakovlev Yak-9	Kirkenes at 500m
162	10./JG 5	17.09.1944	17.41	Yakovlev Yak-9	Kirkenes, low
163	10./JG 5	17.09.1944	17.44	Yakovlev Yak-9	Kirkenes, low
164	10./JG 5	20.09.1944	15.31	Ilyushin Il-2	Kirkenes at 100m
165	10./JG 5	20.09.1944	15.34	Bell P-39 Airacobra	Kirkenes at 800m
166	10./JG 5	25.09.1944	15.46	Bell P-39 Airacobra	Petsamo at 100m
167	10./JG 5	25.09.1944	15.50	Bell P-39 Airacobra	Petsamo at 800m
168	10./JG 5	25.09.1944	16.06	Bell P-39 Airacobra	Kirkenes at 300m
169	10./JG 5	25.09.1944	16.10	Ilyushin Il-2	Kirkenes, low
170	10./JG 5	27.09.1944	11.35	Douglas Boston	E of Vadsø at 5,500m
171	10./JG 5	27.09.1944	11.43	Douglas Boston	E of Vadsø at 5,500m
172-196***	9. or 10./JG 5 between 1943 and 1944, subsequently confirmed by RLM				
197	10./JG 5	16.02.1945	c16.00	RAF Bristol Beaufighter	Ålesund at 4,000m
198	10./JG 5	16.02.1945	c16.10	RAF Mustang	Ålesund at 4,000m

Notes

* No further details could be found relating to Victories 10-12 and 64-65.

** Victories 51ff should, in fact, be 52 ff. This mistake is most likely due to an original error in numbering by the ops room clerk at Petsamo.

*** Victories 172-196 were initially reported by the Navy, checked by the RLM in Berlin and confirmed by them in November 1944.

Appendix 3 Victories scored with Jagdgeschwader 7 'Windhund' ('Greyhound')

Number	Staffel	Date	Time (hours)	Opponent	Location/area
199	1./JG 7 Stabsstaffel	24.03.1945	c12.00	USAF P-51D Mustang	Leipzig-Dresden at 6,000m
200	1./JG 7 Stabsstaffel	24.03.1945	c12.05	USAF P-51D Mustang	Leipzig-Dresden at 6,000m
201	1./JG 7 3. Staffel	28.03.1945	unknown	USAF P-51D Mustang	Stendal region
202	1./JG 7 3. Staffel	07.04.1945	12.15	USAF P-51D Mustang	Wittenberg region
203	1./JG 7 3. Staffel	10.04.1945	14.30	USAF Boeing B-17 G	Oranienburg region
204	1./JG 7 3. Staffel	10.04.1945	14.33	USAF Boeing B-17 G	Oranienburg region
205	1./JG 7 3. Staffel	10.04.1945	14.35	USAF Boeing B-17 G	Oranienburg region
206	1./JG 7 3. Staffel	10.04.1945	14.38	USAF Boeing B-17 G	Oranienburg region

In compiling the above lists I unfortunately no longer had any of my logbooks or performance books available. The data has therefore been assembled from published sources, from the victory and loss lists of Jagdgeschwader 5 and 7 that appear on the internet, from documents and statements kindly provided by former members of these Geschwader, and from my own records and personal recollections. The lists make no claims to be complete or absolutely accurate, and may in some instances err in detail regarding number sequence, date, time, opponent or location.

I would thus welcome any additions, corrections, other relevant material or informed comment.

From	To	Rank	Unit	Employment/ position
01.11.1937	30.03.1938	Soldat	2. Fliegerersatzabteilung 24, Quakenbrück	Basic training
01.04.1938	30.09.1938	Gefreiter	Flughafenbetriebskompanie KG 254, Gütersloh	General duties
01.10.1938	15.11.1938	Gefreiter	Meschede/Schüren	Glider school
15.11.1938	31.01.1939	Gefreiter	Flughafenbetriebskompanie, Gütersloh	General duties
01.02.1939	30.04.1939	Gefreiter	Luftfahrttechnische Schule, Bonn-Hangelar	Technical training
01.05.1939	15.06.1940	Gefreiter	Flugzeugführerschule, Fliegerausbildungsregiment 82, Quakenbrück and Cottbus	A/B flying school
16.04.1940	02.09.1940	Gefreiter	Jagdfliegerschule I, Werneuchen	Trainee fighter pilot
02.09.1940	06.10.1940	Gefreiter	Ergänzungsjagdgruppe, 3. Staffel, Merseburg	Trainee fighter pilot
06.10.1940	10.02.1941	Gefreiter	Jagdgeschwader 3	
from 01.12.1940		Unteroffizier	Ergänzungsstaffel, St Omer-Wizernes, France	Operational training Staffel
10.02.1941	15.04.1941	Unteroffizier	Ergänzungsjagdgruppe 3, 10. Staffel, Brombos and St Jean-d'Angély, France	Wingman
15.04.1941	29.06.1941	Unteroffizier	Ergänzungsjagdgruppe 3, Cracow, Poland	Wingman
29.06.1941	09.09.1941	Unteroffizier	Ergänzungsjagdgruppe 3, Bergen-aan-Zee, Holland	Wingman
09.09.1941	29.12.1941	Unteroffizier	Ergänzungsjagdgruppe 3, Esbjerg, Denmark	Wingman
29.12.1941	22.04.1942	Unteroffizier	III./JG 5, 7. Staffel, Kristiansand, Stavanger, Bergen, Trondheim, Bodø, Norway	Wingman
22.04.1942	15.07.1942	Unteroffizier	7./JG 5, Petsamo, Finland	Element leader
15.07.1942	01.09.1942	Unteroffizier	7./JG 5 detachment, Kirkenes, Norway	Detachment leader
01.09.1942	01.12.1942	Unteroffizier	9./JG 5, Petsamo	Section leader
01.12.1942	30.09.1943	Feldwebel	9./JG 5, Petsamo	Staffel leader
01.10.1943	01.07.1944	Fahnenjunker Oberfeldwebel	9./JG 5, Petsamo	Staffel leader
01.07.1944	06.11.1944	Leutnant	10./JG 5, Petsamo and Gossen, Norway	Staffelkapitän
07.11.1944	19.02.1945	Oberleutnant	10./JG 5, Gossen	Staffelkapitän
05.03.1945	26.03.1945	Oberleutnant	Gruppenstab I./JG 7, Brandenburg-Briest	Conversion training, Element leader
26.03.1945	08.05.1945	Oberleutnant	I./JG 7, 3 Staffel, Kaltenkirchen, Brandenburg-Briest, Oranienburg, Prague-Rusin, Saaz	Staffelkapitän

Appendix 5 Aircraft types flown

Grunau Baby II

Focke-Wulf Fw 44 Stieglitz

Heinkel He 72 Kadett

Arado Ar 68

Arado Ar 96

Gotha Go 145

Junkers W 34

Focke-Wulf Fw 56 Stösser

Focke-Wulf Fw 58 Weihe

Bücker Bü 131 Jungmann

Bücker Bü 133 Jungmeister

Heinkel He 51

Henschel Hs 123

Fieseler Fi 156 Storch

Junkers Ju 87

Messerschmitt Me 108 Taifun

Messerschmitt Bf/Me 109

B-2

E-1

E-3

E-7

F-2

F-4

G-2

G-6

G-10

Messerschmitt Me 262 A-1a

Bibliography

Boehme, Manfred *Jagdgeschwader 7: Die Chronik eines Me 262 Geschwaders 1944/45* (Stuttgart, 1983)

Dietl, Gerda-Luise & Herrmann, Kurt *General Dietl* (1951)

Finkentscher, Wolfgang *Petsamo Ladoga* (Leipzig, 1941)

Girbig, Werner *Jagdgeschwader 5 'Eismeerjäger'* (Stuttgart, 1975)

Henkels, Walter *Eismeerpatrouille, als Kriegsflieger in der Arktis* (Dusseldorf-Wien, 1978)

Jurleit, Manfred *Strahljäger Me 262 im Einsatz* (Berlin, 1993)

Mau/Stapfer *Unter rotem Stern: Land Lease Flugzeuge für die Sowjetunion 1941-1945* (Berlin, 1991)

Mombeek, Eric *Eismeerjäger: Zur Geschichte des Jagdgeschwaders 5, Vol 1* (Linkebeek, Belgium, 2001)

Mombeek, Eric *Eismeerjäger: Zur Geschichte des Jagdgeschwaders 5, Vol 2* (Linkebeek, Belgium, 2003)

Obermaier, Ernst *Die Ritterkreuzträger der Luftwaffe 1939-1945, Vol 1 Jagdflieger* (Mainz, 1989)

Poll, Hans *Das Land der Mitternachtssonne* (Oslo, 1940)

Prien, Jochen, Stemmer, Gerhard, Rodeike, Peter & Bock, Winfried *Die Jagdfliegerverbände der Deutschen Luftwaffe 1934 bis 1945. Vol 4/1* (Eutin)

Prien, Jochen *Die Jagdfliegerverbände der Deutschen Luftwaffe 1934 bis 1945. Vol 5* (Eutin)

Prien, Jochen & Stemmer, Gerhard *Messerschmitt Bf 109 im Einsatz bei Stab und 1./Jagdgeschwader 3* (Eutin, 1997)

Rohwer, Jürgen *Chronik des Seekrieges 1939-1945*

Schramm, Percy E. *Kriegstagebuch des Oberkommandos der Wehrmacht 1939-1945* (Herrsching, 1982)

Smith, J. & Creek, Eddie *Me 262, Vol 1* (1998). *Me 262, Vol 2* (1998)

Thorban, F. W. *Der Abwehrkampf um Petsamo und Kirkenes* (1989)